Identity, Belonging, and Community in Men's Roller Derby

Modern roller derby has been theorised as a gendered leisure context, offering women opportunities for empowerment and growth, and enabling them to carve a space for themselves in sport. No longer a women-only sport, roller derby is now played by all genders and has been heralded as a model of inclusivity within sport.

Identity, Belonging, and Community in Men's Roller Derby offers an insight into how men's roller derby culture is created and maintained, how members forge an identity for themselves and their team, and how they create feelings of belonging and inclusivity. Through in-depth ethnographic study of a specific, localised roller derby community, this book examines how practices of skills capital intersect with different configurations of masculinity in a continual struggle between traditional and inclusive models of sport.

An interrogation of the ways a DIY sport can be seen to be achieved, experienced, and understood in everyday practice, this book will appeal to scholars of men, masculinities, and sport. Additionally, the methodological discussions will be of value to ethnographers and researchers who have had to deal with a disruptive presence.

Dawn Fletcher is a qualitative researcher working in the fields of gender and sport. She has published articles on skills capital and trans inclusion in roller derby and is especially interested in the possibilities for diversity and inclusion in alternative sports.

Routledge Research in Gender and Society

82 Gender Violence in Ecofeminist Perspective
Intersections of Animal Oppression, Patriarchy and Domination
of the Earth
Gwen Hunnicutt

83 Reframing Drag
Beyond Subversion and the Status Quo
Kayte Stokoe

84 Rape in the Nordic Countries
Continuity and Change
Edited by Marie Bruvik Heinskou, May-Len Skilbrei and Kari Stefansen

85 Refracting through Technologies
Bodies, Medical Technologies and Norms
Ericka Johnson

86 Young, Disabled and LGBT+
Voices, Identities and Intersections
Edited by Alex Toft and Anita Franklin

87 Transdisciplinary Feminist Research
Innovations in Theory, Method and Practice
Edited by Carol A. Taylor, Christina Hughes, and Jasmine B. Ulmer

88 Identity, Belonging, and Community in Men's Roller Derby
Dawn Fletcher

For more information about this series, please visit: www.routledge.com/
sociology/series/SE0271

Identity, Belonging, and Community in Men's Roller Derby

Dawn Fletcher

LONDON AND NEW YORK

First published 2020 by Routledge

2 Park Square, Milton Park, Abingdon, Oxon OX14 4RN
605 Third Avenue, New York, NY 10017

Routledge is an imprint of the Taylor & Francis Group, an informa business

First issued in paperback 2021

Copyright © 2020 Dawn Fletcher

The right of Dawn Fletcher to be identified as author of this
work has been asserted by her in accordance with sections 77
and 78 of the Copyright, Designs and Patents Act 1988.

All rights reserved. No part of this book may be reprinted or reproduced or
utilised in any form or by any electronic, mechanical, or other means, now
known or hereafter invented, including photocopying and recording, or in
any information storage or retrieval system, without permission in writing
from the publishers.

Notice:
Product or corporate names may be trademarks or registered trademarks,
and are used only for identification and explanation without intent to
infringe.

Publisher's Note

The publisher has gone to great lengths to ensure the quality of this reprint
but points out that some imperfections in the original copies may be apparent.

British Library Cataloguing-in-Publication Data
A catalogue record for this book is available from the British Library

Library of Congress Cataloging-in-Publication Data
A catalog record has been requested for this book

ISBN: 978-0-367-85680-9 (hbk)
ISBN: 978-1-03-217271-2 (pbk)
DOI: 10.4324/9781003014317

Typeset in Times New Roman
by Wearset Ltd, Boldon, Tyne and Wear

For Paul and the Octopodes

Contents

Acknowledgements	viii
List of abbreviations and glossary	ix
1 Not just a girls' sport	1
2 Community and engagement	25
3 Image and identity	48
4 Belonging and inclusivity	76
5 Barriers to belonging	108
6 Skills capital and acceptable masculinities	132
Index	144

Acknowledgements

First, thanks must go to all of those who supported me through my doctorate: my supervisors Lorna Warren and Tom Clark; my journal colleagues Ruth Beresford and Lauren White; my housemates Jen Hughes, Steve Woolass, Sprocket, and Hendricks; my league the Sheffield Steel Roller Derby, especially the Crucibelles.

In the writing of this book, additional thanks go to my family for giving me the time and space to write without having to worry too much about the other parts of life.

Finally, thank you to all the members of The Inhuman League, past and present, but especially to Fin. I, quite literally, could not have done this without you. I might not see you as much as I would like, but I love you all. Despite any of the difficulties I have laid bare, you are still, and will always be, my very favourite men's sports team. And, yes, I still have the Zom B Cru helmet covers. They are ready and waiting whenever you need them.

Abbreviations and glossary

Bench	Area set aside for skaters who are not participating in the current jam, the line-up manager, and the bench manager.
Bench manager	Person who gives instructions to the skaters participating in the jam. They will often advise skaters on strategy and have an overview of what is happening in the game. They can also call official reviews.
BI	Barrow Infernos. Men's team participating in Tier 1 of British Champs during the 2016 season.
Block	The action of contacting an opposing skater. A block can be positional, where a blocker will position themselves in the way of an opposing skater, or physical, where a blocker will push or hit the opposing skater. In order to be a legal hit, contact must be to a legal target zone, with a legal blocking zone.
Blocker	Skaters who participate in a jam but are not the points scorers are called blockers. They may "block" the opposition in any legal manner, often working together to create "walls" that the opposing jammer will try to break through.
Bout	A game of roller derby. "Bout" carries connotations of choreographed hits, and fighting, so increasingly, the term "game" is used instead.
Boutfit	Outfit a skater wears to participate in a bout or game of roller derby.
Brit Champs	British Roller Derby Championships. Organised roller derby seasonal tournament in the UK, consisting of an MRDA side and a WFTDA side, split into tiers and groups within tiers. Teams compete to win their group, to go on to playoffs, to be promoted to a higher tier for the next season. Each team playing must organise one "home" game per year.

BRSF	British Roller Sports Federation. The official governing body for roller sports in Great Britain, including roller derby.
CTB	Crash Test Brummies. Men's team participating in Tier 2 of British Champs during the 2016 season.
Crucibelles	SSRD's B-Team.
Flat Track Stats	A website with information about roller derby games. Teams submit results of games to the site, which they can then use for rankings, and to calculate the likely score of a match-up between two teams.
Game sanctioning	If a roller derby game is played between two MRDA teams, following the MRDA ruleset, teams can apply for the game to be "sanctioned", meaning that the results of the game will count towards ranking points on the MRDA system. A high ranking means a team could be eligible to compete in the MRDA championships. The WFTDA have a similar system.
HHRD	Hallam Hellcats Roller Derby. Sheffield women's team that split from SSRD in 2012.
Jam	Roller derby games are split into two 30-minute periods. Each period is further split into short bursts of gameplay of up to two minutes, which are called "jams". The line-up manager will send on a new line-up of skaters for each jam.
Jammer	The skater who is the designated points scorer for that jam. They wear a helmet cover with a star on.
League/Team	The league is the wider organisation which encompasses all members, such as The Inhuman League, whereas the team is the group of people who form each team within that league, for example the Army of Darkness and Zom B Cru. In the UK, the terms league and team are often used interchangeably.
Line-up manager	Person who will work with skaters on the bench during a game to decide who goes on track, and in which position, for each jam.
LRT	Lincolnshire Rolling Thunder. Men's team participating in Tier 1 of British Champs during the 2016 season.
MERDC	Men's European Roller Derby Championships. A tournament for the best MRDA teams in Europe. It ran for two years until it was replaced by the Men's European Cup (MEC).
Minimum skills	Skaters must pass a practical minimum skills test before they can play roller derby against another team. This test includes 21 basic skills, which are broken

	down into several elements, and cover style, footwork, speed, safety, and contact skills. Before passing these skills, skaters are often called pre-mins. The Inhuman League ran a minimum skills programme for new skaters called "Dead Meat", a variation on the common (although increasingly contested) use of "Fresh Meat" to refer to new skaters.
Misconduct	A type of penalty a skater would receive for behaving in an unsporting way. Misconduct includes such actions as attempting to deceive an official into giving a penalty to another skater and swearing at officials or skaters.
MRDA	Men's Roller Derby Association. Global association for men's roller derby, based in the USA.
MRDA Champs	Annual tournament featuring the top 12 teams in the MRDA.
Non-skating official	Up to 14 people per game act as non-skating officials (NSOs). These officials time the jams, the game, and skater penalties. They also track which skaters skate in each jam, skater penalties, and the score.
NWO	Manchester Roller Derby: New Wheeled Order. Men's team participating in Tier 1 of British Champs during the 2016 season.
Official review	In each half of a game, teams are allowed one occasion where they can ask the officials to review a penalty call that was made/not made. Shortened to OR.
Open to All/Co-ed	The term co-ed stems from co-educational, meaning men and women together. More recently, steps have been taken within the derby community to remove binary language such as this in favour of terms such as gender inclusive, or open to all (OTA). I use co-ed to refer to historic roller derby, and OTA to refer to modern, mixed gender roller derby.
Out of play block	A type of penalty issued when a skater continues to actively "block" another skater after having been warned they are "out of play", i.e. more than 20ft in front of the foremost pack skater. Shortened to OOP.
Playoffs	Games that are played between the teams who are top of the results table in their groupings to decide which teams will be promoted to a higher tier in British Championships.
Quad Guards	Toulouse Roller Derby: Quad Guards. Men's team based in Toulouse, France.
RCRD	Rainy City Roller Derby. Women's roller derby team. One of the highest performing in the UK.

xii Abbreviations and glossary

Rookie Game	Used to refer to a skater's first game, or mixed games organised to give newer skaters game experience. These games will typically ask for skaters with 0–3 previous games' experience. The term "cherry popper" was previously used, but often considered offensive/ inappropriate, and the term "rookie game" became more widespread.
Scrimmage/scrim	Informal game played during a training session, either against league members or a visiting team.
SDRD	Southern Discomfort Roller Derby. Men's team participating in Tier 1 of British Champs during the 2016 season.
SSRD	Sheffield Steel Roller Derby (known as Sheffield Steel Roller Girls until 2018). Sheffield women's team that was founded in 2008 and has had various links with TIL.
Skate/derby name	Name a skater chooses to be known by on uniforms and in game programmes. This name is often used more widely instead of a skater's legal name.
Skating Official	Up to seven people act as referees per game. Referees wear skates. The head referee (HR) oversees the other referees, calling penalties, and the safety and flow of the game. The HR skates on the inside of the track boundary. Up to three outside pack referees (OPRs) skate around the outside of the track boundary, following the action on track. One jammer referee (JR) per team will track the jammer through the pack. The JR counts points/passes and signals points to the scorekeeper (a type of NSO) to record. One inside pack referee (IPR) skates on the inside of the track boundary, supporting the HR and the JRs.
SSB	Super Smash Brollers. Men's team participating in Tier 2 of British Champs during the 2016 season.
Target/blocking zones	Parts of the body a skater may block with, or to, another skater. Legal zones include shoulders, hips, and thighs. Illegal zones include the head, forearms, back, and below mid-thigh.
Tattoo Freeze	Annual tattoo convention, which features a roller derby tournament.
TIL	The Inhuman League. Sheffield men's team that was founded in 2011. Army of Darkness – TIL's A-Team (name rarely used during fieldwork). Zom B Cru – TIL's B-Team.
TWI	Team West Indies. International women's team that participates in the Roller Derby World Cup. Dr Blocktopus is the team's bench manager.

Abbreviations and glossary xiii

UKRDA | United Kingdom Roller Derby Association. The national governing body for roller derby in the United Kingdom. Not currently associated with BRSF.
WFTDA | Women's Flat Track Derby Association. Global association for women's roller derby, based in the USA.
WFTDA Champs | Annual tournament featuring the top teams in the WFTDA.

Chapter 1

Not just a girls' sport

Roller derby is played all over the world, with teams from 50 nations competing in the Roller Derby World Cup. Although men's roller derby is played by fewer individuals and has been called a "niche sport within a niche sport" (Goodman, 2016), the Men's Roller Derby World Cup had skaters from 24 nations in 2018. It is fair to say that roller derby, a full-contact roller sport originating in the USA, can no longer be considered "women-only". The men who play have been called untypical (Morgan, 2013) and roller derby is thought to be a marginal sport, which attracts people who did not feel that they belonged in mainstream sport. However, sociology has largely ignored men's roller derby up to now. Increasingly, roller derby leagues and communities have seen growing tensions between those who want to foster inclusivity, and those who strive to create a serious, professional sport. It is important to consider the place of men's roller derby within that environment, to explore its inclusive possibilities and what roller derby offers men. The Inhuman League (TIL) was one of the first men's teams in the UK, and the issues it faced mirrored the experiences of other leagues throughout the UK. As the first UK men's roller derby team to explicitly welcome trans and non-binary skaters, the league is a good place to begin.

This book, then, is an ethnography of TIL, centred on the overarching themes of identity, belonging, and community. Within this context, I explore and problematise notions of inclusivity. Despite a desire to be inclusive, which is common to many roller derby teams and other team sports, certain members are permitted more freedom to behave in ways that alienate others. Policies and practices that seek to include everyone, in effect exclude those who cannot perform acceptable masculinity (or within this specific context, a successful roller derby persona). Through a discussion of the impacts of skills capital, I argue that it is necessary to make a choice about who should be included/excluded, and that absolute inclusivity is neither practical nor desirable.

Skills capital functions as cultural or symbolic capital in the Bourdieusian sense (1977, 1984, 1986, 1990a, 1990b. See Fletcher, 2017, 2019). Skills capital, as I have previously outlined (Fletcher, 2019), differs from other forms of symbolic capital (Hutson, 2013; Konjer *et al.*, 2019; Parry, 2016) and from the social (Darcy *et al.*, 2014; Lindström, 2011; Long, 2008) and subcultural (Fairley and O'Brien, 2018) capital that has been theorised through the lens of sport in that it arises from the development of a range of specific skills and competencies. Skills capital does not necessarily confer social capital, and functions independently. Although here I discuss skills capital within the habitus of roller derby and I conceptualise it as accumulated roller derby specific skills, such as footwork and skating skills, or understanding of strategy, or perhaps the ability to hold others' attention to coach them effectively, there is no reason it could not be reconfigured to explore other sport or other environments where a different set of skills is highly desirable. Roller derby is unusual, however, in that the relevant competencies are often gained through prior experiences of sport, such as rugby, or roller hockey. Roller derby was once considered to be a sport for those who do not like sport (Breeze, 2013), but it takes a more serious approach to develop a high level of skills capital, and such individuals are rewarded with power to effect change and imprint their ethos on the team. Issues of inclusivity arise when this ethos includes the adoption of mainstream sports practices.

Acceptable masculinity is a way of theorising the process of acceptance and the inclusion of a range of presentations of masculinity. The concept incorporates both inclusive and hegemonic practices in a way that requires members of a community to be "good enough". I differentiate this from Anderson's (2009) theory of inclusive masculinity, because the more traditional form of masculinity seen here is definitely hegemonic, in the sense in which Connell (2005) uses the term. This allows for the inclusion of difference within a community, and accounts for the continual struggle within this roller derby team between different models of sport, both serious and cooperative. It includes women and non-binary people, if they can display enough masculine qualities, and the inclusion of men who display hegemonic qualities, if they can be moderated by a desired level of skills capital. These concepts offer a lens through which to explore men and masculinity in roller derby in a way that acknowledges the challenges of a commitment to inclusivity. This research owes a debt to Goffman's (1959) concept of the presentation of self and expands upon the idea of identity as a process (Jenkins, 2014).

Although the book is concerned with how the dislocated "ideals" associated with roller derby are experienced in very particular places, as the sport is still unfamiliar to many, some explanation and context is required before turning to an introduction of the research and its setting. Below, I offer a brief history of roller derby, outlining its initial development in twentieth-century USA and its resurgence in the twenty-first century. I also point to areas where the tensions found in my research are present throughout roller derby history.

Once this overall context is provided, I introduce the team itself, exploring its place within roller derby and situating the period of observation within the overall timeline of the team's existence. Methodologically, I extend the understanding of insider research to explore more thoroughly how one deals with a disruptive presence. In the explication of my multiple and shifting roles as a participant, researcher, and official, there is much that offers an autoethnographic perspective, or rather *perspectives*, and so I offer an exploration of my place within roller derby and the team, providing necessary background to the points within the book where I discuss my experiences.

A detailed exploration of the contemporary roller derby community places this team, TIL, firmly in context. I discuss how participants' identities are created through roller derby personas and clothing choices, and how the team image is deliberately crafted by its members, evaluating how both individual and group identities rely upon acceptance by those whose definition of a situation counts. Through detailed exploration of banter, a feeling or experience I call "teamliness", and the acceptance of others, and using many examples taken from observations and interviews, I discuss how a feeling of belonging is important for team members. In considering the reverse of that, a lack of belonging, I highlight some of the potential issues inherent in a commitment to inclusivity. The book concludes with a discussion of how successful performances of a roller derby persona and constructions of community in everyday practice contribute to the development of skills capital and acceptable masculinities, which in turn impact upon the inclusivity of the team, and the sport.

The key contribution of the book lies in the analysis of how tensions between inclusivity and professionalisation play out in men's alternative sport. When the team's focus was on seriousness and competitiveness, established practices of mainstream sport and hegemonic masculinity came to the fore. However, at other times, practices were much more inclusive, such as when skaters demonstrated closeness and intimacy. Consequently, the ethos of the team remained in constant flux. The interplay of skills capital and acceptable masculinities was apparent when highly skilled skaters reproduced practices at odds with the inclusive ethos of the league, yet this behaviour became hidden under a collective definition of inclusivity.

Although academic interest in roller derby is not new, previous works have focused on the phenomenon as a women-only sport. This book acknowledges, for the first time, the men who play the sport. The potential negatives of involvement in roller derby have been explored before, but this book differs in that it engages with theories of masculinities as a lens through which to explore the tensions between inclusion and exclusion, and examines the experiences of previously ignored groups within roller derby: officials and volunteers. Although studies of roller derby have previously explored roller derby personas, this book connects the individual experience more clearly with the wider team and community.

The development of roller derby

The sport of Roller Derby was invented by promoter Leo Seltzer in 1935. The first event, dubbed the "Transcontinental Roller Derby", was held in Chicago, on 13 August 1935. Initially, it was billed as an endurance contest, with teams of two (one man and one woman) skating against others for prize money. Sources differ on exactly how far the teams skated, but it was billed as the distance between New York and San Diego (Coppage, 1999; National Museum of Roller Skating, 2016),

4 Not just a girls' sport

which is just under 3000 miles. Teams skated up to 110 miles a day (Coppage, 1999, p. 5) and the contest lasted somewhere between a month (National Museum of Roller Skating, 2016) and seven weeks (Coppage, 1999). In Depression-era America, this was an attractive prospect, as it at least guaranteed food, shelter, and $25 a week (Coppage, 1999).

Leo Seltzer modified the game over the next three years, increasing team sizes, and playing up the speed and the contact. The popularity of the sport waxed and waned over the years, with boom periods during the 1940s, when it was first televised, and from the late 1950s to the early 1970s, when Leo Seltzer's son, Jerry, had taken over the reins. The Roller Derby, as the Seltzers called it (always with capitalised R and D) had competition in the form of the Roller Games, or the National Skating Derby, run by Bill Griffiths, which was "flashier and more theatrical than the Derby" (Deford, 2014, loc. 334), but ultimately, both versions became less and less successful, and were shut down in the 1970s (Coppage, 1999, p. viii).

Roller Derby and its competition were "sports entertainment": commercial enterprises existing to make money for the organisers. Skaters were "professionals"; they were paid to skate, and though some had other jobs in the off-season, many lived off this money year-round (Deford, 2014). In writing about Jerry Seltzer's Roller Derby, Deford focused on his impressions of the skaters and noted how "a great sense of belonging, as well of place, is evident; there is a strong feeling of community" (2014, loc. 1915). Skaters lived and worked together, and were part of the same group, regardless of the team for which they might be skating. It was more than a job for the skaters and became an integral part of who they were (Rutter, 2001). Thus, notions of identity, belonging, and community have long been regarded as important aspects of roller derby.

In the years since the original Roller Derby closed its doors, there have been numerous attempts to stage a revival, including *RollerGames*, a TV spin-off of Griffiths' version, and the short-lived UK based *Roller Blaze*. In one of the most successful attempts, Stephen Land and Ross Bagwell, having sought advice from Jerry Seltzer, produced the cable television show *RollerJam*, first shown in December 1998. They put together the "World Skating League": skaters who were paid to train to be part of the show (Coppage, 1999, p. 102). The focus was on creating a television show, and the rules were modified to appeal to contemporary audiences, notoriously a heavily banked figure of eight track with an alligator pit in the centre (Mabe, 2007, p. 48). *RollerJam* lasted only two seasons. These attempts to recreate a once successful formula had a similar mix of professional skaters and entertainment for audiences, but there was clearly something missing. It seemed that the glory days of roller derby were gone forever.

Undeterred by the failure of others, in Austin, Texas in 2001, "Devil" Dan Policarpo gathered together a group of women to try to revive roller derby once more.

> A few girls were invited to join in a circus-infused, punk-rock themed version of the game that focused more on staged antics than athleticism. That formula

had already been proven a failure and almost killed the sport again when the man heading up the production [Policarpo] left the idea, the sport, and the skaters behind.

(Mabe, 2007, p. 61)

After Policarpo disappeared with over one thousand dollars of money they had raised, the women he had recruited decided to pursue the plans for a roller derby revival. Styling themselves the SheEOs (a play on CEO or Chief Executive Officer), they created a for-profit business called Bad Girl, Good Woman Productions (BGGW), and set about creating their own version of roller derby. This time, there were no men allowed, and the focus would be on athleticism as much as theatrics – "professional" in the sense of taking the sport seriously, rather than focused on "performance".

Joulwan (2007), a member of the Texas Rollergirls, discusses some of the problems associated with running the league for profit and writes a very personal account of the acrimonious split of the league in 2003, thus acknowledging the gulf between the ethos of the original modern roller derby league and its administration. Jerry Seltzer had talked about the barriers to getting a Derby project off the ground (Coppage, 1999, p. 98), but he had been talking about the idea of a league owned and operated privately and run for profit. He had not been considering a grass-roots plan. BGGW became Texas Roller Derby Lonestar Rollergirls, a banked track league, which continued to run for profit, but the majority of skaters left to form Texas Rollergirls, a flat track league, which was "skater-owned-and-operated" (Barbee and Cohen, 2010, p. 46). This model of ownership is replicated in most flat track roller derby leagues today, under the auspices of the Women's Flat Track Derby Association (WFTDA), created in 2005. This organisation, run by volunteers from member leagues, standardised the rules, instituted a minimum-skills policy, and developed a rankings system. Its motto was "by the skaters, for the skaters" (Mabe, 2007, p. 80). This new mission statement encapsulated the desire to move away from roller derby as a profit-making, commercialised form of sports entertainment towards a Do-It-Yourself (DIY) model, which explicitly distanced the sport from its roots. Though there are many roller derby leagues that are not part of the WFTDA, its ruleset is the most widely used.

The rules of roller derby are quite complex. The current ruleset and accompanying casebook run to 72 pages (WFTDA, 2019a). In reading this book, although a thorough grasp of the rules is fortunately unnecessary, an awareness of the basics is useful. Briefly then, flat track roller derby can be played anywhere there is space to lay a track, though sports halls tend to be the most common venues. For each game, a roster of up to 15 skaters is allowed, plus up to four bench staff. Each game will also have up to seven referees, and up to 13 non-skating officials. Games consist of two periods of 30 minutes, split into a number of sections, called "jams", of up to two minutes each. At the beginning of each jam, five skaters from each team take their positions on track. The track is an oval, with an infield and outfield for referees, and two lines mark the jammer start line and the pivot line.

One skater for each team per jam is designated the jammer: the points scorer. They wear a helmet cover with a star on, and line up behind the jammer start line. The other four skaters line up between the jammer line and the pivot line. They are called blockers, and blockers from both teams form what is called the pack. One of these blockers wears a striped helmet cover; that blocker is the pivot. The pivot is the only blocker who may start touching the pivot line, and if in that position, all blockers must line up behind. When the jam starting whistle blows, the jammers must try to skate through the pack. The first jammer through is signalled lead jammer. Then they must lap the pack and pass the blockers again. When a jammer passes an opposing skater, they earn a point. The blockers' job is to stop the opposing jammer from passing them, whilst also helping their jammer to get past. The lead jammer can "call" the jam at any point, usually after they have scored points, and before the other jammer has the chance to score. Then a new group of skaters will line up on track, and the next jam will start.

Books written about the early days of the modern roller derby revival (Barbee and Cohen, 2010; Joulwan, 2007; Mabe, 2007) might more accurately be termed "love letters" to roller derby, so passionately do these writers feel about the sport. Members are involved in all aspects of running a league and there is much more to it than a dry description of the rules can express. Writers focus on the names and outfits and partying but are also at pains to stress the athleticism. Joulwan (2007) writes about the experience of being a "rollergirl", and the joy of the game, but also of the deep friendships and connections that are made. It is not clear what exactly sparked the growth of this version of roller derby, but it seemingly created the same feeling of belonging as the original Roller Derby. Modern flat track derby quickly gained the attention of other countries, and in April 2006, the London Rollergirls (now London Roller Derby) became the first roller derby league in the UK (London Roller Derby, 2019). Although men were always involved as officials and supporters, these books make it clear that to the writers, roller derby is very much "all-women" (Mabe, 2007, p. 16), or "all-girl" (Joulwan, 2007, p. 3), which represents another break from its roots.

Sociological research on roller derby

Sociological research on roller derby has likewise focused on *Women's* Flat-Track Roller Derby, acknowledging its roots in the Riot Grrrl movement and third wave feminism as a deliberate attempt to create a separate female space in sport (Breeze, 2010; Pavlidis, 2012; Storms, 2008). The concept of "doing gender", explored through ideas such as: construction of identity (Becker, 2010); challenging gender norms (Beaver, 2009; Cotterill, 2010; Peluso, 2010a); and bodily practices (Peluso, 2010a), argues that performances of gender by roller derby participants act to disrupt or challenge the gender binary, or mainstream ideals of femininity and gender expectations, whilst simultaneously reinscribing, embracing or supporting the gender order and heteronormativity (Carlson, 2010; Finley, 2010; Peluso, 2010b). Becker (2009), for example, discusses this

Not just a girls' sport 7

through an analysis of skaters' appearance, both sexualised and athletic, which she argues is non-mainstream. Carlson (2010) argues that roller derby skaters play with their femininity through derby personas, but do not cross gender boundaries. Cotterill (2010) argues that skaters do challenge gender norms, in that "roller derby allows them to be feminine and to engage in socially acceptable gendered activities in new ways" (p. 15), claiming that these skaters "do gender" as a form of edgework (Lyng, 1990), risking their identities at the boundary, but again, stopping short. Finley (2010) suggests that the humour and irony associated with skaters' conscious adoption of sexualised clothing is a way of appropriating pariah femininities (Schippers, 2007), and therefore disrupting hegemony. Peluso (2010b) identifies *"performative opportunities* for women to transgress cultural norms" (p. 5) through bodily practices (a concept similar to Connell's (2005) bodily reflexive practices), but adds that some skaters express concern over the impact of sexualised clothing (Peluso, 2010b). These studies suggest that women in roller derby can either expose the existence of gender norms, or begin to subvert them, through overt expressions of sexuality; but in critiquing third-wave feminism and superficial narratives of empowerment, Whitlock (2012) disagrees, arguing that "roller derby imagines the same ideal woman as hegemonic society just with superficial additives" (p. 16), and claims to have refuted "previous research about the transgressive possibilities of roller derby" (p. 66).

In trying to explore what makes up this female space, the various and conflicting conclusions of researchers strongly suggest that the community of roller derby is "profoundly fractured" (Pavlidis and Fullagar, 2013, p. 19). It is community, nonetheless, and frequently couched within discussion of how roller derby creates a women-only "safe" space, and the focus on its DIY ethos (Beaver, 2012) and "sisterhood" (Cotterill, 2010), several studies explore the nature and extent of inclusivity within roller derby as a whole and its individual league organisations. In a pessimistic account, Cohen (2008) concludes that the supposedly all-inclusive environment is anything but, finding that the only acceptable form of self-expression is one that confirms the counter-cultural ideal – a strict and rigid model of femininity required to be welcome in the roller derby league she studied. Other researchers discuss how "rookies" (new skaters), can feel excluded and marginalised (Krausch, 2009); how all are welcome, but "all" really means the right kind of person (Cotterill, 2010; Finley, 2010). These studies suggest that, although it may be possible to do gender differently within this non-mainstream sport (Gieseler, 2012; Messner, 2002; Sailors, 2013), this possibility is still somewhat constrained, echoing the arguments of West and Zimmerman (1987).

Despite such issues, it is clear in the research that there has been a consistent attempt by leagues to eschew the methods of traditional sports organisations, and focus instead on reflecting a sense of collective identity and community (Beaver 2009), and there are indications that this has worked to support inclusivity in some leagues (Beaver, 2012; Becker, 2010). With reference to Texas Rollergirls, Beaver (2012) states roller derby's organisational form does not "reproduce the hierarchical structure found in other sports" (p. 45). Researchers demonstrate that

8 Not just a girls' sport

"derby welcomes women of all shapes, sizes, and skill levels" (Becker, 2010, p. 12), and there exists a strong belief amongst skaters that there is no "typical" roller derby girl; there is, instead, a space for every woman, especially those who previously struggled to fit in, or who have had no sporting background (Beaver, 2009; Cotterill, 2010; Finley, 2010; Peluso, 2010a). Although it is common for research to suggest these alternative femininities are more desirable in roller derby, Mullin's (2012) research finds a clear acceptance of any type of femininity in the league she studied, including "girly girls". She contrasts Carlson's (2010) study with hers, which "more accurately reflects the current crop of derby girls who may be less 'alternative' and less explicitly engaging in the sport because of its rebellious stigma" (Mullin, 2012, p. 8), and criticises the rebellious/alternative derby girl stereotype. Drawing upon Risman *et al.* (2012), Mullin (2012) suggests roller derby could indicate the possibility of some sort of gendered utopia, where skaters possess a mix of masculine and feminine (p. 20). Similarly, Pavlidis and Fullagar (2014) equate study of female bodies with the realisation of "opportunities for a more just, equitable, inclusive society" (p. 23). It can be said that the motif of "inclusivity" masks the reality that "it is only a certain kind of woman that leagues are targeting for recruitment (read: one that is appropriately sexual and feminine)" (Whitlock, 2012, p. 32). This notion of appropriate femininity is further explored in a study (Chananie-Hill *et al.*, 2012) of the ways in which third-wave feminism (characterised by freedom of expression, inclusiveness, and social justice) is reflected in roller derby and found that, in important ways, it really was not very inclusive at all, "because leagues are women-only, the viewer is encouraged to assume that all players are biological females, so trans men and trans women must be uninterested, invisible, or unwelcome" (p. 42). The "WFTDA's implementation of a gender policy with the hope of promoting inclusion" (Murray, 2012, p. 20) has been noted, however, at the time Murray wrote this, the policy stated that trans skaters must be able to produce on request a doctor's note confirming hormone levels within the range accepted for females (WFTDA, 2011). Far from being "an accepting community in otherwise oppressive cultures" (Murray, 2012, p. 133), the WFTDA had a far less inclusive policy than was possible at the time (UKRDA, 2014).

Breeze (2013) discusses the impossibility of being completely inclusive. Not all skaters want the same thing, so, although there is a level of collaboration, as the league moves towards serious competitiveness, selection becomes also about exclusion. Breeze (2014) argues that this form of exclusion is necessary for the sport to develop, and that "without competition, the chances of roller derby's recognition as a sport are very slim indeed" (p. 173). This idea is echoed further by Paul and Blank (2014), who question whether the unique context of roller derby as an alternative sport can continue in the face of an increasing drive to become mainstream. Breeze (2014) separates her participants' thinking on roller derby into a "like sport" versus "not like sport" dichotomy, with, on the "like sport" side, an increasingly narrow definition of "skater" (p. 187) and increasing pressures to dress like "serious athletes" (p. 204), wherein the "rollergirl" becomes a symbol of not taking the sport seriously (p. 208). These narrow definitions and increasing pressures indicate that the sport is becoming increasingly aligned with the values of mainstream sport, as in the "Just Do It" model explicated by Messner (2002) "as though the institutional center is the place to be" (p. 148).

These ideas suggest that a desire for professionalisation may prove an insurmountable barrier to inclusivity. There is a tension between professionalisation and commercialisation, which can be seen in the conflicting ways theorists discuss roller derby. For example, discourses of DIY models include discussions of sponsors, hierarchies, and commercialisation – concepts that are held to be antithetical to this approach (Beaver, 2009, 2012; Burger, 2012; Krausch, 2009). Donnelly (2012) challenges the assumptions of theorists that women's sport and, hence, roller derby, should be a "reconstruction or transformation" (p. 40) of mainstream sport, and this is reflected in Breeze's (2014) findings that "seriousness is about hegemony and dominant ideology, and a dazzling utopic potential for renewal and radical change is attributed to seriousness' opposite" (p. 199), and so Breeze (2014) explores the way roller derby athletes seek to distance themselves from the past roller derby image, and promote the sport as serious, as "sport rather than entertainment" (p. 115). Being taken seriously suggests a problematic relationship between roller derby, as skaters wish it to be, and professional sports. Pro-sports *are* money-making entertainment: they are commercialised. The continued presence of the boutfit and alter egos, often seen as incompatible with mainstream recognition, may not preclude professionalisation seen in terms of attractiveness to mainstream media and big business sponsorship. It is ironic to note serious professional sports are making moves towards displaying nicknames on jerseys, and having nicknames for players (Newsom, 2013; Paul and Blank, 2014), suggesting that making a show of individuals' personalities, increasingly discouraged in roller derby, is important to mainstream sports.

Men's roller derby and The Inhuman League

Implicit in research on gender in roller derby is the assumption that "gender" can be explored in all its forms with sole reference to female skaters. Few academics have adequately considered male, trans, or non-binary skaters. These "femininity" studies explore how women "do gender", but do not consider how it might be possible for men to also "do gender" in a sport which is considered to be a sport for women, or how roller derby can allow for the existence of masculinities embodied by men.

Modern roller derby may be discussed as a women-only sport, but in practice, it did not remain that way for long. The first men's roller derby team, Pioneer Valley Roller Derby's Dirty Dozen, was created in 2006 (Barbee and Cohen, 2010). After the appearance of several other men's teams, the Men's Derby Coalition (MDC) was founded in 2007 to represent the interests of men's leagues, promoting the sport, and offering support to each other as they developed (MRDA, 2017a). This was renamed the Men's Roller Derby Association

(MRDA) in 2011. From a group of 11 member-leagues all based in the US, MRDA has grown into a larger organisation which offers member benefits such as insurance and an annual competition: the Men's Roller Derby Championships. As of December 2019, the MRDA had 69 member-leagues listed on its website from 14 countries, of which 45 are ranked, having played the required number of "sanctioned" games against other MRDA member leagues. Though initially there was little support within the WFTDA for men's roller derby (Vecchio, 2012), the two organisations began to work more closely together to advocate for the sport of roller derby in all its forms (MRDA, 2017b). Despite gaining in popularity, the growth of men's roller derby was not as fast as that of women's roller derby, and thus the MRDA remained a much smaller organisation than the WFTDA. This, and issues of workload, led to the organisations again separating in 2019 (MRDA, 2019; WFTDA, 2019b).

Gieseler (2012) suggests "that with any marginalised group, specifically the extreme sporting world, there are opportunities to do identity differently away from mainstream controls" (p. 57), an idea previously explored by Messner (2002). Men's roller derby offers such a space. For Murray (2012), "If big, strong and powerful are no longer categorised as masculine traits, then something new is emerging in the way the genders, once binary opposites that privileged masculinity, are constructed, performed, and perceived" (p. 128). However, despite evidence of some blurring of the boundaries between masculine and feminine, Murray acknowledges that genders are still divided, and the binary remains (Murray, 2012, p. 251). Thus far, research has not found evidence of male skaters challenging gender norms.

Conflict between the desires of skaters is ever present, seen in the literature in the tension between the desire for expression of alternative identities and recognition as a serious sport, and this becomes more apparent as roller derby becomes more popular, and people who identify as something other than "woman" fight to find a space to belong in this "women-only" sport. Although mainstream sport may be considered a masculine arena (Gieseler, 2012), these studies suggest that modern roller derby is very much a female endeavour, and what little masculinity is explored, is displayed by women.

Therefore, though this drive to be taken seriously has been explored through observation of women's teams, the research has yet to uncover what male and trans skaters want, and why they play. Connor and Pavlidis highlight "the problematic denial of the role of men in derby" (2014, p. 8), and though they acknowledge the additional tensions and challenges inherent in OTA roller derby, "argue for mixed sex/gender derby as an important step forward for the sport" (2014, p. 5; see also Pavlidis and Connor, 2015). The presence of other genders suggests roller derby still has revolutionary potential, not just for men to "accept women as key leaders and allow themselves to play second fiddle to the women's game" (Copland, 2014, para. 17), which is a questionable assumption in any case, but for skaters of all gender identities to compete in a full contact sport on equal terms, as can be seen in the growth of both OTA teams and gender inclusive MRDA teams.

In 2011, some five years after the appearance of the first men's roller derby team, The Inhuman League was formed during a meeting in a pub. Initially the league consisted mostly of men who had been associated with the established women's league Sheffield Steel Rollergirls (now SSRD), as partners or siblings of SSRD skaters, as referees, or as non-competing members. TIL was one of the first men's teams in the UK, along with London's Southern Discomfort Roller Derby (SDRD), Newcastle's Tyne and Fear (T&F), Manchester's New Wheeled Order (NWO), and Lincoln's Lincolnshire Rolling Thunder (LRT), and were at the forefront of the development of men's roller derby in the UK.

Official recognition as a sport by the British Roller Sports Federation (BRSF) in February 2011 (UKRDA, 2011) had brought a new seriousness to roller derby in the UK. Tensions existed within the roller derby community arising from conflicting desires around the sport's future. Participants variously wanted a commercially viable sport, a professional sport, a sport in which skaters retain control of all aspects of production, an inclusive sport, and a fun, recreational sport. For men's teams, however, roller derby was very new.

For a while, SDRD was the only men's team capable of putting together a full roster, so teams banded together to play games. In September 2011, for example, TIL members teamed up with T&F members to form The Inhuman Fear, beating SDRD by 68 points in that game. By 2012, TIL had enough members who had passed the minimum skills assessment to field a team, and played their first game against T&F, losing by one point. During that year, the team played 16 games, which included travelling to Toulouse to play the Quad Guards, Toulouse's men's roller derby team, and participating in the 2012 Men's European Roller Derby Championships (MERDC), in which they finished sixth out of seven teams (Flat Track Stats, 2017).

The year 2013 was pivotal in the development of TIL. The team had grown in numbers, leading to competition for roster spots. The league's response to this was to create a B-Team, Zom B Cru, which consisted of mostly newer members and a few established members who had not made the A-Team. The A-Team, newly dubbed Army of Darkness, played Birmingham's Crash Test Brummies (CTB) in the first United Kingdom Roller Derby Association (UKRDA)-sanctioned men's game (UKRDA, 2013), and competed in MERDC again, this time finishing fourth out of 15 (Flat Track Stats, 2017). By the end of July, Army of Darkness were fourth in Europe, and Zom B Cru were twelfth (European Roller Derby Rankings, 2014). In terms of rankings, this represents the high point for the league, as both the A- and B-Teams began to slowly slide down the European Roller Derby Rankings, in part due to the founding of more men's teams, and hence more competition.

But there was also tension in the team ranks. The next year was marred by poor performance from the A-Team, disagreements around attendance policies and training, and the eventual disbanding of Zom B Cru in September 2014. The team lost several of their most experienced members, who said they were not being challenged enough, but also many newer teammates who said they were

12 Not just a girls' sport

unhappy that training had become less enjoyable. TIL could no longer sustain two teams, and they could no longer compete against the best men's teams in Europe.

In the winter of 2014, TIL suffered somewhat of a crisis; skaters were dissatisfied for a number of reasons, and many left – either to go on to new teams or give up the sport altogether. The setting I "entered" for fieldwork was quite a different setting to the one I was part of in 2014: there was a different committee, coaches, team management, members, and fewer of each. The TIL Facebook group numbered 23, of whom only 13 were bouting skaters who had passed the minimum skills assessment. Given that a full team numbers 14, this was a far cry from the heady days when TIL boasted an A-Team in the top five in Europe, and a B-Team in the top 15. When the British Championships began in 2015, TIL were in Tier 2, finishing the season mid-table. In 2016, the year during which my observation took place, they won the tier and were promoted to Tier 1 for 2017. Despite this resurgence, the tensions never completely dissipated, and the league continued to be a turbulent place.

My experience

In outlining possibilities for feminist epistemologies, Haraway explains that "only partial perspective promises objective vision…. Feminist objectivity is about limited location and situated knowledge…. It allows us to become answerable for what we learn how to see" (1988, pp. 582–583). Situated knowledges, in Haraway's view, can be objective – more so than the "unlocatable, and so irresponsible, knowledge claims" (1988, p. 583) of positivist, masculinist theorists. Haraway is not advocating relativism but "partial, locatable, critical knowledges" (1988, p. 584), as a preferred, but not perfect, alternative standpoint (Harding, 1986; see also Rich, 1986 and Stanley, 1997).

I can only lay claim to a partial knowledge, and similarly reject positivist objectivity. It is crucial therefore to explore my position within the research: where was I *situated*, and what were the implications for the *knowledge* I could have? As insider researchers suggest, ethnographers must not write themselves out, rather, learning to see themselves as part of the research helps to ground them in the field, and negotiate the challenges of being an insider, which includes insider blindness (DeLyser, 2001; Leigh, 2013; Taylor, 2011). Having an understanding that my vision was partial, and situated, ensured I did not privilege this perspective over those of my participants. My truth was not *the* truth, and I had to take care to separate my personal views from my academic, reflexive understanding of the situation as a whole:

> insider scholars … need to get into their own heads first before getting into those of participants; they need to know in which ways they are like their participants and in which ways they are unlike them; they need to know which of their social identities can advantage and/or complicate the process.
>
> (Chavez, 2008, p. 491)

An awareness of multiple meanings is especially important to a study of roller derby, since "from the perspective of a participant–researcher, the meaning of roller derby is multiple, shifting and not necessarily coherent" (Downes *et al.*, 2013, p. 104). Roller derby can mean different things to different people at different times and places, hence "a commitment to ontological multiplicity is helpful here: roller derby can be and is 'just a sport' at the same time as existing in many other confusing, wonderful, ridiculous and inspiring forms" (Downes *et al.*, 2013, p. 105). It was never just a sport to me; it was a community, an identity, and a source of joy and despair. In an attempt to clarify where I was situated, I explore here my roller derby beginnings, what brought me to the sport, and what I found there.

I first became aware of roller derby in 2010. I saw a flyer inviting new members to join SSRD at a tattoo convention in early October. I went to the introduction session on 16 October, and despite not talking to anyone, I enjoyed it enough to go back. What I had at first thought might be an interesting and slightly different way to get a bit of exercise, became the most all-consuming activity I had ever known. As my involvement continued, I learned new physical skills and the many rules of the sport. I also acquired a new language that revolved around roller derby, and began to refer to things like default strategy, and skate maintenance. I became part of the subculture.

I wrote for a roller derby magazine (Billie Viper, 2011) about how I thought I had found my "tribe", though, in reality, whilst I enjoyed skating, I was not sure I belonged in this group of self-consciously "alternative" people. In the early days, we talked about roller derby as a sport for people who did not like sport (Breeze, 2014); a place for people who hadn't played sports at school and who weren't particularly athletic. It was clear that many of the Sheffield Steel Rollergirls were reflexive about their involvement and that, in part, roller derby was a quest for belonging (Packington, 2012).

Quite a few men joined SSRD around the same time I did, and later went on to join TIL. Initially, TIL had very close connections with SSRD. They trained once a week, on Sunday evenings, after the SSRD training session, and several members of both teams attended both sessions. I had been on the periphery of TIL for a while, being friendly with members, and occasionally attending training sessions, but it was during 2013 that I became much more involved. I had just broken my wrist whilst playing for the B-Team of SSRD, the Crucibelles, and in searching for ways to stay involved, had volunteered to be a line-up manager for a mixed scrimmage that TIL had organised. I enjoyed it so much that, when TIL had advertised for a line-up manager for Zom B Cru, I jumped at the chance.

One of the stories I tell about myself is that this event changed my relationship with roller derby. I was so excited to be voted line-up manager of The Inhuman League's newly formed B-Team, Zom B Cru, and events coordinator not long after. On my return to skating, I felt safer training with the men's team, and went to more of their training sessions than the women's team. I went on to play more games since than before I was injured, but I never regained quite the same confidence as I had before; although I felt strategically more aware, I remained conscious of vulnerability, and was a much more cautious player. I also began to referee with more regularity, becoming an MRDA recognised official in December 2014, and a UKRDA affiliated official soon after. Becoming head referee for my league signalled my unofficial retirement from playing roller derby. Haraway's (1988) argument that knowledge claims must come from a body is echoed by DeLyser (2001), who suggests including the body as research site: having a focus on bodily experiences – and others' interpretation of that body. In such a physical environment as roller derby, this makes sense. My physical limitations have impacted upon my choice of role, my emotional responses have impacted upon how I performed that role, and hence this research begins with the view from this body.

My involvement in the two teams has ebbed and flowed over the years, and I did not manage to maintain heavy involvement with both teams at the same time. Zom B Cru played their last game in June 2014. Due to illness, my attendance at TIL training was patchy throughout 2015. As I started my observation, I was aware that I was not as much an insider as I had been previously. Insider/outsider status, however, is more complex than a binary suggests. In terms of The Inhuman League, ostensibly my position had shifted to that of outsider because, no longer a line-up manager, as a female skater I was, at the beginning of the research, ineligible to skate for the team, and chose not to do so after the change in policy. As a referee, I was also in a sense "outside", both physically, and psychologically. However, during fieldwork I was an associate member, the event organiser for the committee, as well as officiating for them in training and at games. It is important to remember that "in home fieldwork, multiple axes of commitment must be integrated with one's research agenda" (DeLyser, 2001, p. 444), and thus, my fieldwork had to be integrated with both my roles within The Inhuman League, and my role as head referee of the local women's team. This was not always easy; these roles afforded me a level of familiarity with the research site that could be both beneficial and detrimental to understanding and analysis.

It has been suggested that with insider research, "the research process can also reveal harmful behaviours, alter friendships, undermine passion and enthusiasm, and even end DIY cultural participation" (Downes *et al.*, 2013, p. 115). As much as I claimed at the outset that I was prepared for this, I am not sure it was possible to be fully aware of the impact becoming a researcher could have. Ultimately, although my passion and enthusiasm for the sport of roller derby itself remained undimmed throughout the research process, the relationship I had with The Inhuman League *did* change. I am not sure how much this was because of the research element and how much was down to my decision to referee. As an official, it is important to retain a sense of impartiality – to focus on upholding the safety and rules of games, and the mental shift from teammate to official necessitated a certain level of withdrawal. Breeze (2014, p. 193) notes difficulties in focusing on transcribing interviews because of a reluctance to change roller derby from a pleasurable hobby into work, and DeLyser cautions "those of us whose place of research may also be a personal space of refuge would be well advised, before undertaking insider research, to attempt to tease out and contemplate the potential repercussions that professionalizing the personal may have" (DeLyser, 2001, p. 446). However, as a referee, in a sense roller derby was work, and was already in some ways *professional* to me.

The research context

I liked roller derby a lot, but I *loved* men's roller derby; it was less rule-bound and offered more freedom. At the point I joined, men's roller derby had the feel of something new and exciting, and retained the fun and silliness that women's roller derby was increasingly rejecting. Many studies stated that men did not, *could not*, play roller derby, and that it was a women-only sport. These studies spoke to the life-changing impact of roller derby for women, and how women challenged gender norms through this sport. However, the lives of the men around me were also changing, and I could see them challenging gender norms too.

Despite narrow definitions of athletic identities and performance (Messner and Sabo, 1990), men's roller derby offered men significantly more freedom to express emotion without fear, and to develop different kinds of identities. The gender regime (Connell, 1987) of roller derby, holding such different values to the gender order of the institutional "centre" of sport (Messner, 2002) in which hegemonic masculinity is still prized, represented a "crisis tendenc[y]" (Connell, 1987, p. 159), and thus had "greater space for the development of a range of (sometimes even subversive) meanings, identities, and relationships around issues of gender and sexuality" (Messner, 2002, p. xxi), and was a site for doing gender differently.

Prior to my research, there were various articles and blogs posted debating the view that men had no business playing roller derby; that it was a women-only sport, and they should stick to playing their own sports s(Copland, 2014; D'Andrea, 2011; Ford, 2015; Hanna, 2015; Rider, 2014; Rodriguez, 2015). Well-known derby skaters, such as Bonnie Thunders, were outspoken in their disdain for men's derby (Vecchio, 2012). It has been argued that men are limited to masculine performances (Eckert and McConnell-Ginet, 2013) and that deviating from gender norms by performing femininity is considered a risk (Risman *et al.*, 2012). Regardless of the risks they took and the ridicule they potentially faced, male skaters were wearing feminised clothing, and wanting to join in a women's sport.

Doing identity and doing gender is theorised as inescapable (Butler, 1990), and as an ongoing, everyday process (Bricknell, 2005; Connell, 2005; Goffman, 1959; Jenkins, 2014; West and Zimmerman, 1987), and "if we fail to do gender appropriately, we as individuals – not the institutional arrangements – may be called to account" (West and Zimmerman, 1987, p. 146). So, picture the moment when my friend, Phallic Baldwin, wore black hot pants with a green zombie hand on the crotch and got lead jammer to thunderous cheers in the final jam on Zom B Cru's first bout. A man who was not typically athletic could succeed in this sport, and do it in an outfit deemed feminine, and hence, ridiculous. This subject was worth exploring further.

In terms of ethics, I faced two significant ethical issues: by what names would I refer to participants, and how would I handle league members who chose not to participate in the research? I could not promise anonymity to my participants. The roller derby community remains relatively small, and those active within the community often become well known. I took the decision not to disguise the name of the league I was studying because it would be obvious to anyone in the roller derby community, and very easy to discover for anyone outside the community. Similarly, with pseudonyms, I gave participants the choice of being identified by their skate name, or an alternative made-up name. Most participants opted to allow me to use their skate name. Skate names assume a level of importance in skaters' lives, as part of their identity, and are valuable data in themselves. The use of pseudonyms in such a small roller derby group would not guarantee anonymity (Downes et al., 2013), but there are ethical and moral dilemmas present in naming participants. Browne suggests that in the case of her participants who wanted to be named, anonymity implied further marginalisation.

> By naming Pat I may have inadvertently identified other women who may [have] wished to remain anonymous. Conversely, in removing Pat's autonomy to choose whether she was named in the study, I feel I have redeployed the potentially negotiated power relations and not enabled Pat to make her own choice.
>
> (Browne, 2003, p. 139)

I chose to use skate names where participants consented, and alternatives where they preferred; an imperfect compromise.

How to manage members who did not consent to participate was a much thornier issue. Ultimately, I obtained written consent from 24 members of the league and only directly refer to those members. However, difficulty in securing consent from all arose from a lack of certainty about who was a member and exactly how many members we had. In committee meetings throughout the observation, neither the treasurer nor the membership officer could give exact numbers. What constituted membership was fuzzy and ill-defined. Was it payment of dues? There were people who attended training and were rostered for games who had not paid a membership fee in months. There were people who paid a fee but had not been to a training session in months. Attendance was therefore not an accurate marker for membership either. The members Facebook group contained people who neither paid nor attended, and new members who paid and attended were not in the Facebook group. In the end, membership seemed to work on the basis of a feeling of belonging and team management were reluctant to ever explicitly bar an individual from membership. Members who had not given consent are either left out of the account where practical or referred to as "a skater" or "a member".

There is one notable exception to this compromise. One member (interestingly enough, part of the committee who granted me access to begin with) actively refused consent, but it quickly became clear that he played such a dominant role in the group that to write him out would have rendered the observation unintelligible. McKenzie (2017) argues that one of the difficulties of resolving ethical issues involving consent lies in the importance to the data of those who refuse consent. He claims that "to write out individuals from the research would be an impossible task because their impact on the data direct or indirect would be difficult to isolate" (2017, p. 5). McKenzie advocates a frank account of ethical decisions, and an acceptance of compromise. My compromise was that I devised a pseudonym, Donald Thump, and made the decision to only include my observations and others' responses to him, as they were necessary for discussion and analysis. Reading Chapter 4 and Chapter 6 especially, it will become clear how often that was necessary.

After gaining access, I immersed myself into the league as a total participant for a period of a year, training with the team on average twice a week, sometimes participating in scrimmages as a skater, but mostly as a referee. I attended league games, and mixed games in which league members were involved. In addition to this, I attended social events. During these times, I took field notes. Sometimes these were mental notes, sometimes written, to be translated into full field notes as soon as possible after the event. Often, it was not practical to write field notes during training sessions. Joining in contact drills or refereeing scrimmages and games made it impossible to take notes. At times, especially towards the end of fieldwork, I found it useful to be much more obvious about my note-taking. This served as a reminder, for myself as much as the participants, that I was there as a researcher. This enabled me to begin the process of withdrawing from the field.

In terms of method, situational analysis (Clarke, 2005) suited the reflexive standpoint I had taken. Postmodern in approach, situational analysis is a development from grounded theory (Charmaz, 2006; Glaser and Strauss, 1967; Strauss and Corbin, 1998) and seeks to acknowledge the multiple, the fractured, and the shifting nature of a situation. Where Geertz (1973) calls for "thick description" (p. 6), situational analysis yields "thick analysis" (Perez and Cannella, 2013, p. 506). Situational analysis, however, is deliberately flexible. Although Clarke clearly outlines the method and the individual steps and task to be undertaken, situational analysis is deliberately flexible. My prior engagement with the research setting allowed for the use of sensitising concepts (Blumer, 1954, 1969), but by focusing on the *situation* as the unit of analysis, it prevented over-reliance on key informants.

I used preliminary codes for field notes and interviews, in part by hand and also using NVivo. These codes helped to stimulate thinking, which in turn helped mapping sessions be more productive. I created situational maps which included *everything* in the situation. I conducted simultaneous memoing, noting new things in data, areas of inadequate data, and areas of theoretical interest (to support theoretical sampling). The memos I wrote led towards sites of silence, which it was fruitful to pursue. Keeping a running research journal or audit trail – chronicling changes of direction, rationales, analytic turning points etc., was also useful. Maps helped to bring the big picture back into view and encouraged me to notice even small and infrequently occurring aspects. Given the shifting and complex nature of the roller derby community, this method allowed me to think through the "situation" without overly privileging individual participants or positions. I mapped throughout the process of analysis, which ran concurrently to fieldwork.

The key themes apparent as a result of this mapping process are discussed in the following chapters. Chapter 2, on community and engagement, offers both an extended contextualisation of the place of TIL within Sheffield, and the wider roller derby community, and an analysis of how TIL and its members engage with these communities. Chapter 3 explores the processes of identification undertaken by TIL members and the league, focusing on practices of naming, choosing numbers and wearing boutfits as sites of individual identity, and how discourses of "good impressions" and "inclusivity" serve to create an identity of the league. In Chapter 4, I explore how specific practices engender feelings of belonging, focusing on banter, "teamliness", and acceptance. Chapter 5 involves an examination of the barriers to belonging, evaluating, through the experiences of marginal group members, how everyday practices may result in exclusion.

Throughout the data chapters I have tried to maintain a sense of the constant negotiation at work within TIL. Each example I use represents a moment, and though I focus on specifics within the exploration of each moment, there was always more going on than I could hope to replicate. The impact of skills capital and the place of acceptable masculinity are clear throughout the chapters. Participants' focus was on identity as a whole and creating a community: gender and masculinity were part of a larger identity project. The members of TIL were engaged in presenting an image of themselves and the team, which changed continually, but was always something of which they were conscious. They were concerned with feelings of belonging, and their community was important to them. But above all, they were interested in getting on with the business of "doing" roller derby.

Chapter 6 explores this thread in more depth, to consider how notions of "being" and "doing" roller derby run through each of the themes explored in the data chapters. Roller derby is constantly shifting, and so participant and team identities must constantly shift, and this process is never complete. I conclude with a look at how the findings in this book add to the body of knowledge on roller derby and on identity and community. I also suggest some of the implications of this research, and areas where questions remain. I end the book with a postscript, an update of the changes within TIL that takes us to the present moment.

References

Anderson, E. (2009) *Inclusive Masculinities*. London, Routledge.

Barbee, J. and Cohen, A. (2010) *Down and Derby: The Insider's Guide to Roller Derby*. New York, Soft Skull Press.

Beaver, T. D. (2009) Roller derby revolution: Sport as a social movement. *Proceedings of the 2012 American Sociological Association Annual Meeting held at the Colorado Convention Center and Hyatt Regency, Denver.*

Beaver, T. D. (2012) By the skaters, for the skaters: The DIY ethos of the roller derby revival. *Journal of Sport & Social Issues*, 36(1), pp. 25–49. DOI: 10.1177/0193723511433862.

Becker, S. (2009) Fishnets, feminism, and femininity: Gender and sexuality within women's roller derby. *Proceedings of the 2009 American Sociological Association Annual Meeting held at the Hilton San Francisco, San Francisco.*

Becker, S. (2010) Fishnets, feminism, and femininity: Resistance, construction, and reproduction of femininity within sport. *Proceedings of the 2010 American Sociological Association Annual Meeting held at the Hilton Atlanta and the Atlanta Marriott Marquis, Atlanta.*

Billie Viper (2011) Team Spirit. *Inside Line*, 3, pp. 16–17.

Blumer, H. (1954) What is wrong with social theory? *American Sociological Review*, 18, pp. 3–10.

Blumer, H. (1969) *Symbolic Interactionism.* Upper Saddle River, NJ, Prentice-Hall.

Bourdieu, P. (1977) *Outline of a Theory of Practice.* Cambridge, Cambridge University Press.

Bourdieu, P. (1984) *Distinction.* Cambridge, MA, Harvard University Press.

Bourdieu, P. (1986) The forms of capital, in J. E. Richardson (ed.), *Handbook of Theory of Research for the Sociology of Education.* New York, Greenwood Press, pp. 241–258.

Bourdieu, P. (1990a). *In Other Words: Essays Towards a Reflexive Sociology.* Stanford, CA, Stanford University Press.

Bourdieu, P. (1990b) *The Logic of Practice.* Cambridge, Polity Press.

Breeze, M. (2010) There's no balls in derby: Roller derby as a unique gendered sports context. *The International Journal of Sport & Society*, 1(3), pp. 121–133. DOI: 10.18848/2152-7857/CGP/v01i03/54028.

Breeze, M. (2013) Analysing "seriousness" in roller derby: speaking critically with the serious leisure perspective. *Sociological Research Online*, 18(4), p. 23. DOI: 10.5153/sro.3236.

Breeze, M. (2014) *Just a Big, Sexy Joke? Getting Taken Seriously in Women's Roller Derby.* PhD thesis, University of Edinburgh.

Bricknell, C. (2005) Masculinities, performativity, and subversion. *Men and Masculinities*, 8(1), pp. 24–43. DOI: 10.1177/1097184X03257515.

Browne, K. (2003) Negotiations and fieldworkings: Friendship and feminist research. *Acme: An International E-journal for Critical Geographies*, 2(2), pp. 132–146. Available from: http://acme-journal.org/index.php/acme/article/view/690/554 (accessed 3 January 2016).

Burger, U. M. (2012) *Roller Derby and the F-Word – Marketing Feminism, Alternative Femininity or False Consciousness.* MSc dissertation, Edinburgh Napier University.

Butler, J. (1990) *Gender Trouble.* London, Routledge.

Carlson, J. (2010) The female significant in all-women's amateur roller derby. *Sociology of Sport Journal*, 27(4), pp. 428–440. DOI: 10.1123/ssj.27.4.428.

Chananie-Hill, R. A., Waldron, J. J. and Umsted, N. K. (2012) Third-wave Agenda: women's flat track roller derby. *Women in Sport & Physical Activity Journal*, 21(1), pp. 33–49. DOI: 10.1123/wspaj.21.1.33.

Charmaz, K. (2006). *Constructing Grounded Theory: A Practical Guide Through Qualitative Analysis.* London, Sage.

Chavez, C. (2008) Conceptualising from the inside: Advantages, complications and demands on insider positionality. *The Qualitative Report*, 13(3), pp. 474–494.

Clarke, A. (2005) *Situational Analysis: Grounded Theory after the Postmodern Turn*. London, Sage.

Cohen, J. H. (2008) Sporting-self or selling sex: All-girl roller derby in the 21st century. *Women in Sport and Physical Activity Journal*, 17(2), pp. 24–33.

Connell, R. W. (1987) *Gender & Power: Society, the Person and Sexual Politics*. Cambridge, Polity Press.

Connell, R. W. (2005) *Masculinities* (2nd edn). Cambridge, Polity Press.

Connor, J. and Pavlidis, A. (2014) Gendered tension: Roller derby, segregation and integration. *Proceedings of the 2014 Australian Sociological Association Annual Conference held at the University of South Australia, Adelaide*.

Copland, S. (2014) "Roller derby could herald a revolution for gender equality in sport". *Guardian Online*. Available from: www.theguardian.com/lifeandstyle/2014/jun/18/could-the-men-of-roller-derby-become-sports-first-male-feminists (accessed 27 August 2015).

Coppage, K. (1999) *Roller Derby to Rollerjam: The Authorized Story of an Unauthorized Sport*. Santa Rosa, CA, Squarebooks.

Cotterill, M. S. (2010) *Skating the Metaphorical Edge: An Ethnographic Examination of Female Roller Derby Athletes*. MA dissertation, University of Delaware.

D'Andrea, N. (2011) "Five reasons there shouldn't be a men's roller derby". *Phoenix New Times*. Available from: www.phoenixnewtimes.com/arts/five-reasons-there-shouldnt-be-a-mens-roller-derby-6576589 (accessed 27 March 2019).

Darcy, S., Maxwell, H., Edwards, M., Onyx, J., and Sherker, S. (2014) More than a sport and volunteer organization: Investigating social capital development in a sporting organization. *Sport Management Review*, 17, pp. 395–406. DOI: 10.1016/j.smr.2014.01.003.

Deford, F. (2014) *Five Strides on the Banked Track: The Life and Times of the Roller Derby*. New York, Open Road Integrated Media.

DeLyser, D. (2001) "Do you really live here?": Thoughts on insider research. *Geographical Review*, 91(1/2), pp. 441–453. DOI: 10.1111/j.1931-0846.2001.tb00500.x.

Donnelly, M. K. (2012) *The Production of Women Onlyness: Women's Flat track Roller Derby and Women-Only Home Improvement Workshops*. PhD thesis, McMaster University.

Downes, J., Breeze, M., and Griffin, N. (2013) Researching DIY cultures: Towards a situated ethical practice for activist academia. *Graduate Journal of Social Science*, 10(3), pp. 100–124.

Eckert, P. and McConnell-Ginet, S. (2013) *Language and Gender* (2nd edn). Cambridge, Cambridge University Press.

European Roller Derby Rankings (2014). Facebook post 2 July 2014. Available from: www.facebook.com/EuropeanRollerDerbyRankings (accessed 5 November 2017).

Fairley, S. and O'Brien, D. (2018) Accumulating subcultural capital through sport event participation: The AFL International Cup. *Sport Management Review*, 21, pp. 321–332. DOI: 10.1016/j.smr.2017.08.003.

Finley, N. J. (2010) Skating femininity: Gender manoeuvring in women's roller derby. *Journal of Contemporary Ethnography*, 39, pp. 359–387. DOI: 10.1177/0891241610364230.

Flat Track Stats (2017) "The Inhuman League". *Flat Track Stats*. Available from: http://flattrackstats.com/teams/17613 (accessed 5 November 2017).

Fletcher, D. (2017) "Or are you just pleased to see me?": The role of the boutfit in men's roller derby. *Sheffield Student Journal for Sociology*, 1, pp. 120–136.

Fletcher, D. (2019) Skills Capital and Inclusivity in Men's Roller Derby. *International Review for the Sociology of Sport*, Online First. DOI: 10.1177/1012690219855733

Ford, C. (2015) "Why some sports should remain a women's game". *Daily Life*. Available from: www.dailylife.com.au/health-and-fitness/dl-sport/why-some-sports-should-remain-a-womens-game-20150519-gh53a2.html (accessed 14 January 2017).

Geertz, C. (1973) Thick description: Towards an interpretative theory of culture, in C. Geertz (ed.), *The Interpretation of Cultures: Selected Essays*. New York, Basic Books, pp. 3–32.

Gieseler, M. (2012) *Performances of Gender and Sexuality in Extreme Sports Culture*. PhD thesis, University of South Florida.

Glaser, B. and Strauss, A. (1967) *The Discovery of Grounded Theory*. Chicago, IL, Aldine.

Goffman, E. (1959) *The Presentation of Self in Everyday Life*. London, Penguin.

Goodman, E. (2016) "Meet the men of roller derby, a niche sport within a niche sport". *Vice Sports*. Available from: www.vice.com/en_us/article/xybdq7/meet-the-men-of-roller-derby-a-niche-sport-within-a-niche-sport (accessed 27 March 2019).

Hanna, A. (2015) "Roller derby doesn't enforce gender separation and women still rule the sport". *Guardian Online*. Available from: www.theguardian.com/commentisfree/2015/aug/19/roller-derby-gender-separation-women-rule-the-sport (accessed 27 November 2017).

Haraway, D. J. (1988) Situated knowledges: The science question in feminism and the privilege of partial perspective. *Feminist Studies*, 14(3), pp. 575–599.

Harding, S. (1986) *The Science Question in Feminism*. Ithaca, NY, Cornell University Press.

Hutson, D. J. (2013) "Your body is your business card": Bodily capital and health authority in the fitness industry. *Social Science and Medicine*, 90, pp. 63–71. DOI: 10.1016/j.socscimed.2013.05.003.

Jenkins, R. (2014) *Social Identity* (4th edn). London, Routledge.

Joulwan, M. (2007) *Rollergirl: Totally True Tales from the Track*. New York, Touchstone.

Konjer, M., Mutz, M., and Meier, H. E. (2019) Talent alone does not suffice: Erotic capital, media visibility and global popularity among professional male and female tennis players. *Journal of Gender Studies*, 28(1), pp. 3–17. DOI: 10.1080/09589236.2017.1365696.

Krausch, M. L. (2009) Feminism(s) in practice: The sport, business and politics of roller derby. *Proceedings of the 2009 American Sociological Association Annual Meeting held at the Hilton San Francisco, San Francisco*.

Leigh, J. (2013) *Constructing Professional Identity in Child Protection Social Work: A Comparative Ethnography*. PhD thesis, University of Salford.

Lindström, M. (2011) Social capital, desire to increase physical activity and leisure-time physical activity: A population-based study. *Public Health*, 125(7), pp. 442–447. DOI: 10.1016/j.puhe.2011.01.015.

London Roller Derby (2019) "Who are we?". *London Rollergirls*. Available from: http://londonrollergirls.com/who-are-we/ (accessed 27 August 2019).

Long, J. (2008) Sport's ambiguous relationship with social capital: The contribution of national governing bodies of sport, in M. Nicholson, and R. Hoye (eds), *Sport and Social Capital*. London, Butterworth Heinemann, pp. 207–232.

Lyng, S. (1990) Edgework: A social psychological analysis of voluntary risk-taking. *The American Journal of Sociology*, 95, pp. 851–886. DOI: 10.1086/229379.

Mabe, C. (2007) *Roller Derby: The History and All-Girl Revival of the Greatest Sport on Wheels*. Denver, Speck Press.

McKenzie, J. S. (2017) "You don't know how lucky you are to be here!": Reflections on covert practices in an overt participant observation study. *Sociological Research Online*, 14(2), pp. 1–10. DOI: 10.5153/sro.1925.

Messner, M. (2002) *Taking the Field: Women, Men and Sports*. Minneapolis, MN, University of Minnesota Press.

Messner, M. and Sabo, D. (1990) Toward a critical feminist reappraisal of sport, men, and the gender order, in M. Messner and D. Sabo (eds), *Sport, Men, and the Gender Order: Critical Feminist Perspectives*. Champaign, IL, Human Kinetics Books, pp. 1–15.

Morgan, G. (2013) "Bonnie Thunders, roller derby star, on the sport's acceptance of LGBT players". *Huffington Post*. Available from: www.huffingtonpost.com/2013/05/15/bonnie-thunders-roller-derby-gay_n_3280263.html (accessed 27 March 2019).

MRDA (2017a) "About". *MRDA*. Available from: http://mrda.com/about (accessed 5 November 2017).

MRDA (2017b) "MDC discusses future plans. WFTDA encourages men's derby". *MRDA*. Available from: https://mrda.org/11910mdcdiscussesfutureplanswftdaencouragesmensd erby/ (accessed 5 November 2017).

MRDA (2019) "Dissolution of MRDA/WFTDA partnership". *MRDA*. Available from: https://mrda.org/dissolution-of-mrda-wftda-partnership/ (accessed 21 December 2019).

Mullin, K. (2012) *Neither Butch nor Barbie: Negotiating Gender in Women's Roller Derby*. MA dissertation, Loyola University Chicago.

Murray, G. (2012) *The Unladylike Ladies of Roller Derby? How Spectators, Players and Derby Wives Do and Redo Gender and Heteronormativity in All-Female Roller Derby*. PhD thesis, University of York.

National Museum of Roller Skating (2016) "The history of roller derby". *National Museum of Roller Skating*. Available from: www.rollerskatingmuseum.org/roller-derby (accessed 21 December 2016)

Newsom, M. (2013) *All-Women's Flat Track Roller Derby: Gender, Psychoanalysis, and Meaning*. MA dissertation, Louisiana State University.

Packington, E. (2012) "Roller derby saved my soul … O RLY?". *TEDx Sheffield*. Available from: http://tedxsheffield.com/2012/erica-packington (accessed 21 July 2018).

Parry, D. (2016) "Skankalicious": Erotic capital in women's flat track roller derby. *Leisure Sciences*, 38(4), pp. 295–314. DOI: 10.1080/01490400.2015.1113149.

Paul, J. and Blank, S. (2014) Boutfits: A sociological analysis of the fashion and symbolic wear of roller derby attire. *Sociation Today*, 12(1), paras. 1–30.

Pavlidis, A. (2012) From Riot Grrrls to roller derby? Exploring the relations between gender, music and sport. *Leisure Studies*, 31(2), pp. 165–176. DOI: 10.1080/02614367.2011.623304.

Pavlidis, A. and Connor, J. (2015) Men in a "women only" sport? Contesting gender relations and sex integration in roller derby. *Sport in Society*, 19(8–9), pp. 1349–1362. DOI: 10.1080/17430437.2015.1067781.

Pavlidis, A. and Fullagar, S. (2013) Becoming roller derby grrrls: Exploring the gendered play of affect in mediated sport cultures. *International Review for the Sociology of Sport*, 48, pp. 673–688. DOI: 10.1177/1012690212446451.

Pavlidis, A. and Fullagar, S. (2014) *Sport, Gender and Power: The Rise of Roller Derby*. Farnham, Ashgate.

Peluso, N. M. (2010a) "Cruising for a bruising": Women's flat track roller derby as embodied resistance. *Proceedings of the 2010 American Sociological Association Annual Meeting held at the Hilton Atlanta and Atlanta Marriott Marquis, Atlanta.*

Peluso, N. M. (2010b) *High Heels and Fast Wheels: Alternative Femininities in Neo-Burlesque and Flat-Track Roller Derby.* PhD thesis, University of Connecticut.

Perez, M. S. and Cannella, G. S. (2013) Situational analysis as an avenue for critical qualitative research: Mapping post-Katrina New Orleans. *Qualitative Inquiry*, 19(7), pp. 505–517. DOI: 10.1177/1077800413489514.

Proven, R. (2014) The effect of co-ed on the women's game. *Leadjammer*, 9, p. 16.

Rich, A. (1986) *Blood, Bread and Poetry: Selected Prose 1979–1985.* London, Virago.

Rider, L. (2014) Feminism, Roller Derby, and Why Men are not the Devil. *Nottingham Roller Derby.* Available from: http://nottsrollerderby.co.uk/feminism-roller-derby-and-why-men-are-not-the-devil/ (accessed 27 August 2015).

Risman, B. J., Lorber, J. and Sherwood, J. H. (2012) Toward a world beyond gender: A utopian vision. *Proceedings of the 2012 American Sociological Association Annual Meeting held at the Colorado Convention Center and Hyatt Regency, Denver.*

Rodriguez, S. (2015) "The pros and cons of co-ed roller derby". *RollerDerbyNotes.com.* Available from: www.rollerderbynotes.com/2015/04/23/the-pros-and-cons-of-co-ed-roller-derby/ (accessed 27 August 2015).

Rutter, S. (2001) *Demon of the Derby: The Ann Calvello Story.* [DVD] Fireproof Productions.

Sailors, P. (2013) Gender roles roll. *Sport, Ethics and Philosophy*, 7(2), pp. 245–258. DOI: 10.1080/17511321.2012.737012.

Schippers, M. (2007) Recovering the feminine other: Masculinity, femininity, and gender hegemony. *Theory and Society*, 36, pp. 85–102.

Stanley, L. (1997) Methodology matters, in V. Robinson and D. Richardson (eds), *Introducing Women's Studies.* Basingstoke, Palgrave Macmillan, pp. 198–219.

Storms, C. E. (2008) There's no sorry in roller derby: A feminist examination of identity and women in the full contact sport of roller derby. *The New York Sociologist*, 3, pp. 68–87.

Strauss, A. and Corbin, J. (1998) *Basics of Qualitative Research: Grounded Theory Procedures and Techniques* (2nd edn). Thousand Oaks, CA, Sage.

Taylor, J. (2011) The intimate insider: Negotiating the ethics of friendship when doing insider research. *Qualitative Research*, 11(1), pp. 3–22. DOI: 10.1177/14687941 10384447.

UKRDA (2011) "Roller derby recognised as a sport in the UK". *UKRDA.* Available from: http://ukrda.org.uk/2011/02/roller-derby-recognised-as-a-sport-in-the-uk/ (accessed 27 August 2015).

UKRDA (2013) "UKRDA Southern Tournament". *UKRDA.* Available from: https://ukrda.org.uk/2013/04/ukrda-southern-tournament/ (accessed 5 November 2017).

UKRDA (2014) "UKRDA Transgender Policy". *UKRDA.* Available from: https://docs.google.com/document/d/1C_QzK0s3pmmEa49OAJ_1pvhSRxTzbGs1j1BKtpC1vdw/edit (accessed 27 August 2015).

Vecchio, K. (2012) *This is How I Roll.* [DVD] New York, Fork Films.

West, C. and Zimmerman, H. (1987) Doing gender. *Gender and Society*, 1, pp. 125–151. DOI: 10.1177/0891243287001002002.

WFTDA (2011) "WFTDA Gender Policy". *WFTDA.org.* Available from: https://wftda.org/news/wftda-adopts-gender-policy (accessed 2 May 2018).

WFTDA (2019a) "Rules". *WFTDA.com*. Available from: https://rules.wftda.com/ (accessed 21 December 2019).

WFTDA (2019b) "WFTDA statement regarding the dissolution of relationship with the MRDA". *WFTDA.com*. Available from: https://wftda.com/wftda-statement-regarding-the-dissolution-of-relationship-with-the-mrda/ (accessed 21 December 2019).

Whitlock, M. C. (2012) *Selling the Third Wave: The Commodification and Consumption of the Flat Track Roller* Girl. MA dissertation, University of South Florida.

Chapter 2

Community and engagement

This chapter expands on some of the points made in the Introduction to more clearly situate The Inhuman League as a DIY culture within the context of the local community, whilst also exploring links with the wider roller derby community. Exploring the tensions that exist between the league's goals and the impact of outside forces, is the key to understanding why and how practices have been shaped in the way they have.

Everyday practices, routine concerns and sometimes trivial activities that are unremarkable but commonly experienced, regular, and often taken for granted (Morgan, 2011), are intelligible in the "doings" of The Inhuman League. Such practices are active, involve action, and grant agency. This also reflects discussions of identity (Jenkins, 2014) and gender (West and Zimmerman, 1987) in which "doing" is key, and Goffman's theorisation that identity exists in the repetition of performances (1959). Research highlights how practices include thinking and talking in addition to action (Barry, 2018), and marks the contrast between the two (Morgan, 2011), however, the distinction between practices and discourses is not always clear, as they are mutually dependent. This suggests a point of similarity with symbolic constructions of community, which for Cohen (1985), exist in thinking about and talking about, as much as in action.

Roller derby exists, not as a single community, but as a series of linked communities. Individual teams engage with localised or far-flung teams, with national and international governing bodies, and with global and online communities, with little in common except a love (and sometimes hatred) for this ridiculous sport we play. An interrogation of the communities of TIL reveals the thinking and talking, and the actions around which the league constructs their identity.

The local roller derby community

Women's teams

Roller derby arrived on UK shores in 2006, with the founding of the London Rollergirls, now London Roller Derby (London Roller Derby, 2019), but Sheffield's roller derby community began two years later, in 2008. Founded by

26 Community and engagement

Jane-Doe-A-Go-Go, Sheffield Steel Rollergirls (now Sheffield Steel Roller Derby, or SSRD) was the first roller derby team in Sheffield. Initially a very small team, it grew until there were enough members for an A- and a B-Team. Internal tensions, common in roller derby, forced a split in 2012, and Hallam Hellcats Roller Derby (HHRD) was born.

Whilst it sometimes seems like there are residual negative feelings between the teams, they are generally supportive of each other, although most members do not have a great deal of contact. Having said this, there has been a lot of crossover over the years, with members switching teams, and sometimes switching back again, and with members of one team occasionally guest skating in games with the other. In this particular context, community is inextricably linked to a search for belonging (Delanty, 2010, p. 18), and some individuals have crossed team boundaries again and again in search of the right space for them. Thus, it is possible to talk of the Sheffield roller derby community as a wider entity, but also as separate individual team communities.

Many TIL members were connected with these teams also. Bench team Zoya and Wilma were both members of HHRD (although Zoya used to be a member of SSRD), and Nuke and Fin had both been on the bench teams of SSRD and HHRD. Additionally, as TIL drew its membership from a relatively wide geographical area, members had connections with teams from Hull, Grimsby, Leeds, Barnsley, and Mansfield, with members serving as bench team or referees for several women's teams throughout the region. Membership of TIL was often fuzzy, with confusion over the membership status of those on the edge relatively common (as discussed in Chapter 1); however, despite this back and forth flow of members, and a few individuals maintaining dual membership, the boundaries between the teams remained much clearer (Barth, 1969). This had not always been the case. When TIL was created, links were stronger, and the communities overlapped considerably.

TIL's founding members were originally part of SSRD. In 2010, when I joined, there were a few men involved, learning to skate with us, and often becoming referees. At that point, there was no real opportunity for them to play roller derby, and though many of SSRD's members were happy to engage in contact with men at training, some were not. These members were at the margins of the sport, by virtue of being men. Their welcome in an "all-woman" sport was conditional. In an attempt to construct a community where they would feel that they more fully belonged (McHugh *et al.*, 2015; Stone, 2017), these men became keen on forming their own team. By 2011, it seemed that there was enough interest to make it happen. Blocktopus remembers there being around eight or nine people at the first meeting during which TIL became one of the first five men's roller derby teams to be founded in the UK.

> It was recognised as being so close to the start of men's roller derby in the country that we were learning everything very quickly and not really caring about particularly how well we did it. It was sort of, we'll do it, see what

comes of it, try to improve and – but we were very much feeling our way with it.

(Blocktopus Interview, 8 January 2016)

Without much in the way of models to draw upon from the men's roller derby community, TIL maintained a close connection with SSRD, relying on their knowledge to build the team and its structures. As many of TIL had relatives or partners in SSRD, the social circle was initially very similar; they remained part of the same community. Additionally, both teams held training sessions at the same venue on Sunday afternoons and early evenings, and so there was a lot of crossover with skaters joining in each other's training sessions. Despite this closeness, TIL began to strive for independence.

> We did go through a phase where we, I think it's when I were chair, I started to deliberately want to put some separation between TIL and SSRD, 'cos I thought it felt a bit one-sided. They'd been very helpful and supportive, but I also felt it were time for TIL to stand on its own two feet. Um, and to forge its own identity. But it was never – the aim was never to break the links with SSRD, it was just to stop relying on them for everything.
>
> (Daddy Longlegs Interview, 3 October 2016)

At the start of 2013, an influx of new members meant that TIL was big enough to have a B-Team. For a time, this renewed the connection between TIL and SSRD as there were, again, several relationships between members of this B-Team, Zom B Cru, and SSRD's B-Team, the Crucibelles. This sense of community was valued by members and added to the enjoyment of roller derby.

> We were really lucky as well because, er, I hate to sound like a nostalgic arsehole, but, you know, it was a really golden time as well where Crucibelles and Zom B Cru had a real affinity. You know, there was several, sort of, courtships between the two teams and that seemed to really – really bring the two groups together.
>
> (Grievous Interview, 15 January 2016)

Grievous highlights the feeling of togetherness that was apparent during this time. Romantic relationships helped to cement ties between the two teams and build a greater sense of one community. There was a sense of "family feeling", shared values and practices (McHugh *et al.*, 2015), opportunities for reciprocity (Mynard *et al.*, 2009), and shared experiences (Stone, 2017). This simple outward appearance of similarity hid complexities within, and these shared experiences and values were seen differently by different members (Wichmann, 2015), however. The links between The Inhuman League and SSRD were constructed symbolically, but though there was an assumption that they were "fundamentally 'playing the same game'" (Barth, 1969, p. 15), the leagues also existed as spaces of difference

28 Community and engagement

(Cohen, 1982, 1985) where conformity was an illusion (Cohen, 1985, p. 37) and multiplexity (Cohen, 1985, p. 30) was key. Whereas B-Team members discussed a feeling of belonging in the Sheffield roller derby community, A-Team members were more focused on dealing with issues of inclusion and exclusion, with boundary maintenance (Barth, 1969) of special concern.

By the time my fieldwork officially started in October of 2015, many of the original members of TIL had left, and because of dwindling membership, Zom B Cru had been shelved for an indefinite period. The close relationship between SSRD and TIL had faded to the point where the chair, and several committee members, struggled to remember a time when SSRD had offered any support to TIL at all. Whilst ex-members such as Grievous could continue to look at the past through rose-tinted glasses, roles within the teams' structures had changed, and those who remained with TIL now spoke of SSRD from the position of outsider.

When skating together, there were tensions and difficulties in gelling as a single team. TIL held Sheffield Roller Derby scrimmages twice during the period of fieldwork, with skaters drawn from TIL, SSRD, and HHRD. In the first one, I observed a lot of sloppy play from several skaters, which resulted in a disadvantage for the team using these tactics. One skater blocked another enough to cause injury, and this was perceived to be a deliberate, illegal hit, although it was not called as such by the referees. This skater then targeted the offending blocker with several revenge hits, and this style of play seemed to spur others on to be more aggressive.

The second scrim was much friendlier and enjoyable to officiate. I was a penalty box timer, and skaters would chat and joke when they were sent to the box, sometimes disagreeing with penalties, but politely, and with good grace. It is difficult to account for why the mood of each scrimmage was so different, considering there were many of the same people present. Perhaps, because I was a referee for the first and an NSO for the second, my perspective affected the way I read the game. However, in the second game, Hoof was injured, and the scrim had to be stopped for a while until he could be taken to hospital. There was some tension during this stoppage, as some people helped Hoof, whist others just went back to skating.

> Nuke comes back shortly after, saying there is a car blocking the ambulance pathway, and asking if anyone owns a red car; a small red car. People shout out "what kind of car?", "is it blue?" (Coogan) and unhelpful things like that. Thump could potentially just be clarifying, as he drives a red car, but the other questions were clearly facetious. Nuke was annoyed by this and said to Coops on his way out that he didn't need this shit. He had given up his skating time to help sort Hoof out, whilst everyone else who were skating just went back to it and left Hoof to the non-skaters.
>
> (Field notes, Wednesday 27 April 2016)

Although this suggests a certain amount of bad feeling, the skaters continued playing, and were obviously enjoying themselves. The second scrim represents a collective will to ignore the negatives and focus on the positive aspects of skating together. These scrimmages had the potential to bring the teams together more effectively than committee discussions, which focused on the things that were not happening. Although this was recognised by some members of TIL, there were no more Sheffield Roller Derby scrimmages after this point. Lack of action on both sides prevented the togetherness that both teams profess to want.

Still connected to roller derby through coaching the junior team at the time of interview, ex-member Grievous felt that, at times, TIL had been hostile towards SSRD, and that members actively resisted being part of a local roller derby community.

> I approached TIL about the junior derby and tried to get them involved with junior derby, and they've just put up barrier after barrier. You know, they've said in essence, "yes we're interested", but then put up every roadblock possible, erm, and it just seems ... perverse to me, why wouldn't you want to have a good relationship with your sister league?
>
> (Grievous Interview, 15 January 2016)

Grievous interpreted the tensions and difficulties as stemming from TIL members and perceived them to be the ones preventing the two teams from working together. At that time, SSRD members were setting up a junior team, open to all genders. Whilst Grievous felt that TIL members should want to be more involved, TIL committee discussions suggested that, as a junior team was not on TIL's agenda, and as there was a hesitation to be involved due to questions around safeguarding that the chair felt had not been properly addressed, it was better to not be involved initially. The TIL committee were themselves dealing with low membership and low engagement, struggling to get team members engaged in TIL business.

> When I was chair I would look at people and say, why aren't you doing something and I'd be lying if I said it didn't piss me off when I saw people doing nothing, when I saw people who just wanted to turn up to training and that's all they'd like to do or not even turn up to training sometimes, just turn up and expect to play a game. It pissed me off loads and that was one of the major things that we tried to deal with when I was chair, trying, how do you engage people?
>
> (Coogan Interview, 31 May 2016)

Under Coogan's leadership (Coogan was a skater who had no previous connection with any other roller derby team), TIL had become more insular and inwardly focused. TIL were more independent, but they suffered through lack of strong links to other teams, especially at a time when numbers were low, and some members were a little disengaged.

This narrow focus could be seen as a natural development in the construction of the community. Jenkins' (2014) discussion of group identity offers a useful way to explore these changes in TIL. Members were seeking to define the team in a way that granted them independence from the women's league, and in this independence, they sought validation of their identity as a men's league. The problem for TIL, which offers a point of contrast to the literature, is that the league appeared weaker and more fragile when members were so inwardly focused, as discussed in the following sections. In Sheffield at least, roller derby seemed split between women's roller derby and men's roller derby, and it felt like there was a necessity to choose a side. Those of us who straddled that boundary, often found maintaining links with both sides difficult. TIL's relationship to local officials, for example, had also become weaker during this time.

Officials

The phrase "by the skaters, for the skaters" is ubiquitous in roller derby, especially in reference to the sport's DIY roots (Beaver, 2012; Mabe, 2007), as it was part of WFTDA's original mission statement (WFTDA, 2016). Although WFTDA no longer use the phrase, other organisations do. In 2019, the British Champs organisers put out the findings of a survey into the season, and concluded with the statement: "Roller Derby is still by the skater, for the skater, and it's you – all our amazing reps and officials and teams – who really make this work" (British Champs, 2019). Despite an additional reference here to officials, what this phrase allows skaters to do is ignore the contribution of anyone who isn't a skating member of the team: committee members, organisers, bench coaches, line-up managers, non-skating officials, skating officials, photographers, staff, medical staff, volunteers. In most cases, at least some of these roles will be taken by skaters, but increasingly, as skaters take the sport more seriously, they have less time to do other roles and those roles are filled by non-skaters.

Just as community and belonging are intimately connected, there is a clear link between thinking (Cohen, 1985, 1986) and doing (Bennett, 2015; May, 2011), but in *by the skaters, for the skaters*, there exists a clear message that however much you "do" community as a volunteer, you are still marginal. Belief in shared values is an important aspect of community construction (Cohen, 1985) and contributes to "whether an individual *feels* that they fully belong" (Stone, 2017, p. 4). Stone argues that this feeling is enhanced through the structure of an organisation, and that it is an individual feeling that "emerges and disappears within the living of everyday life" (2017, p. 10). The structure of many roller derby organisations privileges skaters over non-skaters. Although community and belonging have been theorised as "a process of becoming roller derby" (Pavlidis and Fullagar, 2014), depending on their role, individuals may find that there are limits as to how roller derby they can become.

This simple phrase, then, positions all non-skating participants in the roller derby community firmly at its margins, centring skaters and the playing of roller derby above all else. It may be thought that this makes sense; roller derby is, after all, a sport. But it is a sport that could not be played at all without officials and

Community and engagement 31

would not exist in the form that it does without the work and support of all the many non-skating participants.

During my time as a member of TIL's committee, there were regular discussions about the lack of officials at training. As discussed in more depth in Chapter 5, I had several experiences that negatively affected my desire to referee for TIL, and fellow referee Andy Social also found continued engagement difficult to sustain. Whilst the discussion in Chapter 5 focuses on the barriers to belonging experienced by officials and volunteers and the emotional responses to those barriers, here I want to explore the structural reasons for a lack of officials. Within Sheffield, there were few dedicated officials. Most people who refereed or acted as a non-skating official (NSO) also skated. This meant that to officiate for another team, a person would have to commit to double the time of a non-official. Also, several of the more experienced skaters/refs in Sheffield were members of TIL, so in order to referee for the team, they had to take time out from skating. In a team with low numbers, this was problematic.

Training times were also an issue for those who would otherwise volunteer. During the period of my observation, SSRD trained from 10:30 to 15:00 on a Sunday, whilst TIL trained from 17:00 to 20:30 on the same day. SSRD did not scrimmage on a Sunday, so they managed more easily without officials, whereas TIL did regularly scrimmage. However, for SSRD members who might have been interested in officiating to commit to attending TIL sessions on a Sunday made for a very long day, especially if they had other commitments. Both teams had a training session on a Wednesday at similar times, so attendance at each other's session was limited. SSRD trained and scrimmaged on a Tuesday evening, and TIL members often attended these sessions for a little extra skating time, and to referee the scrimmage. That it was easier in some ways for TIL members to attend on Tuesdays than it was for SSRD members to attend on Sundays was rarely acknowledged. TIL members, especially the committee, pointed to this varying attendance as proof that they offered more support to SSRD than they received in return, and grumbled about the inequality.

The level of engagement between the teams remained unequal because there were more TIL skaters who were willing and able to referee than SSRD skaters. Inexperienced referees had in the past volunteered at TIL training, only to refuse to return due to poor behaviour and attitude from TIL skaters. Comments in both committee meetings and casual conversation suggested that several TIL members believed that referees should "toughen up" or accept that there would be a certain amount of grumbling or arguing from skaters, but that it shouldn't be taken personally, and referees should rise above it and ignore it. Whilst this appeared to be a widespread belief, in this specific instance it failed to solve the problem. TIL had previously attempted a zero-tolerance approach to abuse towards referees, but though most members were able to modify their behaviour, some were not, and it often only took one negative experience to put off a rookie referee completely.

The lack of officials was flagged as a cause for concern during all the committee meetings I attended throughout 2015 and 2016. However, there was rarely

32 Community and engagement

any concrete progress made towards fixing this problem. In December 2015, I suggested a plan for officiating, with training plans to be shared with referees so that a complementary referee-training plan could be implemented. This never happened, in part because the training group did not like to publish training plans in advance. Coogan wanted to see more support from SSRD and said he had not seen that happen since he had been a member of TIL, but attempts to build bridges with SSRD were limited, and the belief seemed to be that SSRD members should be taking the initiative.

This insistence that members of SSRD, primarily women, do the greater share of emotional labour, reflects experiences that are discussed in both the global roller derby community (WFTDA, 2019) and wider society itself (Burford *et al.*, 2019; Müller, 2018). Coogan and TIL's committee failed to recognise that SSRD members often had more family and childcare commitments than they did and were therefore less able to devote additional time and energy to roller derby.

At times, outside referee support was solicited – usually through contacts members had with officials from other leagues. Referees from Dundee came to Sheffield for TIL's home game in March 2016, and Skate Mail, a local referee, was drafted in to function as HR throughout the summer of 2016, until he moved away. These were temporary solutions at best and failed to help improve the number of officials in the local area. Despite the Dundee referees running a boot camp after the home game, which Sheffield referee school members were encouraged to attend, numbers did not improve. Trainee referees in attendance at both these initiatives were drawn from a wider area, including Mansfield and Wakefield, and these referees took their learning back to their local leagues, rather than to TIL or SSRD. There may have seemed for a time to be a wider pool of referees to draw from, but though they were sometimes available for games or planned scrimmages with other teams, they were rarely available for practice sessions. NSOs are often the most invisible of the officials, and so, despite frequent volunteers from local women's teams, they were acknowledged much less than referees.

TIL as a league consistently failed to recruit and retain officials from a more local area. One local unaffiliated skater asked if they could attend training sessions for free in return for offering support with coaching and officiating, but this request was turned down as it was felt that this would set a precedent for people attending without paying if they helped out in some capacity. Committee members felt that they worked hard and if they still had to pay dues as well, no one else should get free membership. On the one hand, this decision seemed fair, but considering the long-standing concern regarding lack of officials at training, it was either short-sighted or contradictory; TIL members expressed a need for referees, but did not always respond positively to offers to do so. In February 2016, Broot was struggling to pay dues, and suggested that he was intending to focus on refereeing until he was in a better position. Both routine behaviour and ritual involve symbolism that group members ascribe meaning to, marking them as insiders (Cohen, 1985, p. 43), and in dealing with change, these rituals are important to

Community and engagement 33

bridge the disjunction between the familiar and the unfamiliar, enabling a sense of continuity. Often, skaters will choose to referee for a time if they cannot do contact, such as in the case of injury. In this way, the ritual of refereeing becomes a symbol of continued belonging, however Broot was discouraged from doing so and, told he was not needed, was denied even this feeling of belonging. Shortly after this, Broot left the league.

In addition to my and Andy's feelings regarding our place in the league as discussed in Chapter 5, other potential referees have felt less than welcome at times. In August 2016, the partner of a TIL member attended a scrimmage as a referee. She said she had not refereed for TIL in a long time because "someone was being a complete douche" (Field notes, 7 August 2016) when she did, and she decided not to come back. Again, this sort of response suggested some TIL members behaved in a contradictory way when it came to referee volunteers. The argument discussed previously that referees should "toughen up" might have merit in the long term, but the refusal of some TIL members to moderate their attitude towards newer referees had not proven effective in encouraging these referees to return. Additionally, there was little done by the league or its committee to clamp down on this negative attitude, in part because the attitude had originated with one or two members of the committee who did not seem to see the connection.

In my field notes, I frequently recorded a lack of engagement between officials and coaches. Attending officials were often ignored and not given direction or asked to participate until an hour or more into the session. Potentially, an experienced referee would be able to use their initiative to watch drills to focus on their development, but it is unlikely that a newer official would be confident enough to do this, especially given that TIL members tended to call penalties in drills too, often disagreeing with calls made by officials. In addition, numbers at TIL training sessions were often too low to have a scrimmage, so if a referee did attend, there was no guarantee they would be able to practise refereeing a scrim, and they were not informed in advance. This happened occasionally at SSRD sessions too, and volunteers from TIL expressed their frustration with this, not seeming to realise how this same issue affected potential TIL referees.

Sometimes, TIL members officiated too. They stepped out of training to referee a scrim, or they volunteered to referee SSRD training sessions or games. When TIL members volunteered with SSRD, they considered it to be a favour that should be returned, expecting volunteers to then turn up to TIL training, which again ignored the issues around training times. Seen in terms of Mauss's (1990) exploration of gift exchange, the collective entity TIL "gifts" SSRD with time and officiating skills, resulting in an obligation to return the gift. That it was not returned created tension in that TIL members, especially the committee, viewed SSRD as having broken some kind of unspoken agreement. It is also interesting to note that, although I regularly refereed for TIL, I was not seen as an SSRD member returning the favour. This highlights one of the difficulties of simultaneous membership of more than one community.

34 Community and engagement

Running a grass-roots sport

Venues

As briefly alluded to in the previous section, outside forces, specifically venue managers, acted as an additional barrier to Sheffield teams maintaining close links. Venues proved difficult for TIL for several reasons. Sheffield International Venues (SIV) controls many of the available sports halls in Sheffield, and though ostensibly not-for-profit, venues were expensive, and bookings were subject to cancellation if another event was booked for which SIV could charge a higher price. When I initially joined TIL, practices were held once a week at Hillsborough Leisure Centre, taking place after the SSRD session. This meant that numbers were often higher, as SSRD skaters would stay for the TIL session. Also, officials would often attend both sessions. This helped the teams remain closer.

In the early part of 2013, TIL members also attended SSRD-run skills sessions on Wednesdays at Ponds Forge. This meant that new skaters were introduced to roller derby in an all-gender environment, and the small number of new TIL skaters could immediately feel part of something. Grievous remembers these early days fondly.

> But you know, I enjoyed it. I think my first six months I would say was probably the most fun I had at TIL. Partly because I think pre-mins, I see this when I train fresh meat you know it's such a great time because you've got a clear goal ... you're chasing, passing your mins, erm you're not worrying about you know the pressure of being part of the bouting squad or anything like that. It's much simpler really, and obviously it's all new and fun and also you're not kind of involved in all the politics of it either because you're pre-mins.
>
> (Grievous Interview, 15 January 2016)

However, given this and Grievous' comments about "courtships" between TIL and SSRD, it is clear that during his interview he was feeling nostalgic. Other interviewees focused much less on memories of the two teams training together, although Blocktopus and Daddy Longlegs did both discuss venue changes in negative terms. Later that year, TIL Wednesday sessions were moved to a different venue, Paces, further out of town, but cheaper. This was seen by some as part of a deliberate attempt to distance TIL from SSRD, but was also encouraged by some from SSRD to enable them to create a women-only space, as not everyone enjoyed contact drills and scrimmage with male skaters. As part of TIL at the time, and not being privy to parallel discussions in the women's league, Grievous saw the men's team as the driver of this change.

> I mean I definitely missed training with the girls, because to me that was, always felt like what we should be doing, what derby should be. It should be like an inclusive, we're all doing this together. I think it quite upset me how much some of the guys were anti-SSRD, you know, I was like "dude,

Community and engagement   35

we're all playing the same sport, can we not just get along?" But there were elements of the team that were actively resisting sort of being part of … and that's still going on today, you know.

(Grievous Interview, 15 January 2016)

At the time of the change, Nuke was developing his coaching skills,

> The coaching progressed to the point where I became head coach for SSRD and I setup, I was kind of, as I was part of that league and part of TIL, a joint session on Wednesday's for pre-mins which was open to both TIL and SSRD and I committed to developing that. Got coaches in place for and even were sharing the work between the two teams for the financial and coaching responsibility of it.

(Nuke Interview, 22 August 2016)

He had worked hard to develop this session as a space for newer skaters in both teams to learn together. As Nuke was committed to inclusivity in roller derby and wanted to see the men's side of the sport become "open" rather than gender based, this sort of development was important to him. After the change in venue for TIL, Nuke made the decision to continue coaching SSRD rather than attending TIL's Wednesday session. He felt committed to this session, and "[he] enjoyed doing it and [he] thought it went well" (Nuke Interview 22 August 2016).

The change in venue clearly had impacts on individuals within the team, and though it was proposed partly on the basis of cost saving, there were clearly other agendas. The training sessions worked well for a while, but did impact numbers attending, and did separate the two teams, as the skills sessions were now run concurrently, in different parts of the city.

From this point, then, the teams were not training together, although they still shared the same venue on Sundays and there was still a fair amount of crossover in attendance at each other's sessions on this day. The closure of Hillsborough to put in a sprung floor, unsuitable for skating on, meant, however, that both teams had to find a different Sunday training venue. Eventually, SSRD settled on Springs Leisure Centre, whilst TIL moved to Forge Valley. Although at opposite sides of the city, training was now at different times, and it was still theoretically possible to attend both sessions, albeit with the additional complication as discussed in the previous section, of attendance at both leading to a very lengthy training day. Largely because of this, team crossover declined considerably, with no TIL members attending SSRD sessions on Sundays, and very few SSRD members only infrequently attending TIL Sunday sessions. This lack of crossover meant that newer skaters on each team had less opportunity to get to know each other, and already strained links became even weaker as physical distance became symbolic of the emotional distance that had grown between the two teams. In both the "imaginary community" of "the game", and the real community of place (Spracklen, 1996, p. 135) the teams were now separate. Though community is associated

36 Community and engagement

with shared meanings and mutual knowledge (Cohen, 1982, 1985; Spracklen, 1996) there was now a clearer divide between men's and women's roller derby that created tension as different meanings come into conflict.

During the 2015–2016 season, TIL trained at Forge Valley from 8:00 to 10:00 pm on Wednesdays and 6:00 to 8:30 pm on Sundays. They seemed to have built up a good relationship with the managers of the sports hall, leaving equipment in the storeroom, and having laid a permanent track. This saved time at the start of each session, and allowed for more accuracy, as there was a defined track boundary rather than an approximate edge marked with cut up mouse mats, as had previously been the case.

However, the hall was only big enough for training and the occasional scrimmage, as there was no room for outside pack referees. TIL were still able to hold a few games there against other teams, or as part of Sheffield Roller Derby, but it was unsuitable for open events due to its size. TIL could host games that were "closed", and this was useful for training, but the lack of an OPR lane prevented its use for sanctioned games, and the general lack of space prevented "open" events which would attract paying audiences. This limited the league's ability to generate income from games, and therefore, retaining members and recruiting new ones becomes more important.

Another issue with the venue was its location. Although transport links were relatively good, members struggled to get to the venue if they were outside Sheffield or if they relied on public transport. This was discussed within the committee as a poor excuse for not attending. Nevertheless, it remained an issue, not least as regards retaining members.

For open games, then, venue choice was limited, and often expensive to the point that making any kind of profit was difficult. There existed a tension between the desire to have events that were as cheap as possible to run, and the desire to get as many people in the audience as possible. The money made at games through entrance fee, refreshments, and merchandise could be used for subsidising travel, guest coaches, and promoting the team. TIL's 2015 home Champs game was held in Dewsbury, as the venue was significantly cheaper than any in Sheffield. A cheaper venue hire meant TIL could charge less for tickets, which potentially could encourage a bigger audience. This event was a modest success, demonstrating that TIL could organise a game without support from other leagues, but also, it failed to make a profit.

> Overall, I would call this event a qualified success. We did not make a profit on the day, but the loss was small. Venue issues came to the fore, and we were forced to decamp to Dewsbury. Although the leisure centre there is a good roller derby space, it was commonly felt that straying too far from home ground prevented us really making the most of the opportunity to rake in some much-needed funds. It also made organisation more difficult, and attendance (both spectators and potential staffing) lower than it could have been.
>
> (TIL AGM Statement, April 2015)

Members felt that, in future, they would rather hold their home game at home in Sheffield, weighing up the greater venue outgoings with potential for a bigger audience.

This decision proved to be a good one, as TIL did make a small profit from their next home game:

> The home game was more profitable than last year, probably due to being held in our home city, and because of greater involvement of TIL members both in the run up to the game and on the day.
>
> (TIL AGM Statement, April 2016)

This does strongly suggest that greater engagement from league members, including a push on promotion, and a wider variety of stalls and merchandise on offer at the event, meant a greater attractiveness to home audiences. These considerations have always been finely balanced, and regardless of the level of work and input from league members, spiralling venue costs remained the number one barrier to the success of TIL.

The cost of venues represents a significant challenge to the growth of the sport as a whole, and to TIL as a league. Rainy City Roller Derby, based in Oldham, have their own venue, the Thunderdome, an old warehouse they have transformed into a training and bouting space. Although this required hard work over a long period of time from league members, it allowed them to train more often and build their league to the point where their A-Team were playing in Division 1 of the WFTDA, and they had B, C, and D teams. A venue of one's own is a dream for many roller derby leagues, and there was discussion of this within TIL. Although the league had never been in a financial position to consider doing this themselves, there had been many cross-league discussions regarding a warehouse for Sheffield teams.

A training and bouting space of their own would solve many of the venue problems – they would not be so reliant on expensive SIV venues, and depending on location, it could be more convenient for members. One sticking point, however, was the level of engagement that would be required from all league members to make it a realistic prospect. Members who rarely showed up for training were unlikely to give up extra time for the running of a warehouse space. Additionally, it would require good communication and support between the Sheffield leagues, which, given the feelings on both sides, was unlikely during the period of fieldwork.

Doing-it-yourself

Coogan spoke extensively of his views about the sport and what he thought was holding it back: those who join for derby's alternative, DIY image, and not for the sport itself.

> Roller derby comes from a DIY ethos which I'm very familiar with I'm you know I've listened to punk music my whole life you know that whole DIY

thing that you do it yourself, don't rely on anybody else it's all about hard graft ... [but] it's not like it was back in the DIY days.

(Coogan Interview, 31 May 2016)

However, in saying this, Coogan did not make the connection that roller derby still was very much a DIY sport. Although the focus is changing to be less about the peripheral entertainment and more about the athleticism on track, leagues and events are still run by members, often without any kind of sponsorship, and relying solely on fundraising efforts through the events themselves, and merchandise. As chair, he did encourage greater involvement from all members, and often embodied this notion of "hard graft", but in conversation he sought to position roller derby as a sport, not as part of an "alternative" lifestyle. Coogan's view also failed to take account of the showmanship and spectacle that is often part of mainstream sport – that commercial sport *is* entertainment – and so, there are arguments to suggest retaining some of the "sillier" aspects of roller derby.

Another barrier to TIL's growth was the lack of any coordinated approach to promotion and recruitment. In a DIY league, it can be difficult to ensure the right people are performing the right roles, and often people took on a role simply because they were the only person willing to do it. I was TIL's events coordinator for two years despite having no prior experience of events management. During that two years, the sponsorship position was vacant more often than it was filled, recruitment was run by the membership officer, whose time was often filled with chasing non-payment of dues, and non-attending members, and promotion was under the remit of the media officer, which involved running the league's social media sites and not much more.

Although members had ideas, not all were prepared to put the time in, and those that were often did not have the expertise to fully realise these ideas. Committee meetings were often taken up with dealing with day-to-day matters, or with excuses as to why things were not done. Engagement of members was variable. Both Coogan and Frank, as chairs of TIL, struggled to get members involved with supporting and helping to run the league. Both explained that they had never wanted to be chair, and did not believe they were particularly good leaders, but they wanted to give something back to the league, and, each time, were the only ones volunteering to do it, so they were both elected unopposed.

Coogan took over as chair during a difficult period after a lot of members had left, so he saw his role as rebuilding the league; asking what members wanted and taking it from there.

Like, I'd seen two previous chairs and then a mish mash of a lot of shit. And it was always obvious to me that people have no idea what they're doing, they're not listening to the league, they pretend to listen, they say what do you want? Then pretend to listen and then do whatever the fuck they wanted

Community and engagement   39

> to, but it wasn't right for the team. And so yeah, I do think that the way I [led the league] helped.
>
> (Coogan Interview, 31 May 2016)

After discussing what the team wanted, he felt empowered to make decisions on behalf of the league. He could be quite autocratic and justified this by arguing that other league members should step up to vacant roles if they wanted more influence in the league. TIL was more stable by the point Frank took over, and he ran things differently, more democratically.

> You know you've got to try and make it as open to league members as much as possible, so you try and keep them involved in certain situations which are going on and it's difficult to sort of stay impartial as well. Because you are meant to be as impartial as possible. Things get on my nerves as well I want to sort of like tell people what I think is a bullshit, but you've got to try your hardest to sort of not lead people on to things. Or not lead people into decisions. And it's quite difficult to do.
>
> (Frank Interview, 17 August 2016)

Despite differences in leadership style, both chairs tried hard to engage members, and both found it very difficult, with low numbers, and lack of enthusiasm for doing league work outside of skating. With such reluctance on the part of members, it is perhaps not surprising that members also fail to engage with those outside the sport.

Within Sheffield, roller derby did not seem to be widely known or supported outside the central derby community. There were three teams in Sheffield, but engagement both with and from the local community was sporadic at best. Whilst SSRD was involved with national initiatives, such as Sport England's *This Girl Can* campaign, there were no such initiatives for men's sport. Stuntman and Andy Social were involved in fundraising for Sheffield Children's Hospital, and Fin was engaged in the support and promotion of issues of concern to the trans community, but these actions were largely individual, rather than league wide. Teammates supported these efforts but were not engaged themselves. Some members just wanted to skate twice a week and not think about it for the rest of the time. There did not seem to be the same passion for raising the profile of the sport in the men's league. Engagement was minimal.

Engagement with ex-members was also minimal. As membership officer, Jason would occasionally message ex-members to let them know that the door was always open should they want to return, but many ex-members found they had little reason to keep in touch. The majority of current members did not know those who left prior to 2016: high turnover, and low membership led to a lack of continuity and many ex-members had become strangers.

Recruiting new members was another area beset by lack of engagement. In 2013/2014, the committee decided on a large-scale recruitment process they

40 Community and engagement

referred to as "Dead Meat". Interested people were recruited for a 12-week programme to teach them the basics of roller derby and pass their minimum skills. This was the first time the league had approached training in this way. They hired a hall in Stocksbridge, and one member, who owned a skate shop at the time, loaned kit for the new skaters. Dead Meat was a resounding failure. New skaters were not properly integrated into the league, it was expensive to train them, coaches were not always available, and some potential skaters disappeared with hire kit and never returned, overall, the programme lost the team around £1200, money they could ill afford to lose. Very few Dead Meat skaters graduated to the main league. Since then, TIL have ceased recruiting in this way, instead continuing to have members join and train them in an ad hoc way. In any league discussion on recruitment, Dead Meat invariably gets a mention, with one or two members making snide and sarcastic comments. The refrain "ask about buy-back", in reference to a tagline on a recruitment poster offering new skaters loan kit to keep at a reduced price, was often used to derail conversations about the best ways to get new people interested in roller derby.

Although the more recent ad hoc approach was a very slow way of recruiting, members felt it was more successful. Pipkin joined in this way and felt a sense of belonging from the start. New skaters were more successfully integrated into the league and saw gameplay early on, giving them a better understanding of both the league and the sport.

Social media is a valuable tool for recruiting, but it was rarely used to its full potential in TIL. The league had a website, a Facebook page, a Twitter account and an Instagram account. The media officer on committee was responsible for the upkeep of these, and though other members chipped in on occasion, it was largely left to a single person to manage. There were several periods where a member with this responsibility left without passing on any information to others, and so the post was vacant, with very little outward communication happening.

The website changed several times over the years, with the version used during the 2015–2016 season being very basic and containing very little historical information. For example, there was no reference to Zom B Cru at all. This could be seen as the previous media officer, Beat Monkey's, and the committee's, wish to break with the past and focus just on the team moving forward. It could also be an attempt to conceal or suppress the past, and curate the public image of TIL, as discussed in Chapter 3. A community's past may be used as a resource to manage change, and as a "repository of meaning and a referent of their identity" (Cohen 1985, p. 118), but TIL chose instead to break with the past completely, ignoring their rich history, which, though not always pleasant, was interesting, and was sometimes more successful in engaging with the wider community. The discourse of community that TIL were engaged in thinking and talking about here suggested they were an independent group with a strong boundary with little interaction with the wider Sheffield roller derby community.

The wider roller derby community

Beyond the local community, there was a wide world of roller derby; men's, women's, and OTA teams throughout the world, and a number of recognised governing bodies. Men's roller derby is governed by the MRDA worldwide, and the UKRDA within the UK. TIL had been members of the MRDA since 2013. Though they were also members of the UKRDA, they had discussed letting their membership lapse, MRDA membership being considered more important. Membership of either was voluntary but could confer advantages.

The United Kingdom Roller Derby Association (the aforementioned UKRDA) is a voluntary organisation set up to promote the sport of roller derby in the UK. It is run by volunteers from the roller derby community and is recognised by the British Roller Sports Federation (BRSF). During 2016, leagues paid £100 a year for membership.

It was difficult to find information about the inner workings of the UKRDA. As they are a private limited company, information about their directors and accounts should be made public, but it was apparent that much of the publicly accessible information was out of date. The information that could be found suggested that the UKRDA were not particularly active. They raised money through membership dues but had not done anything with that money. As of April 2016, their assets were £7562, a figure that had been steadily rising over the last five years (Companies House, 2017).

UKRDA continued to post on their website occasionally, but other than organising an annual roller derby tournament at the Tattoo Freeze tattoo festival, they were very quiet. As a result of this lack of action, TIL discussed whether it was worth continuing to be members of the association, as they were seeing no return for their money. The connection with BRSF as the governing body recognised by Sport England did open up accessibility for specific funding pots, but these were often not available to men's teams, and in any case, no one in TIL had the time or inclination to apply, and so the potential link between roller derby leagues throughout the UK was the only aspect of the UKRDA that was of value to TIL, and then only as a source of sanctioned games.

In late 2019, I made an abortive attempt to become a director of the UKRDA. Although voted in by member league representatives, and officially appointed Director of PR and Communications/Diversity and Inclusion by the Board of Directors, I resigned after a month. Becoming a party to the inner workings of the UKRDA did not immediately provide adequate reassurance as to the relevance of the organisation. In fact, it quickly became apparent that the UKRDA's finances were in a mess, and the Board spent the first month engaging in a process of boundary work, arguing that one of the Directors who had been voted in should be dismissed because of previous sanctions placed on them by governing bodies including the UKRDA. This strongly suggested that the problems and complexities existing within roller derby leagues was also a feature of governing bodies, and that this community existed in the thinking and talking about as much as, or

42 Community and engagement

probably more than, in the doing. Board members discussed what they felt the UKRDA should or did represent and though there was consensus that it should be relevant and represent the sport, the community was fractured to the point that there was not even the appearance of similarity.

The British Roller Derby Championships, often known as British Champs, or simply Champs, was a national interleague tournament divided into four tiers for women and three tiers for men. The tournament began as the End of the World Series, a competition between six women's teams based in the Midlands. Rebranded the following year as the Heartland Series, it grew over two years to 24 teams. The first British Roller Derby Championships in 2015 featured 72 teams, including, for the first time, men's teams (British Champs, 2015).

Although it ran with the support of the UKRDA, they were separate organisations, and British Champs was funded through entry fees (UKRDA, 2014). Although the first season did feature UKRDA-sanctioned games, due to the silence of that organisation few games were sanctioned by them in 2016, in fact, TIL had not had a game sanctioned by them since September 2015 (Flat Track Stats, 2017).

British Champs had its share of controversy in the roller derby community. Again, it was difficult to find out anything about the organisers, or what happened to the entry fees. During the season, leagues took financial responsibility for putting on games, but Champs paid for the Playoffs, which was a two-day event held to decide which leagues would be promoted and which demoted for some tiers. Entry fees to the competition were £72.50 per league, and in 2016, 86 teams took part (66 women's teams, and 20 men's teams). It was unclear what this entry fee was spent on. In addition, the organisers issued demerits for leagues who failed to supply officials or rosters on time, and games were forfeit under certain circumstances, such as if players were fielded who were not on the published roster. A forfeit game resulted in a 300–0 victory to the other team. This caused problems in that teams finished in the relegation zone whilst performing better than teams who benefitted from a forfeit. Also, the lack of transparency of the organisation meant that some leagues received demerits or had games forfeited where they felt it was undeserved.

The organisation of Champs was a little opaque, and it was difficult to be certain who was in charge, and who made the decisions. Tournament and Tier head officials were publicised on the website, but beyond that, it was silent. Roller Derby on Film experienced difficulties with the British Champs organisers with their photography waiver, which he said was "bizarre" and "ridiculous", being very restrictive and showing a lack of understanding of how photographers work. He suggested that the organisers would not listen to his concerns until the top names in the sport responded to and supported his position. This does suggest a hierarchy within the sport, where those with a talent for self-promotion got heard more than others and underscores how difficult communication with Champs could be.

Despite these issues, many leagues continued to engage with Champs, as did TIL, because it offered a season structure and a guaranteed five games a year

Community and engagement   43

against opponents of a broadly similar standard, and only one of those would be a home game, which reduced the financial burden considerably, whilst still allowing for gameplay. TIL took part in all seasons of British Champs. In 2015, they were put in Tier 2, winning three out of their five games, losing only to Manchester's New Wheeled Order, and Barrow Infernos. Both teams went up to Tier 1 in 2016. TIL stayed in Tier 2, going on to win four of their five games, and at the end of the 2016 season, were promoted to Tier 1 for 2017.

The MRDA ran along the same lines as WFTDA. Member leagues made the decisions: the organisation was democratic, and volunteer led. Not everyone was happy about this.

> We keep on getting shit and stuff through MRDA you know they're supposed to be our governing body saying, we're looking at these rules and we're thinking about changing them, we'd like your opinion. And it's like oh for fuck's sake really. You know yeah, I've talked about listening. You need to listen but there's a point then when you listen too much. You need to get a good idea, you need to go forwards with it, test it out if you've got a good idea. We get so much stuff through on the TIL page from MRDA and they're not leaning in any direction, they're just wanting the teams to pull them forwards and it's the wrong way of going about it.
>
> (Coogan Interview, 31 May 2016)

Coogan believed MRDA should be run along the same lines as his tenure as chair of TIL: canvas member opinion, and then get on with the job. TIL struggled to keep up to date with MRDA and UKRDA requirements due to lack of interest in the role of representative for the team. In May 2015, the plan was to merge the roles, so there would be three people representing TIL in both organisations. By mid-2016, TIL were still having difficulty in filling these roles.

MRDA required engagement from member leagues, so leagues had representatives on the MRDA forum who were expected to take part in discussions and vote on behalf of the league. Although this was not an especially onerous task, it generally fell to members who were already part of the committee, so already taking on the bulk of the administrative work. But without members on the forum, TIL were excluded from discussions affecting the men's roller derby community, isolating them from the wider organisation. MRDA membership fees were £175, but without the engagement, TIL received little return on this investment, as sanctioning games (which opens the door to involvement in MRDA tournaments) required engagement on the forum.

Although several members of TIL were not very involved in wider debates, there were those who felt passionate about the future of roller derby, and specific issues bound up in that future. In December 2015, the committee discussed the nature of TIL as a men's, co-ed, or open league; the latter being the preferred model – that is, people were selected on ability. They argued that the MRDA non-discrimination policy gave them the lead to be much more gender inclusive.

44 Community and engagement

As UKRDA policy stated that women could only play for one league and Champs would not allow mixed teams, the decision was made to contact both to raise the issue and ask for their take. By mid-2016, there had been no response from UKRDA. The committee said that any further discussion or plans would need to be discussed with the whole membership, but it was clear that this meant potentially withdrawing from UKRDA membership and/or the British Champs competition.

Nuke was keen for TIL to go down the "open" route, believing that a policy that selected skaters on ability rather than gender was a better way to organise the league (this is discussed further in Chapter 3). He saw both British Champs and UKRDA as standing in the way of that, because both organisations stated that a skater could not compete for teams in both the men's and the women's tiers, despite the tiers remaining separate. He explained:

> So, I wouldn't have a problem with somebody being in a women's league also being in an open league and very few people I talk to share that viewpoint. And Champs and UKRDA also don't share that viewpoint.
>
> (Nuke Interview, 22 August 2016)

In fact, MRDA and WFTDA said the same thing, so Nuke's view had very little support in the wider community. He did argue that MRDA was the most inclusive of all the organisations and would require only a change of focus to become "open" rather than "men's". This would go some way to solving the issue of non-binary skaters having to choose which gender they most identified with, as there was no organisation specifically for them; there was men's and there was women's, more recently referred to as MRDA-aligned and WFTDA-aligned in an attempt to be less binary, but still skaters had to decide which one was the best fit. This changing environment had a positive impact within TIL, however, allowing Fin to join, and also allowing cisgender women to join the team, if MRDA roller derby was where they preferred to be.

This chapter highlights some of the difficulties of running a grass-roots league, and indeed, sport. The boundary work the TIL committee engaged in had a number of impacts throughout the local roller derby community, serving to push certain groups and individuals towards the fringes of the team. In this there did seem to be a gendered aspect, although it was not the only way in which a lack of understanding of inclusion needs was evident.

The committee showed a lack of concern for time commitments, which impacted more on women who were more likely to have substantial caring commitments and less on the men who were often single. Three members became fathers during my fieldwork, however, and in each case, they took a substantial amount of time out from league work, without complaint. The marginalisation of officials in the roller derby community was compounded at TIL training because the venue was smaller, meaning they did not have space to conduct their own training in a way they did at SSRD training. Attitudes towards referees were demonstrably worse when referees were new and/or female. Lower income and

Community and engagement   45

financially disadvantaged skaters faced marginalisation if they relied on public transport, and therefore failed to make training on time, or at all.

Ties of belonging were important to TIL members. The failure of Dead Meat indicated what happened when people did not have those ties. Members struggled to understand why it failed, when SSRD's similar new intake system had proven successful time and time again. Holding Dead Meat training sessions in a venue far out of the city centre emphasised the above issues making access limited to a privileged few. Additionally, these new members were isolated and separated from the main league.

Engagement, or rather the lack of it, was an issue not just for TIL, but for the roller derby community as a whole. There was strength in numbers, but the fractured nature within leagues, between leagues from similar geographical areas, and between leagues and governing bodies acted as a substantial stumbling block on the path to the development of the sport. Roller derby was still a relatively new sport, and people joined for many different reasons. Lash (1994) writes about community as chosen and reflexive, May (2011) says belonging is dynamic and relational, and Bennett (2015) theorises belonging as a practice, something people do. Yet some members did not consider what they were doing to be community at all. For them, it was just a sport, just exercise. They accepted roller derby was "for the skaters" but had yet to come to terms with the idea of roller derby also being "by the skaters". So, although TIL existed in the form it did because of a collective internal definition of what and why they were (Jenkins, 2014), the same action, the same practice, had different meanings for members (Cohen, 1985) and although individuals shared a nominal identity, that of TIL member, they "did" this membership differently.

The discourse of "independence", for example, meant something different to successive league chairs. For Daddy Longlegs, independence meant maintaining ties with other leagues, but not relying on them; having clear leadership; and the ability to run their own events. Coogan's notion of independence required becoming insular, withdrawing from the community, and closing themselves off from "outsiders". The strained links between TIL and other Sheffield leagues, and officials, impacted their ability to put on events and the success of those events. TIL appeared weaker when the league was inwardly focused, and the wider communities and organisations like the UKRDA, Champs, and MRDA also clearly struggled with engagement levels. I would argue that the strength of the roller derby community lies not in clearly defined boundaries, but in the many linked communities: the multiplexity (Cohen, 1985). A failure to adequately recognise this was a weakness, and so ties with SSRD, with officials, and with potential recruits also became weaker.

The chair of TIL was usually the one with the power to define a situation, control the discourse and influence the ethos of the league. This was especially apparent if the chair was also a skater with high skills capital, such as Coogan. His determination to move away from roller derby as an alternative sport, and to focus on the performance of the team as a sports team rather than a community, negatively impacted not just the strength of the community, but ironically, the strength of the team as well, as engagement suffered, and fewer members were taking on league work. Additionally, such clear boundaries meant that more people existed at the margins, and so were less inclined to feel part of TIL, which meant they were less inclined to engage. Moreover, the way the league moved towards a more traditional sports model during this time, meant that discourse and practice both became less accepting. Although league members liked to believe that TIL was very inclusive, during the first part of my fieldwork, this was not the case. In later chapters, I explore examples from these months, which highlight the impact of traditional, mainstream models of sport, but I also explore the impact of changes that took place in the latter half of fieldwork, after Frank became chair. In Chapters 4 and 5, I return to the practices members engage in to create a sense of community, and the ways some members, especially officials, can experience barriers to feelings of belonging. Before that, in Chapter 3, I turn to a discussion of how the identity of the group developed over time and explore how the identities of individual members are constructed.

References

Barry, B. (2018) (Re)fashioning masculinity: Social identity and context in men's hybrid masculinities through dress. *Gender and Society* [Online], 30 May, 1–25. DOI: 10.1177/0891243218774495.

Barth, F. (1969) *Ethnic Groups and Boundaries*. Boston, MA, Little Brown.

Beaver, T. D. (2012) By the skaters, for the skaters: The DIY ethos of the roller derby revival. *Journal of Sport & Social Issues*, 36(1), pp. 25–49. DOI: 10.1177/0193723511433862.

Bennett, J. (2015) "Snowed in!": Offbeat rhythms and belonging as everyday practice. *Sociology*, 49(5), pp. 955–969. DOI: 10.1177/0038038515589299.

British Champs (2015) "Tournament history". *British Championships*. Available from: www.britishchamps.com/tournament-history/ (accessed 1 September 2017).

British Champs (2019) "2019 Survey findings". *British Championships*. Available from: https://docs.google.com/presentation/d/1wNXMXAzwE7J4M9hQXE97T8wfJuoB NdT7DXbikjpx04s/edit?fbclid=IwAR1OpOR3A24Jaqajlzi0s80jVcJDsy0sqT_u8ku 3botTD1jINz-vTZDF28w#slide=id.p1 (accessed 1 November 2019).

Burford, J., Bosanquet, A., and Smith, J. (2019) "Homeliness meant having the fucking vacuum cleaner out": The gendered labour of maintaining conference communities. *Gender and Education*, 32(1), pp. 86–100. DOI: 10.1080/09540253.2019.1680809.

Cohen, A. P. (1982) Belonging: The experience of culture, in A. P. Cohen (ed.), *Belonging: Identity and Social Organisation in British Rural Cultures*. Manchester, Manchester University Press, pp. 1–19.

Cohen, A. P. (1985) *The Symbolic Construction of Community*. London, Routledge.

Cohen, A. P. (1986) *Symbolising Boundaries: Identity and Diversity in British Cultures*. Manchester, Manchester University Press.

Companies House (2017) "United Kingdom Roller Derby Association Limited". *Gov. UK*. Available from: https://beta.companieshouse.gov.uk/company/07614295 (accessed 1 September 2017).

Delanty, G. (2010) *Community*. London, Routledge.

Flat Track Stats (2017) "The Inhuman League". *Flat Track Stats*. Available from: http://flattrackstats.com/teams/17613 (accessed 5 November 2017).

Goffman, E. (1959) *The Presentation of Self in Everyday Life*. London, Penguin.

Jenkins, R. (2014) *Social Identity* (4th edn). London, Routledge.

Lash, S. (1994) Reflexivity and its doubles: Structure, aesthetics, community, in U. Beck, A. Giddens, and S. Lash (eds), *Reflexive Modernization: Politics, Tradition, and Aesthetics in the Modern Social Order*. Stanford, CA, Stanford University Press, pp. 110–173.

London Roller Derby (2019) "Who are we?". *London Rollergirls*. Available from: http://londonrollergirls.com/who-are-we/ (accessed 27 August 2019).

Mabe, C. (2007) *Roller Derby: The History and All-Girl Revival of the Greatest Sport on Wheels*. Denver, CO, Speck Press.

Mauss, M. (1990) *The Gift: The Form and Reason for Exchange in Archaic Societies*. London, Routledge.

May, V. (2011) Self, belonging and social change. *Sociology*, 45(3), pp. 363–378. DOI: 10.1177/0038038511399624.

McHugh, T. F., Coppola, A. M., Holt, N. L., and Andersen, C. (2015) "Sport *is* community": An exploration of urban Aboriginal peoples' meanings of community within the context of sport. *Psychology of Sport and Exercise*, 18, pp. 75–84. DOI: 10.1177/1049732318759668.

Morgan, D. H. J. (2011) *Rethinking Family Practices*. Basingstoke, Palgrave Macmillan.

Müller, M. (2018) Emotional labour: A case of gender-specific exploitation. *Critical Review of International Social and Political Philosophy*, 22(7), pp. 841–862. DOI: 10.1080/13698230.2018.1438332.

Mynard, L., Howie, L., and Collister, L. (2009) Belonging to a community-based football team: An ethnographic study. *Australian Occupational Therapy Journal*, 56, pp. 266–274. DOI: 10.1111/j.1440–1630.2008.00741.x.

Pavlidis, A. and Fullagar, S. (2014) *Sport, Gender and Power: The Rise of Roller Derby*. Farnham, Ashgate.

Spracklen, K. (1996) *"Playing the Ball": Constructing Community and Masculine Identity in Rugby: An Analysis of the Two Codes of League and Union and the People Involved*. PhD thesis, Leeds Metropolitan University.

Stone, C. (2017) Utopian community football? Sport, hope and belongingness in the lives of refugees and asylum seekers. *Leisure Studies*, 37(2), pp. 171–183. DOI: 10.1080/02614367.2017.1329336.

UKRDA (2014) "UKRDA's role in British Championships". *UKRDA*. Available from: https://ukrda.org.uk/2014/11/ukrdas-role-in-british-championships/ (accessed 1 September 2017).

West, C. and Zimmerman, H. (1987) Doing gender. *Gender and Society*, 1, pp. 125–151. DOI: 10.1177/0891243287001002002.

WFTDA (2016) "Mission Statement". *WFTDA.org*. Available from: https://wftda.org/mission (accessed 2 May 2018).

WFTDA (2019) "WFTDA statement regarding the dissolution of relationship with the MRDA". *WFTDA.com*. Available from: www.wftda.com/wftda-statement-regarding-the-dissolution-of-relationship-with-the-mrda/ (accessed 21 December 2019).

Wichmann, A. (2015) Participating in the World Gymnaestrada: An expression and experience of community. *Leisure Studies*, 36(1), pp. 21–38. DOI: 10.1080/02614367.2015.1052836.

Chapter 3

Image and identity

I joined The Inhuman League during its most successful period to date: The A-Team were fourth in Europe, and we had a successful B-Team. Members worked to create and maintain a public image as a friendly, "nice" team, but within the team there were tensions, which became increasingly apparent as time went on. There was a divide between the A- and B-Teams, and a divide between those who wanted to be "serious" and "professional", and those for whom roller derby was a fun hobby. Over a period of several months, almost a dozen members left – mostly either skaters who wanted to push themselves further and felt other teams would be better for them, or skaters who did not like the increased seriousness and team politics, and so dropped out of the sport entirely. This meant that the B-Team had to be disbanded, and the league had to think about redefining itself, not just to outside observers, other teams, and fans, but from within. Taking from Jenkins (2014) the idea of identity as the capacity "to know 'who's who' (and hence 'what's what')" (Jenkins, 2014, p. 6), and using Goffman's (1959) concept of impression management, this chapter is an attempt to capture the self- and public image of members of TIL and the whole league; to explore how these identities were developed and maintained, an attempt which also recognises identity, or identification, as a process, rather than a thing one has (Goffman, 1959; Jenkins, 2014).

I begin with a discussion of choices skaters made that contributed towards the development of an individual roller derby identity, examining the practice of selecting a skate name and a number, and exploring the impact clothing choices had. These aspects of roller derby have been discussed in both academic and non-academic texts and are often gendered – being presented as a way for women in the sport to subvert gender norms, through the creation of a "tough"-sounding name, for example, or hyper-sexualised clothing. The suggestions from these texts are that such choices are not open to men in the same way (Murray, 2012), and my own observations support the argument that, especially in terms of clothing, men were often ridiculed for dressing in creative ways. Including data from my ethnography, and from a pilot study into "boutfit" (outfits worn for a roller derby bout, or game) choices, I explore how men used names, numbers, and boutfits to express their masculinity, and femininity, in ways which were just as successful at calling into question accepted gender norms.

In the second part of this chapter, I explore discourses (Foucault, 1972) within the team that were focused on the image members wished to create of themselves as a collective. Many of these discourses involved the desire to make a good impression, and to develop a positive image for the team. Through impression management, the league variously positioned itself as "calm", or as the underdog. Importantly, the league continually attempted to foster the impression that it was inclusive, and hence a space to welcome difference. I discuss how a commitment to inclusivity worked in practice more thoroughly in Chapter 4, but here I focus on the *discourse* of inclusivity and how it was used to build a picture of what the league believed about itself, and the image it wanted to project to the rest of the roller derby community.

Data from interviews was especially pertinent in exploring perspectives of image and identity. I conducted 16 interviews with both current and ex-members of The Inhuman League, and one non-member. Including ex-members facilitated a more thorough analysis of group dynamics, and the development of athletic identities, through discussions with those who were "unsuccessful" (Pavlidis and Fullagar, 2014). I sought consent for interviews separately, identifying individuals I wanted to interview partly on the basis of availability and interest (interviewees were often self-selecting) and partly according to a very basic sampling process, which entailed seeking out participants who were new members, high-level skaters, and less experienced skaters, in addition to ex-members and volunteers, in an attempt to include as wide a variety of experiences as possible. Interviews took the form of life histories, focused specifically on sport, and their time with TIL. They were deliberately conversational, and semi-structured in the sense that I had an interview schedule or map which outlined specific questions I was interested in asking, but interviewees were encouraged to take the conversation in any direction. We explored ideas around inclusivity, gender equality, and professionalisation. As I transcribed each interview, I sent a copy to the interviewee to confirm they were happy with it. One interviewee requested I redact a specific comment about another member, and one requested I reword a phrase he used because of a concern that his point might be misunderstood. Given the potential for harm, I agreed to the omissions. The interviews were transcribed, and coded, and then analysed alongside field notes within a situational analysis framework (Clarke, 2005).

Interviews enabled me to gain insight into how members created their identities, into how they maintained or challenged perceptions (Kleinman *et al.*, 1994). As an interviewer, I had access to feelings, ideas, and thoughts, either hidden or not shown, in the research setting (Okely, 2009), and interviews offered a way to interrogate the silences and absences of the group setting. Most of my interviewees were male, and cross-gender interviewing had its own challenges. Ortiz (2003) found that gender was negotiable in the field, and that one way of "doing gender" (West and Zimmerman, 1987) was through "muted masculinity" (Ortiz, 2003, p. 608), which enabled him to be thought of as an acceptably incompetent outsider. Although the gendered context of my interviews was different, my largely male

50   Image and identity

interviewees performed "knowledgeable" identities (Pini, 2005), thus allowing me to also position myself as "acceptably incompetent", despite being an insider. Through this strategy, participants were more open to sharing their thoughts. Additionally, recognising and accepting that I was not in control of the direction the interviews took (Browne, 2003), allowed me to focus instead on attempts to understand how and why the participants responded in the way they did.

In addition to the gendered context of interviews, it was important to consider the impact of friendship and insider knowledge. The interviewees were mostly friends and fellow team members, a situation that brought with it its own set of challenges, and required a different approach (DeLyser, 2001). It is for this reason that I decided to use a more conversational interview style; to allow for the potential to say "This is how it was for me. How was it for you?" to explore the different responses to the same situation, rather than pretend I was not present. In many interviews, questions were met with "well, *you* know, of course", or similar. It was also necessary to begin interviews with the disclaimer that we may have already discussed topics or questions before (Chavez, 2008; DeLyser, 2001), but that I was interested in hearing their thoughts again.

There were benefits to interviewing friends. As a less formal arrangement, these interviews were more flexible, and there was greater potential for rearrangement (Browne, 2003). Also, it became possible to reward participation in a myriad of intangible ways. I was able to offer participants rewards for their time such as dinner, or time spent with my dogs (Grievous, in particular, found this to be a fair trade). Interviewing those I had a personal relationship with in either my home or the homes of participants, with friends and partners present allowed for a more natural dialogue, and for the inclusion of their responses also. However, due to the additional emotional factors inherent in conducting fieldwork and interviews with friends, I propose that clear processes and boundaries to the research are vital. Situational analysis provided those processes for my research.

Names and numbers

One of the ways members maintained an identity was through skate names and numbers. The concept of the skate name, or roller derby persona, has arguably entered the public imaginary more effectively than the sport itself. Names are written about on popular blogs and websites, and in academic articles about the sport. Popularised in books published by and about roller derby participants (Barbee and Cohen, 2010; Joulwan, 2007; Mabe, 2007), this formulation involves the idea that skaters are normal, everyday *women* "by day", and take on an alter ego or fictitious persona "by night". This interest in the reasons for choosing and using a skate name has spilled over into academic texts. In sociological work on roller derby, there are many discussions of the meanings these names hold for participants (Carlson, 2010; Finley, 2010; Hern, 2010; Mullin, 2012; Murray, 2012; Parrotta, 2015) and, frequently, discussion of how and why naming practices are important. Each number is unique within a team, and each name is unique within the sport (or was until participant numbers grew so large as to make this unfeasible and unrealistic). Through the means of choosing a new name and number for themselves, skaters are said to carve out a new identity within the team and the sport.

Popular publications document the use of derby names as part of skaters creating a "persona": a fictional version of themselves displaying admired, and desired, traits. Skate names have been discussed as a mechanism for engaging with and fighting against hegemonic ideals of gender, ethnicity, and class (Chananie-Hill *et al.*, 2012; Finley, 2010). Researchers argue that the creation of a derby name or persona enables skaters to perform a partially fictionalised identity, which may be more "masculine" than their real self, and allows them to redefine themselves in a way that is empowering (Chananie-Hill *et al.*, 2012; Cohen, 2008; Hern, 2010; McDonald, 2013; Mullin, 2012). Carlson (2010) claims skater names question emphasised femininity, both resisting and reproducing gender norms, through their use of both feminine and masculine descriptors, also finding that "skaters refer to each other almost exclusively by their derby names at practice, at bouts (where the public knows them only by their derby names), and outside of practice; most skaters do not know each other's actual names" (p. 433).

In 2015, Frogmouth Clothing released a Graphical Taxonomy of Roller Derby Skate Names, introducing it in a blog on their website. This blog discussed the roller derby world as "diverse, informed, and creative: a global group of women drawing power and inspiration from everywhere—and especially from other powerful, inspiring women, both real and imagined" (Frogmouth, 2015). The blog fails to account for the names chosen and used by men: Jason Slaysthem, Dodger Moore, David Hasslehoof, and Bollock Obama, whose names feature in the taxonomy, are all men who have played for TIL. A later blog entry suggests that "skate names reveal a lot about the culture of the sport, and the women who play it, including the fact that a lot of them are geeks, and many are science fiction fans" (Frogmouth, 2015). These writers connect the practice of using "alter-egos" with women's roller derby and ignore the men in the sport. This omission fails to recognise how naming works differently in men's roller derby. In TIL, members often did not take names as seriously as the literature would suggest women do, nor did they show respect for each other's choices of name, instead naming practices became subject to banter and power relations.

A roller derby identity always involved negotiation between the claimed identity and the one you were given, and some performances (Goffman, 1959) were more successful than others. Jenkins (2014) suggests the difficulty of changing names, but within TIL there was the added difficulty of disrupting one's own narrative without that disruption being in turn disrupted by teammates. Several skaters' real names were used interchangeably with their skate names, several other skaters had skate names that used their real names as a basis and were often called by a shortened form of these names, which was basically their surname. Sometimes, using a skater's real name was a way of signalling a long friendship, or a close friendship (Blocktopus, for example, tended to use real names, especially

52 Image and identity

for members he was close to during his time at TIL, like Stuntman) but at other times, it was a signal of a refusal to engage with that skaters' identity or persona. Frank-N-Hurter, Skate Mail, and Dr Blocktopus were examples of members and ex-members whose real names were usually used.

Goffman views success in carrying off a performance as a matter of "creating or projecting a definition of a situation" (1959, p. 235). But Jenkins insists that it is not so simple, and there must be a consideration of power, and an understanding of whose definition counts in any one situation, and any performance must be validated by those with power (Jenkins, 2014, p. 44). In the case of some members, such as Phally and Pipkin, attempts to name themselves failed, as their names were imposed by the rest of the group. In both cases, these skaters were given their names by others, after spending time thinking of alternatives. Phally, or Phallic Baldwin, was given this name by Stuntman, and it stuck immediately. Pipkin had been known as such in previous employment, and members actively resisted his attempts to choose a new name. Members who lack the power to name themselves are, without exception, those with low skills capital.

In contrast, one TIL member decided to change his name and be known on the official roster by his surname, but other members continued to use his skate name, Beat Monkey, or a variation of that (most notably Cunt Monkey or Beast Donkey). Despite nicknames and personas being an integral part of roller derby history, skaters have always discussed the idea of using their real names as a way to legitimise the sport (Malick, 2012).

> But most rollergirls believe that derby names are here to stay. "We still continue to make the public take us seriously on our own terms…. Choosing our own names is a big part of our culture that won't disappear any time soon, and is a time-honoured sports tradition – from Babe Ruth to Ocho Cinco."
>
> (Barbee and Cohen, 2010, p. 158)

In some ways, the use of real names could be seen as a resistance to the roller derby "ethic", and an embracing of traditional sports ideologies. It is perhaps no coincidence that in TIL, the skater most interested in using his real name was the most serious and competitive skater.

What happened within The Inhuman League was a satirising of the process of naming in derby itself. Individuals' attempts to create a specific identity were deliberately subverted or disrupted. Skaters who gave themselves a potentially innocent moniker were subject to the dubious mercies of teammates intent on subverting this innocence. Frank-N-Hurter, so called in reference to the Rocky Horror Show character Frank-N-Furter, with an additional nod to the violent nature of the sport, was another skater who was rarely called by his derby name. Instead, he was referred to by such names as Wank-N-Squirter, or Frank-N-Wank, or simply by his real name. Names could be an area of conflict between personal choice and league or community policing, with several community blogs discussing unacceptable derby names (Ginger Snap, 2011). Within TIL, publicly unacceptable

Image and identity   53

aliases were often bestowed upon members in a deliberate rejection of this policing. However, in public, Bollock Obama sometimes used the alternative name B. Obama so as not to cause offence, usually when junior teams were playing. The alternative names given to Frank and Beat Monkey were only used during training and within the league, and both this practice and Bollock's decision reflect efforts to create a good impression, discussed later in this chapter.

It was clear that there was no suggestion of creating an alter-ego as such, more that naming reflected an existing aspect of identity, as with I Am Broot: "G/Broot is self-explanatory … tree huggerish looking vegan comic art nerd, bit of gentle giant … etc." Often names were linked with favourite films – for example, Dorny Darko (from the 2001 film, *Donnie Darko*) and Stuntman Psyk (from the character Stuntman Mike in Quentin Tarantino's 2007 film *Death Proof*) – or the love of a bad pun (Brian Damage). Frequently, these names ended up shortened to whatever was easiest for teammates to shout on track, and so the initial reason behind the name was lost, as Dorny Darko became Dorny, and Stuntman Psyk became Stuntman. Skaters chose names because it was allowed, even expected, but they did not seem to feel the name was part of some semi-fictionalised identity; rather, it was a nod to some small part of themselves, or something they liked – in many of these cases the embracing of an already existing identity as a film geek.

My own naming history reflects similar ideas. After wrestling with several options, I decided to call myself Billie Viper. I thought it was a strong roller derby name: it takes the name of a well-known actress (at least in some circles) and adds a hard-hitting slant. I envisioned being called Viper. Tough, mean, and capable of lashing out quickly and viciously. All the things I am not. Teammates called me Billie. I hated it. It was just not me, and I could not buy into the need to create some fictional identity, I just wanted to be me – but on skates. As I had introduced myself as Bob in the beginning (an old university nickname), it was easy enough to revert to that instead. Officially, I was Bobus Maximus, but it was always shortened to Bob. Given that I also use this name outside of roller derby, it does not function as a different persona, or even a nickname especially. It is just me – but on skates.

Finley suggests that "names of teams are also signs of a clever irony that indicates to spectators that they are performing something unusual. Often the names are parodies of community monikers" (2010, p. 377). The Inhuman League's name (so called in reference to Sheffield band the Human League) reflects this idea. Despite practices of its members having in many ways gone past the idea of irony and the performance of something "unusual", in the early days, TIL played up the zombie element of the name, making promotional videos using skaters as zombie characters, and naming the B-Team Zom B Cru (a stylised version of the words zombie crew, highlighting the "B" for B-Team). Some members chose names reflecting this theme; on becoming line-up manager for Zom B Cru, I adopted the name Dawn of the Dead, containing both my real name and the name of a zombie film released the same year I was born, 1978 (also the number I chose). More recently, however, TIL members had discussed rebranding and

54   Image and identity

choosing a different name, arguing that outside of the immediate community, it would be unclear what The Inhuman League was.

In addition to choosing a skate name, members also chose a number. Whilst skate names were to some extent optional, for members who wished to play the sport, a number was essential as it was this identifier that would be used by referees and in game statistics. Numbers could also be quite a personal thing. Beat Monkey

> chose 808 after the Roland drum machine that was instrumental (fnar) in the early development of hip hop and techno. That's when I was Beat Monkey. Was going to change to 16, after footballer Roy Keane ... but realised I'd grown attached to 808.

Skaters had to learn to respond to their number, so it made sense that over time, skaters became attached to them, at least in an auditory way; whether that necessarily translated to an emotional attachment is debatable.

People in skaters' lives were also commemorated through numbers. Frank's number, 514, was "based on the birthdays of [his] children". Broot chose 318 because it "was [his] sister's birthday" He explained "She passed away around the time I first gave skating a try and when I saw my first live game". Sometimes, skaters chose a number based on some aspect of their identity, which might be either something they felt strongly about, such as Fin's choice of 1010 "because I'm obviously hilarious and thought having something binary would be a fun contrast. Also – in roman numerals it translates as 'MX' which is the title which I choose to go by", or some otherwise inconsequential detail, like Dorny, who "was originally 4x as I race 4x/4cross but again just going for a simple 4", and Damage "6.6e-34 is Planck's constant which is both a vital astronomical figure and a good description of my first year in roller derby".

Sometimes skaters liked to have an obvious link between their name and number, like Dodger Moore, who "originally came up with 007 for my number (love Bond films) and then tried to combine a Bond name with something relating to derby". These choices seemed to have less to do with sport, or mocking sport, and more to do with wanting to highlight some part of their lives, whether that be a person who was important to them, a piece of popular culture, or part of their identity; choices that were more about everyday lived experiences than political commentary.

Numbers, like names, could be policed in a way that stifled creativity. In November 2014, the WFTDA announced that from December 2015, skaters would no longer be able to use alphabetic characters as part of their roster number. Jason Slaysthem expressed disappointment with this. When asked about his number he said "0N1 because I was on a mission, stupid rule change stole my thunder so 041". Rule changes such as this aligned roller derby more closely with mainstream sports and seriousness and made it more difficult for skaters to be as subversive as they would like.

Image and identity   55

Boutfits

In the views and experiences of male skaters in relation to costumes or outfits worn for roller derby, the sport provided an alternative to the mainstream in terms of gender expression, despite arguments to the contrary (Beaver, 2009). When worn by men, boutfits subverted both gender norms and norms of sport. The conflict inherent in this subversion arose as a result of the risk skaters faced from wearing boutfits. Some skaters negotiated by wearing "sports" leggings, and some resisted by wearing hot pants. For skaters with greater skills capital, there was less conflict, less risk, and more ability to subvert these norms. Whatever their choices, clothing formed a big part of skaters' public image.

Like in women's roller derby (Becker, 2010), in men's roller derby, skaters sometimes chose outfits which could be called sexualised, or feminised, whilst still being athletic. Such skaters risked condemnation more than women in roller derby, because men are not expected to be recipients of the gaze (Mulvey, 1975), and sports participation from men typically confirms masculinity (Messner, 1988). The transgressive and performative opportunities to challenge gender norms through dress have been discussed only in terms of women (Peluso, 2010a, 2010b; Whitlock, 2012), and the professed acceptance of all bodies implies all *female* bodies. As stated earlier, few roller derby studies have considered male, trans, or non-binary skaters.

Although "doing gender" has been theorised in women's roller derby as a form of edgework (Cotterill, 2010; Lyng, 1990), the ways in which men "performed" gender in roller derby could be an even greater challenge to gender norms and thus a greater risk. The men I encountered in roller derby had entered a female space and had to risk their accumulated social and symbolic capital in order to become part of the community and play the sport. The practice of roller derby could "involve a clearly observable threat to one's physical or mental well-being or one's sense of an ordered existence" (Lyng, 1990, p. 857), albeit not in the way Lyng originally conceptualised. Performing a roller derby identity involved control and the exercise of skill, and participants' responses suggested that they were engaged in a commitment to get close to the "edge" in some ways, and that such risk could be necessary for their wellbeing. This was often seen in terms of dress, and the boutfits men chose to wear.

The experience of roller derby players more closely reflects Robinson's (2014) theorisation of "risky practices", where

> risk is evident … in terms of how masculinity is displayed in relation to men's vulnerability, should they "get masculinity wrong" through their choice of shoes. And yet, risky footwear practices also allow them to express creativity though their choice of shoes and the sensory pleasures associated with that agency.
>
> (p. 152)

Robinson explores how men negotiate their masculinity through footwear and suggests that there is a choice between fitting in and being original (p. 162). This is a useful lens through which to explore men's boutfit choices in roller derby. In an extract from a previously published work (Fletcher, 2017, pp. 129–130), I consider how participants in my research used boutfits to express themselves:

> Several skaters see boutfits as requiring "courage" and potentially offering a "thrill". Some respondents said they would like to wear a boutfit, or a more outlandish boutfit than they currently wore, but they lacked the confidence, which is often discussed in terms of body confidence. One respondent, Boon, expressed a negative view of boutfits in general but added "I probably would wear a boutfit for a friendly scrim if I plucked up the courage!" Comments like this suggest that, at times, negative responses do themselves stem from a lack of comfort with one's body. Others suggest that wearing a boutfit can *give* a skater confidence; boutfits are "freeing" and, wearing them, skaters experience "acceptance" of who they are. Rather than "edgework", the ability to express aspects of their identity otherwise kept hidden is more important:
>
> > My boutfit is the expression of my personality that I have to keep toned down during most of my public life. I came to terms with my more feminine personality a long time ago and so I relish the opportunity to wear more feminine clothes in public
> >
> > (Prof. Chaos)

In this extract, then, participant responses suggest that dressing in a way that reflects being comfortable with oneself can be an act of courage, especially when that means wearing clothing that might be deemed feminine. In a society in which men are expected to be masculine, and femininity is seen to be somehow lesser, this perspective can be understood. This courage and the risk that participants take could also be seen in the choices made by non-cisgender, non-heterosexual skaters, as seen in this extract, also from Fletcher (2017, p. 130):

> Not all participants in men's roller derby are cisgender, heterosexual men, and therefore this space also allows marginalised and less privileged identities to be expressed too:
>
> > I wear a boutfit that would be described as feminine because my gender is non binary and this allows me to express that. They simply allow me to feel more normal within myself in a context that won't ridicule me for doing so.
> >
> > (Professor Killa Hertz)

This non-binary skater values places to express themselves fully, in a way not possible in wider society. For them, roller derby is an accepting, inclusive community, they enjoy experimenting with femininity, and their experience is positive. The choice of whether or not to wear a boutfit represents what Robinson refers to as a "repertoire of possibilities", which can "resist and challenge normative masculinities" (2014, p. 164). One respondent, for

Image and identity   57

example, discussed his boutfits choices as, in part, a reaction to working in a masculine environment:

> I "came out" as a pansexual male at last year's *Clam Slam* which is a queer focused derby event held annually during pride week in Toronto. Since then I've sported the Pan flag on my helmet and I love it. I work in a very masculine male dominated industry and feel that when I put on the tights and derby gear it's very freeing. I'm happier that way. I like wearing boutfits, so I feel they are a great way to express yourself as you really are.
>
> (Papa Koopa)

In these examples especially, queer and non-binary skaters were able to express their gendered identities more freely within the roller derby community than they felt able to elsewhere. For them, the risk of doing gender differently was worth it (Risman *et al.*, 2012).

Of all the past and present members of TIL, Phally was the skater who experimented with boutfits the most. He explained how this came about as a result of skaters' nerves, due to the upcoming B-Team debut game, in May 2013.

> So, everyone was a bit scared and I remember talking to Rex, and saying, "Oh no, we'll just keep it light-hearted and just try and keep peoples' spirits up" 'coz he was captain and I was vice-captain. So one of the jokes that we'd come up with was wearing the Phally pants, I was like, "Oh, I'll just wear hot pants", and then it was you and Maid I think that just kept adding to the joke and, I don't know where the idea of the zombie hand came from, but it was just like wouldn't it be funny if there was like a zombie hand just sort of cupping the balls and stuff and Maid went away and made them and I remember seeing them the week before in a picture on Twitter and it came up saying, "Real men wear hot pants" or something like that and I sort of went, "Oh fuck [laughs], I've got to do that now".
>
> (Phallic Baldwin Interview, 25 January 2016)

What started as a joke, quickly became part of Phally's identity, and although he thought it was silly, and a laugh, there was a serious point in there, that if women could do it, why not men? There was also resistance to it from the beginning, with people telling him not to. We discussed how, once it became expected that Phally would wear hot pants, he decided to do something else. This culminated in him going through three costume changes at one event. Phally's choice of boutfit, which often involved colourful hot pants, sometimes worn over equally colourful leggings, but most often not, represented a subversion of his previous identity. This allowed him to behave in ways he would not have done before.

> I probably wouldn't have done half of the ridiculous stuff that we've done like, wouldn't have really been into the jokes as much and stuff like that. Starting off I was incredibly shy and quite withdrawn really and it's one of those where

58 Image and identity

> meeting lots of people and doing lots of things and travelling to other cities and playing with lots of people sort of brought me out of my shell a little bit.
> (Phallic Baldwin Interview, 25 January 2016)

Wearing a boutfit forced attention on Phally, and he had to negotiate the conflict this caused from team members, some of whom were supportive, and some of whom accused him of not taking the game seriously. In resisting attempts to police his mode of dress, he also resisted the increasingly dominant discourse that roller derby was a "serious" sport, and that, as athletes, skaters should not wear costumes; although engaged in sport, he risked his sense of masculinity through his refusal to submit to the dominant discourse, instead revelling in the carnivalesque presentation of self (Bakhtin, 1984).

For some of these men, playing with gendered expectations through boutfits represented a rejection of appropriate sporting performances. Bodies matter, and these were male bodies engaged in sport and athleticism, which is a social and body-reflexive practice that confers masculinity upon a body (Connell, 2005; Messner, 1992), and they were also dressed in hot pants, and glitter and sparkles, etc. For some of these men, Wellard's exploration of "body-reflexive pleasures" (2012, p. 28) offers an additional understanding.

The possibilities of this presentation of self are not accepted in the literature on roller derby. Murray (2012) reiterates the idea that feminine dress in men is a risk to their status or capital and argues that "boutfits are only transformative for women" (2012, p. 140). This is clearly not necessarily the case. Members of TIL other than Phally, also received negative feedback, and had to struggle against criticism. Although his boutfit was not as showy as Phally's, 4D was particularly forceful in his rejection of that criticism.

> I know it's such a tiny point. I mean it's not really relevant, but the amount of times that it gets mentioned about people, men wearing leggings and, oh yeah, cos Zoya doesn't like it. What's the point? I turned round to her and I was like, well they don't restrict my movement and they keep me cool. Would you rather I overheat cos if I overheat, I'll lose my temper. And if I lose my temper, I'll hit someone. I will just.... When she said it. The last time she said it, she was wearing leggings. And I very nearly turned round and went how dare you? Look down. I was like, why is it alright for you? Is it because I have a penis? I'm sorry. I'm pretty certain I didn't choose that either cos I didn't pick my, you know?
>
> (4D Interview, 16 August 2016)

4D enjoyed playing with gender expectations, and actively resisted expectations of dress, on occasion deliberately choosing see-through leggings to provoke a response. He enjoyed anticipating the reaction of his bench manager, outspoken in her dislike of leggings on men, and keen to ban them, if he were to take her at her word.

Image and identity 59

I've got some – I've got some, although granted then I'd be just wearing lycra instead, but they're like tight shorts, that I wear under my leggings. I was at the game – And I was like, well I can take them off [laughs] take them off and wear the other ones and go, there you go [laughs] There you go, what problem did you just solve? Made it worse, didn't you? Made it worse, you know.

(4D Interview, 16 August 2016)

Although there was a sense of anger in 4D's comments, it was clear that he found humour and pleasure in the situation, much like Phally did. This speaks to the newfound confidence of these skaters, in their appearance, and their abilities.

Nuke was similarly confident, but he outlined the possible downsides of this conflict between a pro-leggings and anti-leggings stance, and the risks inherent in sexualising men. At the end of our interview, Nuke said "I'm surprised you didn't ask me about my shorts". The truth is that I forgot, but we did discuss them then. Nuke mentioned his TIL award for "best shorts", but said that he did not think it was really an award worth mentioning; that people of all genders should be able to wear what they want as long as it is within the rules of the game.

I don't think it's really what we should be commentating on and if I'm, I'm very comfortable with who I am, but if I wasn't, which somebody in the team could be, and they chose to wear that as an expression of themselves, and suddenly they are getting commentators at international games bringing it up and they're getting like, people when they turn up to a skate event and people turn their backs on them and tell them they have to wear something different, and they can't even look at it. Which has happened to me but like, I mean, it's not really an acceptable thing to do that to people.

(Nuke Interview, 22 August 2016)

Goffman's concept of front (1959), and Jenkins' account of institutions, which set out "the way things are done" (2014, p. 160), both suggest that there are areas of life where the status quo is accepted, and it is difficult to imagine how to recreate them in a different way. In imagining a different way of performing the identity of the sportsman, wearers of boutfits did not fit the expected parameters of that social role, and hence faced ridicule as a means of control. Boutfits could be risky, with sanctions, such as a potential loss of capital, if the line between "okay" and "not okay" was crossed. In practice, this meant clothing that was "too penisy" (Xavier Bacon). Skaters were deemed to be getting masculinity wrong if they wore clothing that was too short, or too tight. It did not matter if these clothes were allowed in the rules of roller derby, and it was not entirely clear why skaters had faced censure for specific choices. Elsewhere, I have argued that "tight" may be "associated with femininity, or homosexuality, and therefore seen as negative" (Fletcher, 2017, p. 131), despite the advantage gained from the increased freedom of movement over baggy shorts.

60   Image and identity

What is evident is that the risk faced by skaters was not universal. There seemed to be at least three ways of negotiating identity through boutfits. Less experienced skaters, and those with less skills capital, like 4D and Phally, faced increased censure for wearing boutfits many considered to be "silly" and were thought to be preventing the sport from becoming recognised as legitimate. They positioned boutfit choices as a "joke". Skaters with less masculine capital, those who were comfortable with their femininity, or who were not cisgender men, like Professors Chaos and Killa Hertz, seemed more comfortable taking this risk and found the experience brought a sense of freedom. Skater with a high level of skills capital, however, did not experience boutfits as risky. In fact, several of them had *increased* levels of capital as a result of the respect they received from other men (Fletcher, 2017). Chemic-Al and Jonathan R, for example, discussed how much they enjoyed putting on their boutfits, and the "fun" of playing the sport, and Broot and Boon talked about boutfits reflecting the courage and skill of skaters.

It is important to note that at the 4 Nations Tournament, and the Men's World Cup, male skaters chose to tone down their appearance, and skaters who would normally wear boutfits did not. So, it seems that when playing as part of their national team, skaters did submit to the discourse that suggests that boutfits were incompatible with taking the sport seriously. Female skaters were increasingly under pressure to dress like "serious athletes" (Breeze, 2014), and at high-level events, male skaters were also beginning to experience a similar pressure, which in turn impacted on the "risks" associated with resistance to this pressure. The conflict between roller derby as a fun hobby and as a serious professional sport was ever-present, and more visible in discussions of boutfits, which frequently polarised opinion, as this extract from Fletcher (2017, p. 133) demonstrates:

> Taking things seriously is a big concern. More than risk, being professional is key. Mid-level skaters are dismissive of boutfits, preferring instead a more regimented uniform. Respondents clearly distinguish between "uniform" and "boutfit". Uniforms are professional and serious, and engender team spirit. "Unprofessional" dress, i.e. a boutfit, can be seen as detrimental and viewed negatively, as "a throw-back, unprofessional and an unnecessary distraction" (Veggie Kray). In contrast to the views of high-level skaters, skaters who have a negative view of boutfits have suggested that boutfits might physically "hinder performance" (Dead Hardy), although this view is more likely to be expressed towards new or low-level skaters. Phallic Baldwin explains that "there have been times where I have been accused of not taking things seriously because of the boutfits". It is common for those who dislike them to associate boutfits with a lack of seriousness, and this can be seen as harmful to the growth of the sport.

The view that harm may be caused to the development of the sport by skaters continuing to wear boutfits was supported by both Veggie Kray and Dead Hardy, but this ignores the rich vein of showmanship that runs through professional and commercial sports.

This second extract from Fletcher (2017) indicates the link between professionalism and seriousness more clearly:

> There is a sense that boutfits are comical and should only be worn for "fun" games, and also a fear on the part of those who enjoy wearing boutfits, that there will be moves towards banning them in the sport. Some teams have already gone down this route, with one skater explaining that "quite a few people have asked why I don't wear leggings anymore. I am a team player, and this is the view my team has now taken."
>
> (Brawl Jukes)

> These changes appear to be happening in the name of "professionalism". There is a very specific notion of what "professional" means. Whilst Chemic-Al refers to "getting paid" as the indicator of becoming professional, several other participants suggest the important factor is outsider perception of the sport; that *recognition* is key to becoming professional – or being taken *seriously*. Being professional is equated with seriousness, which is taken to necessitate the absence of the "fun" aspects that made the sport of roller derby different to major sports. Seen through the lens of seriousness, boutfit choices are risky because they are seen to actively prevent the sport from becoming legitimised, serious, and professional. Many participants appear to take it as read that this was what skaters *should* strive for.
>
> (pp. 133–134, emphasis in original)

This highlights the tension that continued to exist between skaters such as Phally and 4D, who enjoyed the fun, showy aspects of the sport, and those who insisted such aspects be toned down, or removed entirely. Coogan was a good example of someone who wanted the sport to be more serious, and he subscribed to the view that professionalism ought to be the goal:

> Roller derby came from the whole DIY aesthetic doing it yourself, you know, women, you know, women in fishnets and hot pants and costumes and, we need to distance ourselves away from that to a certain extent.
>
> (Coogan Interview, 31 May 2016)

There were, however, pockets of resistance to this idea. Continuing his discussion of leggings, 4D explained that "I'm still going to try really hard at training but that doesn't mean I can't have a laugh while doing it" (4D Interview 16 August 2016), and Grievous compared the "fun" aspects with the "serious" aspects of the sport, with a sense of regret.

> Some skaters associate boutfits with fun…. You look at fresh meat and they love the fact they get to choose new names and wear leggings and hot pants, and they love all of that. Then you look at champs and half the girls are

changing their names to their proper names, and they're all wearing completely matching kit down to socks and helmets and....

(Grievous Interview, 15 January 2016)

As ways of discussing boutfits, risk and capital suggest that attempts to disrupt and subvert mainstream narratives of sport and athletes were worth pursuing. Conversely, professionalism and seriousness were discourses which themselves sought to disrupt these subversive attempts to challenge norms. This limited how and for whom boutfits could be transformative. Below the surface, these issues were undoubtedly concerned with creating a positive impression of the sport; there were, however, a multiplicity of ways that a "positive impression" was envisioned within the roller derby community, and TIL was no exception.

Good impressions

Several discourses became apparent through study of TIL, including officiating, strategy, winning, competitiveness, teamwork, skills development, professionalism, inclusivity, and recruitment. One of the most important discourses or positions that was clear in the research was the need to make a good impression. What constituted "good" was changeable, but whether it was for an individual, the league, or roller derby as a whole, impression management (Goffman, 1959) was key. Within TIL, creating a good impression was less about dress, and more about behaving in appropriate ways. Creating a good impression of the sport was seen as important by several of the participants, though there were different positions taken on what activities and focus might help to create a good impression: fun, welcoming, and inclusive, or serious, challenging, and athletic. Thus, a "good" impression was inextricably connected with the identity TIL wished to project, part of the symbolic construction of this community (Cohen, 1982, 1985, 1986), the symbolic universe (Berger and Luckman, 1967), or the "story which a collectivity tells about itself, the world and its place in the world" (Jenkins, 2014, p. 163). There were several occasions where this was done through carefully curating an event in the aftermath to de-emphasise specific occurrences, to downplay actions which might be considered to create a bad impression. The TIL committee as a group veered between following up instances of poor behaviour – or brushing them under the carpet, ignoring certain behaviours. or making excuses for them. In this way, team members whose behaviour was "beyond the pale" (Goffman, 1959, p. 88) were still part of the team. But not every member. Skills capital played a part in the decision of who could remain part of the team and who could not.

The dominant discourse cycled between a traditional sports model and an alternative model, whilst subordinated and hidden discourses never disappeared (even when, as with the *Zom B Cru* discourse, they were actively silenced, this discourse only rose to the surface during successful times). Discourses were constantly changing and shifting, through a process of negotiation and a struggle for power. Through disruption and cycles of traditional and alternative models the league showed signs of arriving at a workable model for inclusivity. Such a model continued to be problematic, however.

During its history, the league changed in positive ways, refocusing due to loss of members. Things changed rapidly and frequently. The league was in constant negotiation and a state of flux. At times, it could be seen that individuals were attached to a particular discourse, such as Coogan's conviction that roller derby should strive to be serious. However, skaters also shifted positions. Discourses rose and fell as power shifted. The league was more inclusive when it was more self-consciously "alternative". It was certainly a better place for referees at this time. When not so serious, the league had a better reputation in the community, and more positivity.

When I began the observation with TIL, the dominant discourse used by team members to describe the team was one of calm. Team members discussed how they were calm, and this manifested in them "playing their game" on track. This meant playing according to the strategies and tactics they had drilled, and not allowing themselves to be distracted by mind games from the opponents, or forced into forgetting their strategies, and responding to the tactics of the other team.

In Fletcher (2019), I discuss a scrimmage I refereed in November 2015, between TIL and the Crash Test Brummies (CTB), which I and the other referees experienced as anything but calm. The game was rough, with

> skaters frequently shout[ing] about penalties they thought we had missed. This shouting seemed to coincide with a greater use of revenge hits, and silly behaviour. On blocking an opponent hard, one CTB blocker mimed crying before skating off. The mood coming from TIL seemed to be rubbing off on CTB. At least, I saw it as TIL being the main instigators, with Thump the lead. By the second half, even Hoof was playing aggressively and unpleasantly, giving unnecessary hits.
>
> (Field notes, Sunday 22 November 2015)

Although the game was unpleasant to officiate, and we had discussed the possibility of calling a halt to it more than once, afterwards both teams talked as though it had been a model of sportsmanship. "Clinical" was a term used by CTB's bench manager. Skaters discussed how "heads were calm", and they had "played their game", a view the line-up manager reiterated to me some time later. I have discussed how these terms had often been used within TIL as a way of creating a good impression (Fletcher, 2019), but "calm" was a way of conceptualising gameplay that adhered to a traditional masculine model of sports (Messner, 2002).

Goffman suggests that "while a team-performance is in progress, any member of the team has the power to give the show away or to disrupt it by inappropriate conduct" (1959, p. 88). However, within TIL, "inappropriate conduct" took on a different meaning. Aggression, shouting and yelling, and un-strategic hits could be termed unsporting behaviour, and yet were part of playing their game

64   Image and identity

for TIL, and thus were part of the discourse of calm. To underline this, a scrimmage held the week before this one, in which the team were much less excited and passionate, at least from a referee's perspective, yielded no such discussion. TIL lost the game badly, and the post-mortem suggested skaters had lost their heads, not played their game, and effectively disrupted the show, which again contrasts sharply with my reading of the game, as in this example regarding Beat Monkey's jamming:

> He's clearly exhausted, and not getting through. Still on his initial pass. At one point he falls hard – no penalty to anyone though. He looks hurt – I hesitate over whether to call the jam, but he gets back up and carries on. He's covered in sweat and looks on the verge of tears but doesn't give up.
>
> (Field notes, Sunday 15 November 2015)

One might argue that here Beat Monkey demonstrates good sportsmanship. He did not win, but he tried his best, and kept going. Calm, then, referred to winning – to the Lombardian ethic (Messner, 1992), not to being a good sport.

In addition to calm, "passion" was another term used to discuss such styles of gameplay, featuring anger and aggression that was seen in different ways depending on a skater's place in the team. Coogan, for example, as a proponent of the traditional sports model and a bearer of high skills capital found passion to be a good thing when he joined TIL, whereas Grievous, with less capital and a less traditional sporting background, experiencing the same moment, saw something very different, and had to be persuaded not to leave immediately (Fletcher, 2019).

> Err, yeah it was interesting, I mean my first ever Sunday session, Thump starting screaming and hollering at Dutchman and then threw his helmet against the wall and cracked it or something, and that was like my first ever Sunday, so that was quite a baptism of fire into TIL. Erm, and then I had, you know, err, Nuke and Oblivion trying to convince me to not leave because it wasn't always like that [laughing] so that was a bit kind of oh, okay. But everyone was like, oh, it's okay, he does that sometimes don't worry about it.
>
> (Grievous Interview, 15 January 2016)

TIL concealed the behaviour of Thump and kept him as their "dark secret" (Goffman, 1959) because it was incompatible with the inclusive image. Stuntman said more than once that he did not understand why no one else ever called Thump out on his nonsense, and that what he wanted was for people to talk to him and not just skulk off; that he wanted to be asked what he wanted and then sent off back to his corner. Other members, however, did not feel able to confront him directly.

Despite his behaviour, Thump was still part of the team. Given the negative impact his behaviour had on others, several members expressed surprise that this was the case, especially as it had previously resulted in members leaving:

I think it was potentially, certainly Thump and Pa Corr getting more say in what was happening. And people for whatever reason going along with it, and yeah perhaps not challenging it as much as it should have been.... The main reason that I suspect is that people just didn't want the hassle of having to deal with speaking up about it and then just having the piss taken out of them relentlessly. Or just being told they're an idiot and slowly driven out of the team because they had said something against the direction in which the team was taking at the time.

(Blocktopus Interview 8 January 2016)

The calls to challenge this behaviour were never formalised, and so the committee could easily ignore them. For the first part of my observation period, Thump was part of the committee, and therefore in a position of power over others in the team. Added to his already high levels of skills capital, this meant his place in the team was very secure, granting him the freedom to impose his ideas and ways of thinking about sport on the league, and so, "one of the problems when you have someone like Thump who's so focussed, comes from an individual sport like ... Tai Kwon Do, there's no value besides being good at the sport" (Oblivion Interview, 19 August 2016). Thump, in conjunction with Coogan, had the accumulated power and capital necessary to take the league further towards aggression and violence in line with expected sporting masculinity (Wellard, 2016). Being too skilled to risk losing, this non-conforming (Jenkins, 2014), inappropriate, and embarrassing (Goffman, 1959) behaviour, was possible because of this member's secure group membership.

As the observation continued into the 2016 season, the discourse of calm was replaced by another, similar in that it focused on how TIL wanted to be seen, not necessarily how they were. TIL had lost several skaters, and for many games in the season, they played short. Instead of the usual 14 skaters on the bench (as it was at the time), TIL mostly played with ten or fewer. During the visit to Brussels to play a mini tournament, the descriptor #Magnificent7 was coined by the team; a shared symbol (Cohen, 1985) that allowed team members to believe they saw things differently from other communities (Jenkins, 2014). Whereas other roller derbyists might consider playing with seven reckless, TIL were brave heroes – a diminutive David taking on the Goliath that was most of Belgium's national team. Seven skaters went to Brussels, one was injured in the first jam of the first game, and therefore TIL played two games with six skaters. Despite playing so short, they held the second game to an overtime jam, against a team comprised mainly of Team Belgium skaters. This performance garnered a lot of respect from the opposing teams and the audience. So much so, that TIL returned as "heroes", and this discourse became the dominant one for some time.

The question remains, for whom was this impression management undertaken? In part, it was for the general public and the roller derby community at large. But it was also clear that it was for the identity of the group and for individuals' identity:

a performance of professionalism and sportsmanship, however unconvincing that performance might sometimes be, to allow individuals to see themselves as athletes. These performances formed part of the everyday practices of being a TIL member, demonstrating the importance of shared beliefs and ideals, or at least the illusion of such (McHugh *et al.*, 2015).

According to Goffman, a team's position is unanimous, but they are secretive about the way this unanimity was arrived at (1959, p. 93). Team members wait for the official word before taking a stand, "maintaining the line during a performance" (1959, p. 94). Contrary to Jenkins' point, this does not necessarily mean that team members believe they see things the same way, but that they maintain the front that this is the case. When in a group, or teams, individuals are engaged in creating a performance together, and therefore, there is a communal backstage area where the public performance is created.

Off the track, in TIL's communal backstage area, it was important to some members of the team to foster an impression of being supportive to others. During a committee meeting, Coogan expressed a desire to see more support from SSRD, claiming it had not happened since he became a member of TIL. The discussion turned briefly to all the ways TIL had offered support, and the ways SSRD had not. This was an example of how Coogan was keen to present a positive impression of TIL, even within the team, though it was not so important to him to foster good impressions of roller derby as a whole, keen as he was to denigrate SSRD. Grievous expresses a different view on this:

> I think it quite upset me how much some of the guys were anti-SSRD, you know, I was like "dude, we're all playing the same sport, can we not just get along?" But there were elements of the team that were actively resisting sort of being part of … and that's still going on today, you know, I've had conversations with people at SSRD where they said that they've tried to erm they've tried to work with TIL, you know, on venues and seeing if the two can work together to get a cheaper deal on venues, you know, that kind of thing. And TIL have just been completely unhelpful.
>
> (Grievous Interview, 15 January 2016)

When this drive to create a good impression was threatened, the committee acted to preserve its reputation. At times, my research and the interviews I planned created tension. In one committee meeting (11 April 2016), I was questioned about why I wanted to interview ex-members, committee members suggesting such views were irrelevant. Interestingly, another topic under discussion at this meeting was the plan to delete the current committee Facebook group and start a fresh one with the new committee. This was on the grounds that new committee members did not need to read about difficulties and arguments that had occurred in the past – a similar argument to the one I had been presented with. It seemed that these discussions stemmed from the same desire to hide negative aspects from the team, and from outsiders (Adler and Adler, 1987).

A rather different example of impression management concerned new member, Fin. Previously a member of one of the local women's teams, Fin self-identified as non-binary, and had recently been struggling with issues around gender identity. In a discussion at the time of signing the consent form for this study, we discussed difficulties around anonymity and how, as TIL's only non-binary member, it is likely that (see Marsh, 2013; Meagley and Youth Radio, 2017) identification would be easier. Fin acknowledged, and was comfortable with, that likelihood but it did raise ethical issues. The roller derby community prides itself on being welcoming and inclusive to all genders, and as a member of that community, I wanted to be able to show how inclusive and supportive TIL was towards Fin, as an example of a non-binary skater. As a close friend, also, navigating the line between good research and maintaining a good friendship at times required additional reflexivity and a greater sensitivity to context. I want to briefly explore how "inclusivity" functioned as a discourse within TIL, and how Fin's experience of belonging in the league was used as a marker of how inclusive TIL had become.

Throughout 2016, TIL slowly changed identity from a men's league to an inclusive league. This occurred as a direct result of Fin joining, and in many ways, Fin was the driver for change. For some time, Nuke had spoken of his desire to see men's derby rebranded to "open" derby, welcoming skaters of all genders, stating his belief that whilst there was a need to have safe spaces for female athletes under the banner of the WFTDA, this was not so necessary for men. He wanted to find out about the UKRDA policy on women playing in men's Champs games. He said, "I just want a situation where people with ability can play together". Such discussions regularly arose on roller derby groups and blogs throughout the community. There were many differences of opinion and the issue was, and remains, highly contentious. Although several within TIL were in general agreement with Nuke, the possibility of women playing was still an issue for some. Bench crew Wilma and Zoya played for TIL in a game against the Super Smash Brollers in December 2015, but not everyone in the team was happy about it. Jason felt uncomfortable with the idea of women playing, and for a short time took a step back from TIL management because of this. Fin, still with SSRD at the time, was upset and angry about the idea of cisgender women taking advantage of a loophole in a policy designed to support marginalised identities.

When Fin asked to join TIL, Jason expressed initial reservations about their membership and whether they could play for TIL. In a committee discussion, Jason suggested that we should ask the league if Fin should be allowed to join. This suggestion was roundly rejected by the rest of the committee as unnecessary. As a committee member at the time, I cited the MRDA non-discrimination policy, which explicitly includes non-binary and transmasculine members:

> MRDA does not and will not differentiate between members who identify male and those who identify as a nonbinary gender (including but not limited to genderqueer, transmasculine, transfeminine, and agender) and does not and

68 Image and identity

will not set minimum standards of masculinity for its membership or interfere with the privacy of its members for the purposes of charter eligibility.

(MRDA, 2015)

Other committee members agreed that Fin was eligible to join, and the decision did not require input from all league members, but that they could join through the same process as any other prospective member might. Despite this initial concern, Jason since became one of the most welcoming and supportive of Fin's teammates and made no mention of any remaining doubts he may have had. Also, although members did suggest that they may have to discuss the presence of a non-binary skater on the team with prospective opponents, this gradually seemed to have been forgotten, with Fin welcomed as a skater the same as any other.

Fin's membership of TIL allowed the league to position itself as highly inclusive. The only Tier 1 "men's" team with a non-binary skater during the 2016 season, TIL could say they were the most gender inclusive league in Tier 1. More recently, Fin's joining opened the way for other non-cisgender men to join, including trans skaters, and cisgender women skaters. The presence of cisgender women in men's roller derby was itself a controversial issue, as many felt that the MRDA non-discrimination policy opened membership to all bar cisgender women, and pointed to the MRDA not differentiating "between members who identify male and those who identify as a *nonbinary gender*" (emphasis added), whilst others argued that since the MRDA "does not and will not set *minimum standards of masculinity* for its membership" (emphasis added), cisgender women were welcome. But Fin's membership indirectly suggested that the league would not necessarily accept people as they were; they may be subject to change – in itself a disruption of identity. This was seen, not in the case of Fin, who was themself disrupting their own identity (Le Fin, 2016), but through the experiences of Jason, who had to change, to become more accepting and to negotiate his feelings around transgender and female players on his team. This allowed for the possibility of change from a purely *men's* roller derby to an *open* model, "Open to All", or "OTA", as Dorny referred to it; a team that could become a safe space for trans and non-binary members (Morris and Van Raalte, 2016).

The interplay of team and self-image

This ethnographic account reveals that an understanding of "who's who and what's what" (Jenkins, 2014) is of central concern. Both individuals and collective were engaged in a continual process of "becoming" roller derby (Pavlidis and Fullagar, 2014), whilst always aware of the consequences of getting that wrong. Individual practices fed into group practices and vice versa. Collective or organisational identities were messy and shifting. What was and was not "okay" was in constant flux. This required constant redefinition and renegotiation on an individual level, whilst these individual changes impacted on the collective identity.

An identity is always subject to change. It can only ever be "good enough" or "acceptable", and these terms necessitate the acceptance of change. My participants were not just "doing" masculinity, they were doing roller derby. The risk was not only of getting masculinity wrong, but also of getting roller derby wrong. In the beginning, it was easier, as they were in a sense *creating* roller derby. The more the rules changed, the harder it was to keep up. It is difficult to pin down the shifting nature of identifications within a linear narrative, and to discuss the interconnected nature of the individual and the collective in a way that shows that they impact on each other at the same time. Nevertheless, in an attempt to impose order on the disorderly, this discussion will consider first the individual, followed by the collective.

Throughout this chapter, identity has been discussed as a self-conscious process. Within the process of "becoming" roller derby, there was, in Jenkins' (2014) term, the nominal identity – being a member of a roller derby team, and the categorisation as a blocker, jammer, referee etc. There was also the virtual identity: the experience of being a roller derbyist. This nominal identity encompassed a multitude of virtual identities, which were practical and negotiable. This allowed for similarity and difference to be included within the nominal identity. Getting roller derby wrong was a concern, and there were penalties for that, but there was not just one way to be roller derby, to get it right enough to be considered "acceptable" or "good enough". However, these identities were never finished, and there was no stable ground on which to stand. Bourdieu argued that to be successful in a habitus is to develop a "feel for the game" (Bourdieu, 1990a, p. 61), but the game kept on changing. In the interplay of the immediate group and the wider community, there were many holes for the unwary to fall into. Avoiding getting it wrong meant being always open to change.

Through the construction of this community, shared rituals and symbols were used (Cohen, 1985), creating a symbolic universe (Berger and Luckman, 1967), which allowed members to believe they saw things the same (Jenkins, 2014). Roller derbyists performed the ritual of choosing a name (or, as in the cases of Phally and Pipkin, had one chosen for them) because that was the way things were done. Names were public and visible and allowed categorisation as a member. There was a recognition that this might not always be the way things were done, so names were worn lightly. Because roller derby names were an addition to, rather than instead of, a given name, change was easier. My participants did not see roller derby as a way to craft a specific identity or persona that differed from their core identity, rather it was an extension of this. The names were a necessary symbol of belonging to the community, and became part of the nominal identity. In practice they were used, but equally they were sometimes ignored, or subverted. Skaters had already experienced an enforced change of numbers to more closely align the sport with the mainstream. They recognised that the way things were done could easily become the way things used to be done. Thus, the process of naming and numbering became subject to ridicule and rejection, becoming an object of banter. This refusal to take things seriously is visible in much of the individual identity work of team members.

Boutfits, including fishnets, tutus, hot pants, and face paint, were the way things used to be done. Subverting gender norms by use of these costumes was considered acceptable for women, though it was always a greater risk for men, as men's use of boutfits was considered silly and unacceptable (Murray, 2012). The risk inherent in wearing boutfits was not due only to these attitudes to men's attempts to subvert gender norms and norms of sport, but also in subverting the way things should be done. Some men saw boutfits as freeing, they were a necessary part of their embodied identities, but they were also deviant. Jenkins argues that non-conforming behaviour from secure members of a collective is more likely (2014, p. 152), and this is reflected in the way that skills capital within roller derby afforded some men the freedom to continue to wear boutfits without censure, which is comparable to the way Anderson (2009) argues that masculine capital affords athletes greater freedom to transgress norms. Less secure members were taking a greater risk, but when employed as a joke (by Phally or 4D, for example) this practice was easier to carry off than when it was done seriously. This reflects Thurnell-Read's (2011b) analysis of self-parody performed by stag participants wearing feminine clothing. Equally, wearing boutfits was getting roller derby wrong. This "deviance" was sought out by some who deliberately wore the "wrong" clothes. They were categorised as not taking derby seriously enough, or, ironically considering how ubiquitous boutfits were in the beginning, not "proper" roller derby.

In TIL, identity was shifting and plural; members were creating and maintaining a series of identities, for example Beat Monkey's process of becoming a serious competitive skater was reflected in his desire to be known by his legal name. His experience also demonstrated the negotiation, and the conflict and disruption often involved, in that his nominal identity (Jenkins, 2014) – the identity that he chose for himself – was not necessarily taken up and accepted by his teammates, and so his virtual identity (Jenkins, 2014) continued to be Beat Monkey, or a variation thereof. Potentially, skaters' habitus (Bourdieu, 1977, 1990a, 1990b) and the impact of an individual's background and life experiences, offers a partial explanation as to why members did and saw things differently.

Skaters equated names and boutfits with frivolity and tended to align themselves either with or against that. These choices clearly involved impression management (Goffman, 1959). Skaters attempted to present an image of themselves, which might or might not be accepted by others. The success of the "performance" was very much in doubt. Although Goffman (1959) talks of the importance of not being taken in by one's own performance, it often appeared as though skaters found it easier to see through others' front rather than their own. Jenkins' (2014) suggestion that knowing ourselves is at least equally as difficult as knowing others seemed to hold here.

It is impossible to give one definitive description of The Inhuman League, because it changed so much over the last six years. The league was in a constant state of flux, with dominant discourses changing and shifting as different aspects of the sport became more or less important. The community continued to exist despite changes of membership and members moving between groups (Barth, 1969). Despite change being initially unpopular, community members adjusted, and new ways of working became normalised. As I discuss certain "moments" within the lifecourse of the league, it must be understood that its identity was not static, that in my attempt to pin down what was happening, I inevitably flatten out experiences that were never simply one thing at a time. Nevertheless, my participants' discussions suggested that the year during which I completed my ethnographic observations could be split into two key periods with specific dominant discourses. Cohen (1985) argues that communities exist in the thinking as much as the doing, although does acknowledge that boundary construction is only one part of a community, and that it also involves self-identity (Cohen, 2002). These discourses represent the thinking done within TIL regarding the type of community they were, but also how members sought to frame the group identity.

The "calm" phase I observed from the beginning of fieldwork (November 2015) until around April 2016 was focused on making a "good" impression. Coogan was chair and Thump was vice, and they ran the league in a rather autocratic style, seeking to control the public impression, as seen in their response to my desire to interview ex-members outlined in the introduction to Chapter 3. On track, the league played aggressively, and unsporting conduct was common. The "transitional" phase began as Frank took over as chair. Fin joined, and the team became more "open" and inclusive. Frank ran the league in a much more democratic style. The changes in management coinciding with the discourses present during these periods strongly suggest an element of power involved. The chair of TIL was the one whose definition of a situation counts (Jenkins, 2014), and so understandings of how the league should be positioned differed with leadership styles. Coogan's tenure as chair was characterised by a more traditional approach to male sports, whereas Frank led a more inclusive league.

Dominant discourses, however, worked to disguise conflict. Those who disagreed with the direction of the league tended to remain silent. It was difficult to account for those silences, and so discourses seemed to shift organically. Sometimes, a catalyst for change was obvious, as the league responded to demands from outside the organisation, as in the case of Fin's request to join – although, as this shows, such changes often mirror changes taking place within the organisation. The idea of inclusion links this discussion with the context setting of Chapter 2. Under Coogan, TIL was insular and separate, but under Frank, the league sought to strengthen links within the wider community much more. In Chapter 4, I explore the ways TIL strove to become an inclusive league and discuss the practices of belonging engaged in by members.

References

Adler, P. A. and Adler, P. (1987) *Membership Roles in Field Research.* Newbury Park, Sage.

72 Image and identity

Anderson, E. (2009) *Inclusive Masculinities*. London, Routledge.

Bakhtin, M. M. (1984) *Rabelais and His World*. Bloomington, IN, Indiana University Press.

Barbee, J. and Cohen, A. (2010) *Down and Derby: The Insider's Guide to Roller Derby*. New York, Soft Skull Press.

Barth, F. (1969) *Ethnic Groups and Boundaries*. Boston, MA, Little Brown.

Beaver, T. D. (2009) Roller derby revolution: Sport as a social movement. *Proceedings of the 2012 American Sociological Association Annual Meeting held at the Colorado Convention Center and Hyatt Regency, Denver*.

Becker, S. (2010) Fishnets, feminism, and femininity: Resistance, construction, and reproduction of femininity within sport. *Proceedings of the 2010 American Sociological Association Annual Meeting held at the Hilton Atlanta and the Atlanta Marriott Marquis, Atlanta*.

Berger, P. L. and Luckman, T. (1967) *The Social Construction of Reality*. London, Allen Lane.

Bourdieu, P. (1977) *Outline of a Theory of Practice*. Cambridge. Cambridge University Press.

Bourdieu, P. (1990a). *In Other Words: Essays Towards a Reflexive Sociology*. Stanford, CA, Stanford University Press.

Bourdieu, P. (1990b) *The Logic of Practice*. Cambridge, Polity Press.

Breeze, M. (2014) *Just a Big, Sexy Joke? Getting Taken Seriously in Women's Roller Derby*. PhD thesis, University of Edinburgh.

Browne, K. (2003) Negotiations and fieldworkings: Friendship and feminist research. *Acme: An International E-journal for Critical Geographies*, 2(2), pp. 132–146. Available from: http://acme-journal.org/index.php/acme/article/view/690/554 (accessed 3 January 2016).

Carlson, J. (2010) The female significant in all-women's amateur roller derby. *Sociology of Sport Journal*, 27(4), pp. 428–440. DOI: 10.1123/ssj.27.4.428.

Chananie-Hill, R. A., Waldron, J. J., and Umsted, N. K. (2012) Third-wave Agenda: Women's flat track roller derby. *Women in Sport & Physical Activity Journal*, 21(1), pp. 33–49. DOI: 10.1123/wspaj.21.1.33.

Chavez, C. (2008) Conceptualising from the inside: Advantages, complications and demands on insider positionality. *The Qualitative Report*, 13(3), pp. 474–494.

Clarke, A. (2005) *Situational Analysis: Grounded Theory After the Postmodern Turn*. London, Sage.

Cohen, A. P. (1982) Belonging: The experience of culture, in A. P. Cohen (ed.), *Belonging: Identity and Social Organisation in British Rural Cultures*. Manchester, Manchester University Press, pp. 1–19.

Cohen, A. P. (1985) *The Symbolic Construction of Community*. London, Routledge.

Cohen, A. P. (1986) *Symbolising Boundaries: Identity and Diversity in British Cultures*. Manchester, Manchester University Press.

Cohen, A. P. (2002) Epilogue, in V. Amit (ed.), *Realizing Community: Concepts, Social Relationships and Sentiments*. London, Routledge, pp. 165–170.

Cohen, J. H. (2008) Sporting-self or selling sex: All-girl roller derby in the 21st century. *Women in Sport and Physical Activity Journal*, 17(2), pp. 24–33.

Connell, R. W. (2005) *Masculinities* (2nd edn). Cambridge, Polity Press.

Cotterill, M. S. (2010) *Skating the Metaphorical Edge: An Ethnographic Examination of Female Roller Derby Athletes*. MA dissertation, University of Delaware.

DeLyser, D. (2001) "Do you really live here?": Thoughts on insider research. *Geographical Review*, 91(1/2), pp. 441–453. DOI: 10.1111/j.1931-0846.2001.tb00500.x.

Finley, N. J. (2010) Skating femininity: Gender manoeuvring in women's roller derby. *Journal of Contemporary Ethnography*, 39, pp. 359–387. DOI: 10.1177/0891241610364230.

Fletcher, D. (2017) "Or are you just pleased to see me?": The role of the boutfit in men's roller derby. *Sheffield Student Journal for Sociology*, 1, pp. 120–136.

Fletcher, D. (2019) Skills capital and inclusivity in men's roller derby. *International Review for the Sociology of Sport*, Online First. DOI: 10.1177/1012690219855733.

Foucault, M. (1972) *The Archaeology of Knowledge and the Discourse on Language*. New York, Pantheon Books.

Frogmouth (2015) "A graphical taxonomy of roller derby skate names". *Frogmouth*. Available from: www.frogmouthclothing.com/blogs/frogmouth-blog/48307907-a-graphical-taxonomy-of-roller-derby-skate-names (accessed 19 April 2016).

Ginger Snap (2011) "Derby names: Not ready for prime time". *Derbylife.com*. Available from: www.derbylife.com/2011/09/derby_names_not_ready_prime_time/ (accessed 6 June 2016).

Goffman, E. (1959) *The Presentation of Self in Everyday Life*. London, Penguin.

Hern, L. (2010) On a roll: Empowerment and the construction of femininity in the derby girl revolution. *The International Journal of Sport and Society*, 1(2), pp. 59–69. DOI: 10.18848/2152-7857/CGP/v01i02/54014.

Jenkins, R. (2014) *Social Identity* (4th edn). London, Routledge.

Joulwan, M. (2007) *Rollergirl: Totally True Tales from the Track*. New York, Touchstone.

Kleinman, S., Stenross, B., and McMahon, M. (1994) Privileging fieldwork over interviews: Consequences for identity and practice. *Symbolic Interaction*, 17(1), pp. 37–50. DOI: 10.1525/si.1994.17.1.37.

Le Fin, T. (2016) *Switching Teams*. [Film] Sheffield, E.D.E.N. Film Productions.

Lyng, S. (1990) Edgework: A social psychological analysis of voluntary risk-taking. *The American Journal of Sociology*, 95, pp. 851–886. DOI: 10.1086/229379.

Mabe, C. (2007) *Roller Derby: The History and All-Girl Revival of the Greatest Sport on Wheels*. Denver, CO, Speck Press.

Malick, D. (2012) *"This Is Not Your Parents' Derby": How Women's Flat Tack Derby is Challenging Gendered Expectations in Institutionalized Sport*. BA dissertation, Warren Wilson College.

Marsh, D. (2013) "Sexist language: It's every man for him or herself". *The Guardian Online*. Available from: www.theguardian.com/media/mind-your-language/2013/oct/18/mind-your-language-sexism (accessed 21 July 2018).

McDonald, J. (2013) "It's not breeding that 'I'm an athlete' arrogance": Roller derby and the construction of local celebrities, in A. A. Colvin (ed.), *The Performance of Celebrity: Creating, Maintaining, and Controlling Fame*. Sydney, Interdisciplinary Press, pp. 37–48.

McHugh, T. F., Coppola, A. M., Holt, N. L., and Andersen, C. (2015) "Sport *is* community": An exploration of urban Aboriginal peoples' meanings of community within the context of sport. *Psychology of Sport and Exercise*, 18, pp. 75–84. DOI: 10.1177/1049732318759668.

Meagley, D. and Youth Radio (2017) "All your questions about gender-neutral pronouns answered". New York, Teen Vogue. Available from: www.teenvogue.com/story/they-them-questions-answered (accessed 21 July 2018).

74 Image and identity

Messner, M. (1988) Sports and male domination: The female athlete as contested ideological terrain. *Sociology of Sport Journal*, 5, pp. 197–211. DOI: 10.1123/ssj.5.3.197.

Messner, M. (1992) *Power at Play: Sports and the Problem of Masculinity*. Boston, MA, Beacon Press.

Messner, M. (2002) *Taking the Field: Women, Men and Sports*. Minneapolis, MN, University of Minnesota Press.

Morris, J. and Van Raalte, J. (2016) Transgender and gender nonconforming athletes: Creating safe spaces for all. *Journal of Sports Psychology in Action*, 7(2), pp. 121–132. DOI: 10.1080/21520704.2016.1184732.

MRDA (2015) "MRDA Non-discrimination Policy". *MRDA*. Available from: https://mrda.org/resources/mrda-non-discrimination-policy/ (accessed 7 June 2015).

Mullin, K. (2012) *Neither Butch nor Barbie: Negotiating Gender in Women's Roller Derby*. MA dissertation, Loyola University Chicago.

Mulvey, L. (1975) Visual pleasure and narrative cinema. *Screen*, 16(3), pp. 6–18. DOI: 10.1093/screen/16.3.6.

Murray, G. (2012) *The Unladylike Ladies of Roller Derby? How Spectators, Players and Derby Wives Do and Redo Gender and Heteronormativity in All-Female Roller Derby*. PhD thesis, University of York.

Okely, J. (2009) Response to Amy Pollard. *Anthropology Matters*, 11(2), pp. 1–4.

Ortiz, S. (2003) Muted masculinity as an outsider strategy: Gender sharing in ethnographic work with wives of professional athletes. *Symbolic Interaction*, 26(4), pp. 601–611. DOI: 10.1525/si.2003.26.4.601.

Parrotta, K. L. (2015) *The Politics of Athletic Authenticity: Negotiating Organizational Change and Identity Dilemmas in Women's Flat Track Roller Derby*. PhD thesis, North Carolina State University.

Pavlidis, A. and Fullagar, S. (2014) *Sport, Gender and Power: The Rise of Roller Derby*. Farnham, Ashgate.

Peluso, N. M. (2010a) "Cruising for a bruising": Women's flat track roller derby as embodied resistance. *Proceedings of the 2010 American Sociological Association Annual Meeting held at the Hilton Atlanta and Atlanta Marriott Marquis, Atlanta*.

Peluso, N. M. (2010b) *High Heels and Fast Wheels: Alternative Femininities in Neo-Burlesque and Flat-Track Roller Derby*. PhD thesis, University of Connecticut.

Pini, B. (2005) Interviewing men: Gender and the collection and interpretation of qualitative data. *Journal of Sociology*, 41(2), pp. 201–216. DOI: 10.1177/14407833 05053238.

Risman, B. J., Lorber, J., and Sherwood, J. H. (2012) Toward a world beyond gender: A utopian vision. *Proceedings of the 2012 American Sociological Association Annual Meeting held at the Colorado Convention Center and Hyatt Regency, Denver*.

Robinson, V. (2014) Risky footwear practices: Masculinity, identity, and crisis. *NORMA: International Journal for Masculinity Studies*, 9(3), pp. 151–165. DOI: 10.1080/18902138.2014.950501.

Thurnell-Read, T. (2011b) Off the leash and out of control: Masculinities and embodiment in Eastern European stag tourism. *Sociology*, 45(6), pp. 977–991. DOI: 10.1177/0038038511416149.

Wellard, I. (2012) Body-reflexive pleasures: Exploring bodily experiences within the context of sport and physical activity. *Sport, Education and Society*, 17(1), pp. 21–33. DOI: 10.1080/13573322.2011.607910.

Wellard, I. (2016) Gendered performances in sport: An embodied approach. *Palgrave Communications*, 2, 16003. DOI: 10.1057/palcomms.2016.3.

West, C. and Zimmerman, H. (1987) Doing gender. *Gender and Society*, 1, pp. 125–151. DOI: 10.1177/0891243287001002002.

Whitlock, M. C. (2012) *Selling the Third Wave: The Commodification and Consumption of the Flat Track Roller Girl*. MA dissertation, University of South Florida.

Chapter 4

Belonging and inclusivity

Chapter 2 explored the concept of community in roller derby and considered some of the ways members of The Inhuman League (TIL) engage with those communities, whilst Chapter 3 engaged with practices of individual and group identities. This chapter focuses on how members create a sense of belonging within the immediate community of the league – one that holds the greatest importance for them. Belonging is a practice, something people do (Bennett, 2015) rather than a thing they have, and is subject to change (May, 2011). Individuals are, therefore, active in how they create a sense of belonging, for themselves and for others. This is relevant for a discussion of roller derby, since participants have to develop a sense of the field or habitus (Bourdieu, 1990a, 1990b), and this is also a process that requires action. Thus, belonging is an everyday practice, a process of becoming, which Pavlidis and Fullagar (2014) argue is continual in that it requires constant renegotiation. For Pavlidis, roller derby was about "giving her a place where she felt accepted and loved and was able to be with others with whom she could identify" (Pavlidis and Fullagar, 2014, p. 69), but it was never that simple. In response to May, Pavlidis and co-author Fullagar highlight the multiplicities, which complicate matters of belonging. This multiplicity is also in evidence within TIL, both between members and in the contradictory beliefs and values held by individuals as they work on finding spaces to belong.

Such a focus on "doing" belonging also involves a discussion of inclusivity. Whereas Chapter 3 explored the use of the term "inclusive" as a discourse, this chapter explores how inclusivity and belonging were achieved in practice. In terms of sports, Anderson (2009) theorises more accepting environments lacking in homophobia and increasingly open to gay men as demonstrating inclusive masculinity. Inclusive masculinity theory has been explored further by others (Piedra *et al.*, 2017) but although it is often argued that these environments are more inclusive, the focus remains on cisgender men. Other researchers, however, have explored sex-integrated sports and the potential they offer for women to be included in these spaces (Channon *et al.*, 2016).

Approaching from a different angle – that of women's sports including men – roller derby has been identified as a sport which offers significant opportunities to be inclusive, given its focus on providing space for women, often with bodies

Belonging and inclusivity 77

that are non-stereotypically athletic (Rannikko *et al.*, 2016). Researchers position roller derby as inclusive, with several studies indicating that it is a sport that welcomes all types of women (Alexander, 2016; Carlson, 2010; Farrance, 2014). This is reflected in the articles written for popular publication by community members, who are very keen to position roller derby as inclusive in terms of gender; as a space for all whether cisgender or transgender (Copland, 2014; Flood, 2013; McManus, 2015; Morgan, 2013). Despite this, there are areas of tension, such as that between the drive towards professionalism and seriousness, and the fun, alternative culture of roller derby's roots. There is a "tendency towards homogenization in roller derby" (Pavlidis and Fullagar, 2014, p. 108), seen especially in high-level teams, as difference is flattened out to become thin, white, and athletic skaters who "really like sport" (Breeze, 2015, p. 2). Here I explore how men's roller derby has the potential to offer something different, something more like the inclusivity that women's derby used to aim for.

The chapter is split into several sections, to enable focus on a specific range of practices. First, I discuss the use of banter, jokes, and insults to examine how a feeling of belonging is created through language (Haugh, 2014). Banter is often theorised as a masculine way of communicating (Nichols, 2016), and therefore it is absent from existing literature on roller derby, but I argue that in men's roller derby it occupies a significant place in the practice of belonging. Next, I discuss how camaraderie and "teamliness" develop a sense of closeness and consider specific events where this is evident. Then I explore how belonging is, in theory, open to everyone through an acceptance of others' quirks and differences.

Although this chapter acknowledges some of the ways practices of inclusion are inseparable from *exclusion* (Jenkins, 2014), I do not dwell on this here. Instead, I pick up these threads in Chapter 5. Participants had a great deal to say about belonging, and their feelings of being part of something worthwhile, and it was clear that (as in my own experience) though the community was not perfect and some skaters I interviewed had left the team or the sport, the good times were what they chose to remember and focus on.

Banter, jokes, and insults

The successful performance of banter functioned as a symbol of belonging to this community (Cohen, 1985), and was one of the most apparent, regular practices. Messner (1992) refers to research that shows "women have deep, intimate, meaningful, and lasting friendships, while men have a number of shallow, superficial, and unsatisfying 'acquaintances'" (p. 91), linking this with the idea of "antagonistic cooperation", and arguing that even within teams and friendships, sportsmen are ultimately competing against each other (p. 88). Within TIL, banter could be used as a form of contest: a battle of wits. However, often it was not antagonistic, rather it was performed as a way of expressing that a group of people were the same, and skill in the use of banter confirmed that individual's place in the team.

78 Belonging and inclusivity

Often considered a masculine trait, which is frequently sexual in nature (Nichols, 2016), banter was also used by women within TIL.

Messner regards the denial and denigration of gayness and femininity as an important aspect of locker room culture (in Messner and Sabo, 1994), but also maintains that covert intimacy may exist, and suggests the importance of not judging men's relationships by the standards of women's. Having spent an amount of time in roller derby locker rooms with The Inhuman League, I argue that roller derby does not explicitly reproduce this practice; rather, there are distinct types of banter that reflect a range of masculinities. Insults were only used towards insiders; jokes, ridicule, an instruction to "fuck off", were all types of communication reserved for members of the team (Plester and Sayers, 2007), or those people that team members hoped would join. Politeness was for outsiders. Despite this, and in contrast to Messner's findings and research into humorous language more specifically, the most frequent banter in TIL was neither sexist nor homophobic (McCann *et al.*, 2010), and did not overtly sexualise women (Kotthoff, 2006). Instead, the banter that took place would often tend towards the abstract and eclectic.

> It became a sort of running joke that everything was my fault and a few times a session I'd be asked something, I'd answer, and then be told, "Fuck off, Phally". And I've not actually had that for quite a while until I saw Bollock the other day. First time I've seen him in about two years. I was like, "My God Bollock, it's been so long", to which he replied, "Fuck off Phally, I thought you were dead".
> (Phallic Baldwin Interview, 25 January 2016)

This abstraction, and the use of inside jokes, marked the boundary between members and non-members.

Of all members, Phally seemed to be the butt of the most jokes. He explained the origins of a few of the longest running.

> The shitting in bins I still don't understand. It was just something Pa Corr came out with one day. I was stood talking about something, and he just went, "Phally shits in bins", and then it became a thing, and it was like, "Right, brilliant".
> (Phallic Baldwin Interview, 25 January 2016)

Pa Corr was also instrumental in jokes about Phally stealing dolly mixtures and Michael Bublé CDs. These jokes stemmed from the same away game, and so created a sense of belonging and togetherness. Understanding the jokes, and sometimes being the subject of them worked to foster a sense of belonging in that members shared the same experiences and could relate to them in similar ways, thus emphasising a *feeling* of belonging (McHugh *et al.*, 2015; Stone, 2017).

Initially, I struggled to understand and accept this, finding banter from Jason in particular difficult to deal with when in fact this was his attempt to show that he considered me to be part of the team, and his regular refrain of "all right, fuckers" indicated he had missed everyone. The outcome of such a misreading of practices of belonging is further explored in Chapter 5, but this example shows how I, at times, misread banter as non-genuine, when in practice, the feeling and intention behind the words was what mattered.

> Training was nice and friendly. Even Jason wasn't being a dick with constant banter today. I think I need a bit of nice, genuine conversation at the start of every encounter – "hi, how are you?", "I'm fine", "what've you been up to?" sort of thing to reaffirm that I'm accepted/wanted before the banter. Which is strange, because I think the banter is used as a sign that a person is welcome and fits in. Funny, huh? I guess it's something to think about some more.
>
> (Field notes, Wednesday 30 March 2016)

Dorny's partner, another skater, told me that away from the group, he was all dad jokes, but in TIL, he was "all bants, bants, bants, the banter bus, whatever" (Field notes, Sunday 7 August 2016). This suggests that individuals behaved differently when part of the group; that there was an effort (whether conscious or unconscious) to fit in. Lack of success in banter could result in alienation. Broot was never able to engage in banter, being seen by the rest of the group as *too* odd. Foul Out Boy also expressed frustration at his inability to engage successfully in banter, and eventually left the team, citing lack of enjoyment, but stayed involved in the sport. These examples are suggestive of the importance of banter to positive experiences. Efforts to fit in went so far as developing a persona for use within the group, which was established through the use of specific types of banter. This active way of creating a persona mattered much more than naming choices.

The way Zoya negotiated the masculine/feminine boundary was illuminating. She frequently engaged in banter, even beginning a round, but then would pull back and say the conversation, and the talkers were "disgusting". This was an integral part of the image of herself that Zoya created, along with the dislike of, and attempt to ban, male skaters wearing leggings. During Coogan's tenure as chair, TIL committee meetings featured a lot of banter. Coogan tended to select one thing about a person, and then run with it. Some things seemed to be fair game, but then others were not touched, so the banter was focused on areas the target themselves could also laugh at, rather than being genuinely hurt. For me, it was men in shiny pants and any reference to Zom B Cru. Like Zoya, the persona I portrayed in training negotiated the masculine/feminine boundary. In contrast to Zoya, although I engaged in banter on occasion, I was far more often the recipient, usually from Coogan. I publicly championed men wearing leggings (Fletcher, 2014a, 2014b), and, part of my identity within TIL was as ex-line-up manager for TIL's B-Team, Zom B Cru. These were the aspects that Coogan usually picked up on. In one committee meeting, Coogan suggested playing some lower-level games to give newer members experience. He said, "not a Zom B Cru game, Bob, wring those knickers out" (Field notes, Monday 11 January 2016). In describing me as the subject rather than object of this sexualised banter, Coogan effectively subverts the expectation of locker room talk. These examples suggest that banter

80 Belonging and inclusivity

was a way of demonstrating the validation of a member's self-identity, marking them as part of the community (Dynel, 2008).

Coogan did make sexualised jokes, but they were directed at everyone, and often at himself, such as when he landed on his wheel at training:

> Coogan discussed getting a skate wheel "right up the anus". We joked about this, and I asked what type of wheel, suggesting he must have done it before for it to slip right in. Dorny said it was only an Adonis [a brand of wheel smaller than standard], and we laughed about building up from an Adonis right through to a longboard wheel.
>
> (Field notes, Sunday 10 April 2016)

Thump was the only other member I witnessed make sexualised jokes aimed at female members (Field notes, Sunday 17 January 2016), but I was also told that he behaved very differently when coaching the women's team, which suggested that this behaviour was for the benefit of other men (Field notes, Sunday 28 February 2016). Fin believed that Thump was always trying to force an alpha male competition with Coogan, but that Coogan always deflected and did not engage. I was unconvinced, seeing the contest of wits – who could make the most debased comment – as an alpha battle, not an attempt at deflection. Also, this battle of wits disrespected other members, such as when it was engaged in, loudly, whilst another coach like Nuke was explaining a drill (Field notes, Wednesday 23 March 2016).

Frank and Woody framed one game as a "dick-measuring contest" (Field notes, Sunday 28 February 2016), and banter could be seen in the same way. During one scrimmage, an LRT blocker told a TIL blocker "I've got something for you", accompanied by a thrusting gesture (Field notes, Sunday 15 November 2015). LRT totally dominated this game. Their behaviour here was a contrast to the previous time the two teams faced each other. In that game, one of LRT's skaters complained that a TIL skater was sexually harassing him on the start line. I was part of the referee crew for that game, and to our shame we laughed it off and did nothing. However, we believed at the time that this was because LRT were not dominating the game as much as they had expected and were unhappy about it. In engaging with other teams, it seemed that sexual banter was used to intimidate, it was unsporting. For TIL members, when the recipient of sexualised banter, the usual response was to amp it up further than the other person until they gave up, either through lack of imagination to think of something more extreme, or through discomfort. This response could be read as a display of masculine bravado, but it could also be seen as what Murphy (2017) terms "humour orgies", in an attempt to create group solidarity. It seemed that the enjoyment was as much in the wordplay as what the words themselves signified. Such language reveals an attempt to differentiate TIL from women's roller derby. Using sexualised and extreme banter created a distinction between SSRD and TIL through contrasting communication styles. The lack of homophobic discourse also marks a point of difference with mainstream sports (Messner, 2002).

Whilst in Brussels, the team shared photos of the trip on the public fan page, including a montage of everyone's passport photos. I jokingly complained that mine was not included, showing it to the group who agreed it was an awful picture. Later, we were talking about Josef Fritzl (sentenced to life for rape, incest, murder, and enslavement, after imprisoning his daughter in a basement for 24 years) and I suggested that my passport photo looked like Fritzl's wife. Stuntman responded, "No. Fritzl's wife was attractive". There was a shocked silence at the table, and mutterings that Stuntman had gone so far as to not be funny anymore. I think even he was a bit shocked at what he had said. There was a sense that the boys were expecting me to be upset, but I laughed and acknowledged that it was very funny, and since it was such a good feed line, it would have been disappointing if no one had taken advantage. I both became more part of the group and gained respect through taking the banter and insults in good humour. Later, we called at an off licence and Stuntman deliberated for ages over the choice of a bottle of wine or cans of beer, only to have his bag break, and his wine bottle smash in the gutter. His look of sadness was such that I could not help but laugh and tell him it was karma. Afterwards, it was understood that every time he was mean to me, a bottle of wine died. Thus, we created a feeling of togetherness and belonging that functioned in the same way as Bublé CDs, dolly mixtures, and shitting in bins did for Phally.

References to my research were common, with Stuntman seeming particularly interested, often peering at my notebook when I was writing field notes during training sessions. This became more common after Brussels, since Stuntman and Fin and I had bonded, partly through banter, as discussed above. Skaters drew my attention to particular things that happened or were said. During a jumping drill conducted with more than a usual air of silliness and innuendo, Stuntman shouted to me "KD was jumping me the whole way round – Chester Fiddledicks. Write this down" (Field notes, Wednesday 29 June 2016). I laughed and did as I was told, moments such as these enabling my researcher identity to "belong" more definitively. Sometimes, skaters used my identity as researcher to call into question others' masculinity:

> Groups of three for "minute of pain" [a stationary hitting drill]. Coogan is left with Bollock and Fordy. He says, "I hate you all". Bollock says "Stuntman, do you want to join this group because Coogan is a pussy? Bob, you should write that down."
>
> (Field notes, Sunday 3 July 2016)

Comments such as these were said in awareness that I was writing about masculinities, and thus support Nichols' (2016) argument that sexist banter could be used deliberately in the knowledge that they should know better. In the same session,

> I dropped my book. Stuntman said something I didn't hear and then giggled. I said what, whilst holding my pencil poised above my notebook. Fin said

"verbatim: oh, look, you've dropped it. What a nob." Fin also said something about it being almost like dropping a bottle of wine.

(Field notes, Sunday 3 July 2016)

Writing this account, I recall the same sense of joy I felt at the time. The laughter that accompanied the banter took the sting out of words that could look harsh when written down.

Once I understood the banter as a form of mock impoliteness (Haugh, 2010; Haugh and Bousfield, 2012), I felt much more comfortable with it. The ease with which newer members such as Pipkin engaged in banter does suggest it is more common for men to use this style of conversation, and my lengthy learning process might have a gendered aspect. In addition, the inclusion of banter related to my practice of researching indicated that members had accepted and validated my identity as a researcher; it was now part of my persona, and this acceptance indicated a successful performance of identity (Goffman, 1959; Jenkins, 2014).

My field notes indicate that banter, especially sexual banter, was usually started by Coogan, and less often, Zoya. In Coogan's absence, Jason would start the banter. In one session where Coogan was absent, "Jason said 'I like to show people things, usually my penis'. Without Coogan, that was an hour and 40 minutes into the session before somebody actually mentioned the word penis, which was quite unusual" (Field notes, Wednesday 6 July 2016). Not everyone felt that the banter was always positive or useful, however. During a team meeting, Frank suggested that the banter had been getting away from the team, commenting that "a bit of fun is fine, but keep it down" (Field notes, Sunday 21 August 2016). Beat Monkey added that this was important in games as well, explaining that he was hyper-competitive, and needed to take it seriously, finding the banter and jokes frustrating, and stressing the need to stay focused. This was a change that reflected TIL's increased desire to perform well and chase success as a team, although experience suggested that the banter was a key part of team bonding and when members of the team felt a greater sense of belonging they performed better, so this new sense of seriousness could ironically prove risky in terms of team morale and performance.

> Frank said that sessions need to be harder and reiterated the house rules about focus during training, keeping banter/chatter down so that coaches can be heard and concentration upheld.
>
> (Team Meeting Minutes, Sunday 21 August 2016)

The meeting did not reflect on the source of the banter, and it is interesting to consider that the previous Sunday's training session was almost completely without banter, missing Coogan, Jason, Zoya, and another member who frequently led banter. It is also worth noting that this same member interrupted the flow of the meeting with banter.

Belonging and inclusivity   83

After the meeting, the banter toned down, but did not stop. On the way to a game in Newcastle, we joked and bantered about not being allowed to banter (Field notes 27th Aug 2016), and we made bets about how quickly the banter ban would be broken.

> Coogan still can't do a session without mentioning penises. I'd referred to the "no banter" decision from the team meeting in the car on the way here, and Hoof had said we'll see how long that lasts with Coogan around, although Hoof was surprised it had taken Coogan over an hour to say something.
>
> (Field notes, Wednesday 7th Sept 2016)

The following week, banter levels were still subdued, with only Coogan and one other member saying anything, although others laughed. By October, banter levels were again rising, although with Coogan on leave after the birth of his child, it was largely non-sexualised. In the same way that there is greater freedom for doing identity (and gender) differently away from the centre of sport (Messner, 2002), spaces outside the centre of the community offered some freedom from hegemonic practices. Certainly, the banter between Hoof, Phally, Stuntman, and sometimes Fin and Bollock was less self-consciously "masculine" than the word-play between Coogan and other members.

Stuntman suggested that roller derby could help people through tough times, and Fordy said it made bad days better. Roller derby helped individuals to meet new people and brought diverse groups of people together under a common interest. Although Coogan argued that the team was not friend club, for some, it was. There was a sense of being made welcome; an open and supportive feeling that kept people coming back. The sense of "teamliness" and camaraderie was important, and when training had a "collegial" feel, members felt more relaxed and valued. Though training included inside jokes and banter, which were a part of that friendship, the drinks after training were widely considered to be a better place for it, and were highly valued for the way they helped the league to feel like a community. The silly, off-topic banter played a greater role in bonding the team than the serious tactic discussion, or discussing past glories (this, especially, could have an alienating impact on those who were not part of the team or the event being discussed. That, or they found it boring). The sort of discussion everyone could join in and follow seemed to be the most inclusive. Language functioned as a symbol in the community (Cohen, 1985). New members, who were not able to join in with tactical discussions, or tales of past glories, could engage with banter, and thus develop a sense of belonging and loyalty to the team. Those newbies who felt involved in this way tended to stay longer than those who did not.

Again, writing up this chapter, it is the more abstract humour I miss. There was a joy in the wordplay, and, ironically, an undertone of *kindness* that suggested Phally, Stuntman, and Hoof in particular said horrible things because they liked each other; but were also unafraid to be genuinely kind too, which ensured the banter was rarely taken to be cruel.

It's more of a team now

> Well, I seem to think about this – this – Inhuman team now, is, it's that with this team, I feel would have my back. Whereas the team before – I don't know how they worked. Because they would say, "We're just a bunch of guys who come together to skate." I feel like this is a team now.
>
> (Stuntman Interview, 13 September 2016)

A sense of fun and camaraderie was important. Interviewees experienced this differently, period and duration of membership being an important factor in how they perceived it. With the participants I interviewed after they had left the team, it was possible to detect nostalgia and selective recall. A common trajectory seemed to be that someone joined the team, and for the first six months, everything was wonderful and new and exciting. "It's much simpler really, and obviously it's all new and fun and also you're not kind of involved in all the politics of it either" (Grievous Interview 15 January 2016). Then team politics became apparent, and there was a period when the member struggled to balance enjoyment and disillusionment, which could continue for long periods of time. After this, a member would either reconcile themselves to the reality of being involved with the team, or they would leave. The participants who were ex-members at the time of interview tended to have quite a negative emotional response to the circumstances of their leaving, which contrasted strongly with their fond memories of early membership. In this section, although difficulties are acknowledged, I focus mainly on the positives discussed in interviews, on the ways in which members felt like they were part of a team, in contrast to Chapter 5, in which I focus on some of the ways members might feel excluded.

During interviews, participants suggested that feeling like a team was important to them. TIL was established in 2011, created by a group of men who had mostly been involved with women's team SSRD, as partners of SSRD members, or referee members. In those early days, as discussed in Chapter 2, there was a lot of crossover between the two teams. Not being able to afford more than one session a week, TIL members also skated at some of SSRD's practices, where they often joined in with contact drills. Participants who were TIL members during those early months referred to the close association between the two teams in largely positive ways, but the issue of mixed gender training did arise. As SSRD advertised itself at the time as being a women-only team, there were those who felt uncomfortable training with the men.

> We went through a phase where it almost felt like SSRD I suppose didn't know whether they wanted to be with us, or not with us. I think it was, from what I understand, it was maybe one or two issues with some of the blokes going down to Tuesday training.
>
> (Daddy Longlegs Interview, 3 October 2016)

Although I was a member of SSRD at the time, I do not recall any formalised discussion on this issue, just a widespread assumption that it was "some of the blokes" who were a problem. Specifically, perhaps, those few men who threw themselves into the contact part of the sport with a little more enthusiasm than some of the female members were prepared to deal with. Nevertheless, the teams remained close until measures to become more independent came from TIL.

This desire to be independent came at the cost of close links with the women's team, but was felt to be necessary for TIL's development. Dr Blocktopus discussed how "the adventure of building something" was important in fostering a sense of community.

> In terms of atmosphere, it was fun … it was recognised sort of as being so close to the start of men's derby I guess in the country that we were learning everything very quickly and not really caring about particularly how well we did with it, it was more we'll do it, see what comes of it, try and sort of improve and, but we were very much feeling our way with it, I mean, there was no sort of structure to new skaters coming along and doing a minimum skills programme and learning minimum skills and then going on to scrimmages and then going on to bouting, it was basically you'd turn up, you would skate for a few weeks, if you hadn't fallen flat on your face then the next week you'd be scrimmaging with everybody and then....
>
> (Blocktopus Interview, 8 January 2016)

There was a sense that there was a lot of freedom in the early days of TIL; there were few pre-conceived notions of how men's roller derby should be, and there was not a lot of structure to the team or the training sessions. Though developing through links with SSRD, TIL ran things differently, and at first it was much less structured, it "wasn't too serious. It wasn't full of athletes" (Daddy Longlegs Interview, 3 October 2016). Going to the pub after training featured in several accounts from those who had been members in the beginning. Members discussed the excitement of doing things for the first time.

> Uhm, I think that first year was – was really special, because it felt something new and exciting and there wasn't all the, "Right we need to be this." It was, "We're playing Roller Derby. We're men playing Roller Derby. This is kind of not overly accepted and things. But we're doing it. We're having fun and we went to all these places and met all these people. It was great, you know."
>
> (Stuntman Interview, 13 September 2016)

Members were engaged in constructing a community and gained pleasure from that as much as in playing the sport. They were constructing boundaries between TIL and others. In part, this was imagined (Cohen, 1986), with the difference between TIL and SSRD a deliberate point of separation. But the boundaries were also tied to a sense of belonging, of being in it together (Delanty, 2010).

Opinion was, and in some areas, remained, divided about men's roller derby. As Stuntman alluded to here, men playing roller derby was not universally accepted by women's teams. As mentioned in the Introduction, it was sometimes argued that roller derby was a women's sport, and that men should go and find their own, or that the men's game was inferior to the women's (Murray, 2012), and it was sometimes possible to detect a fear that men's derby could potentially eclipse women's in popularity and coverage. Although there were members of SSRD who felt that way, TIL had a lot of support from women, and involvement could bring "joy" (Oblivion Interview, 19 August 2016).

When asked about their favourite moments in TIL, most interviewees talked about one of three European events, which Coogan characterised as "tours". The first one of these was a trip to Toulouse, France, to play the men's team there. What made this important to interviewees was the newness of playing, of being the first people to do something and therefore the result not mattering.

> Again it was, yeah it was a bit of a trip into the unknown ... it was sort of the adventure of it and, and also with there being so few teams and no real ranking system for the guys, it didn't really matter because we were still gonna be the top five in Europe because there are only five teams.
>
> (Blocktopus Interview, 8 January 2016)

> The Toulouse trip was amazing, just because it felt so exciting. That was the first international men's roller derby bout or something like that. Our first game played in mainland Europe. I can't remember – something exciting – whatever. I remember being driven into the arse end of nowhere. We thought we were gonna get murdered and then we played a game. One of the most chaotically badly reffed games I've ever been in. And I know lots of blokes who'll moan about reffing in roller derby. But this was something.
>
> (Stuntman Interview, 13 September 2016)

Conversations about the Toulouse trip also include the recurring theme within TIL of playing with fewer skaters than usual. The standard number was 14 (and is now 15), but TIL frequently played with fewer than ten skaters.

> It was the first men's bout played outside of the UK and it was a big fucking deal. We went over with eight skaters we finished with four. Blocktopus was delirious with flu, somebody broke, my moron of a husband got *nine* penalties.
>
> (Oblivion Westwood Interview, 19 August 2016)

TIL experienced a difficult middle period. After a very successful showing at the 2014 Men's European Championships, where they finished fourth in Europe, TIL had a disastrous game against Southern Discomfort Roller Derby, the top men's team in the UK, where five people fouled out (Daddy Longlegs Interview, 3 October 2016). Early enthusiasm and enjoyment gave way to disillusionment for many, and it became clear that members wanted very different things, and over a short period of time, several of the team's most experienced and skilled players left, along with many newer players, the experiences of whom will be discussed in the next chapter. This left a much smaller group of skaters, with much less collective experience than previously, to rebuild the team.

During the 2016 season, there was a feeling that this had been successful.

> After that I started to see a bit more of the roughness of TIL, shall we say, they are loud and rude and made dirty jokes and it was great. Yes, there's a lot of camaraderie, I think you get the occasional bickering. It passes but most of it is just people just having a laugh. You get all the lads of TIL wanting to have a laugh. The guests, too. I think a lot of people feel comfortable in these scenarios that we make because it's not we have to do this or make it overly strict, it's more friendly.
>
> (Frank Interview, 17 August 2016)

Although, as pointed out earlier, some members felt that TIL was not "friend club" (Coogan Interview, 31 May 2016), friendship was an important part of membership for others. Also, at times, there seemed to be a certain defensiveness about the size of the team; how smaller was better, and enabled the friendships to thrive.

> The big thing for me is everyone – everyone seems to be really good friends with each other. 'Coz it's such a – 'coz now, we're such a small team. Everyone knows each other. Everyone knows how each other plays. Everyone – a lot of them turn up to training regularly. You know, so everyone's on the – everyone's roughly on the same page or there about, you know. And everyone's – really friendly to each other, the bench is happy and I just skate around with a huge grin on my face. Apparently, I am the happiest member of TIL. That's what Zoya has said anyway. Apparently I just grin my way around the track. I just gormlessly grin when I am sat on the bench waiting for my – waiting for my jam you know.
>
> (Hoof Interview, 22 June 2016)

This negotiation of team identity occurred frequently as members insisted the team was better at the time of interview than it had been in the past. Stuntman, who was a member in the beginning, left during the middle period, and joined again for the 2016 season, said "I feel this is a team now" (Stuntman Interview, 13 September 2016), where previously, he argued, it was more individualistic. This demonstrated a need to remain positive about the team, despite the many changes that had occurred: a need to maintain the outward image that the team was strong and together, and of one mind (Goffman, 1959).

Sometimes, this positivity required a rewriting of history. From April 2013 to June 2014, TIL was big enough to have a second, or B-Team. Called Zom B Cru, this team gave newer members a chance to play, and less experienced skaters a chance to develop leadership skills. Over this period, Zom B Cru played at nine events, including one European tournament. Despite its success, Zom B Cru, as the second team, bore the brunt of the team exodus, and had to be disbanded in September 2014, with one member demanding "I don't want to even hear the words Zom B Cru" (EGM, 29 September 2014). In responding to change, TIL members employed a sort of ritual to enable some sense of continuity (Cohen, 1985). Seen here, one of these rituals involved TIL divesting itself of the past to focus on moving forward (also seen in the decision to delete the committee Facebook group, as discussed in Chapter 3).

Removal of information about Zom B Cru from the league website functioned as a symbol of this focus on the future. Rather than the past being used as a resource in the management of change, as Cohen (1985) argues, within TIL the past was deliberately obscured and forgotten. However, members viewed this differently, and not everyone was so keen to forget the past. Despite this attempt to move on, Zom B Cru was fondly remembered, mostly by ex-members. For these participants, the existence of the B-Team recaptured some of the excitement of the early days.

> You know we had like Friday night skate sessions in the car park where you just take a crate of beer down and skate, or you know parties at the cocoon and that kind of thing so yeah so that was, that was wonderful. I mean that was what I really kind of expected derby to be.
>
> (Grievous Interview, 15 January 2016)

Zom B Cu was remembered in terms of being able to take the game less seriously, having fun and a laugh, focusing on the experience rather than the win, (Blocktopus Interview, 8 January 2016; Daddy Longlegs Interview, 3 October 2016; Phally Baldwin Interview, 25 January 2016). It allowed for a range of experiences and goals within the one wider league. The A-Team was becoming more ambitious and striving to be more serious and competitive. Zom B Cru provided a space to do derby differently, and to allow newer members to experience that sense of excitement that original members experienced in the beginning, including the close ties with the "sister" league.

> When we had an A and a B-Team I felt that it had a quite good balance to it and the B-Team seemed to have a really good time, I mean A-Team was doing great things. The B-Team was clearly having a better time than A-Team was. They had more fun; they enjoyed it.
>
> (Nuke Interview, 22 August 2016)

There were moments when the whole team came together, and a real sense of "teamliness" was evident. One of these examples is what was commonly known as "the Phally jam". In May 2013, Zom B Cru played their first game. We were ahead, so as line-up manager, I asked Phally if he wanted to jam. In what turned out to be the last jam of the game, Phally was awarded lead jammer and completed

Belonging and inclusivity 89

lap after lap to thunderous cheers from everyone in the sports hall. It was one of the moments that Phally remembered with most clarity. He recalled that all of TIL, and many of his friends were there, watching him jam; something he normally did not do. He enjoyed the surprise element of it, and the chance to shine, whilst being comforted by the security of being so far ahead in points, that he was not risking the game. He remembered which blockers were in the wall, and how much trust he put in them to make his job easy.

> I'm like, "Aah, this is brilliant", and then looking at the clock going, "I'm really tired now, still a minute to go," came round again, fucking like, "I'm sure it's been longer than 30 seconds, like how – how is there still time on the clock" and going around. By the end I was like, "I am knackered", just like – [laughs] Um, and then the whistle went, and uh, I remember Pa Corr ran onto the track and basically – picked me up and like threw me on the floor and was screaming at me, and like all of my mates were just so like, "Holy shit", like, "Phally jam that's the best".
>
> (Phallic Baldwin Interview, 25 January 2016)

Phally's memories highlight how important Zom B Cru was to the skaters on this team. They weren't the most athletic or serious, and often had not had success in sports prior to this. Certainly Phally had not played sport much at school, or at all since, and here he was centre stage, his description showing a physical challenge, but a real sense of excitement and enjoyment that captured the attention of the crowd as much as any "serious" sporting occasion might do, and Oblivion believed it "was the most together TIL has ever been. I feel like Phally has a way of bringing people together, 'cause he has such a kind heart that he just unites a team" (Oblivion Westwood Interview, 19 August 2016). Stone (2017) argues that feelings of belonging ebb and flow, and moments such as this, and the way memories of them were shared, highlight again that TIL was not just a sports team.

Emotions ran high at events where the team travelled together and stayed one or more nights. These shared experiences (Stone, 2017) were good opportunities for team bonding. The pleasure skaters had in recalling the visit to Toulouse was mirrored by recollections of the Zom B Cru visit to Malmo, talked about so much afterwards, that those who did not go got completely sick of it, demanding we stop, giving rise to the oft-spoken "what happens in Malmo, stays in Malmo".

BLOCKTOPUS: I enjoyed certainly going to Malmo, and doing the competition with Zom B Cru was good fun.
DF: Tell me about it. Pretend I wasn't there.
BLOCKTOPUS: Am I allowed to tell you?
DF: Of course you are. What …?

90   Belonging and inclusivity

BLOCKTOPUS: I'm under the impression that what happened there stayed there.

(Blocktopus Interview, 8 January 2016)

Despite the connotations of this phrase – the deliberate similarity to "what happens in Vegas stays in Vegas", the visit was not really "going hard" (Coogan Interview, 31 May 2016), in terms of both drinking and socialising, and playing roller derby. It was about shared experiences, and shared emotions. It was an opportunity for getting to know your teammates better, for spending time together and creating inside jokes, and also, about doing something new and exciting.

As well as fun, "nice" was a word frequently used to describe this event; not a word typically associated with athletic events or "lads on tour" (Thurnell-Read, 2011):

> Well, that was just good, you know, it was a laugh. No one was taking it too seriously, there was just, it was just a sense of lads on tour just kind of having a laugh. But then you also had the added fact that we had Maud, we had Mouche there, so it kind of made it feel quite nice in that sense as well rather than just a "woah, boys" kind of thing. It was just nice, you know, that was a real kind of part of what derby – you know.
>
> (Grievous Interview, 15 January 2016)

Skaters enjoyed the lack of enforced jollity or manufactured "roller derby saved my soul" aspect (Packington, 2012), and enjoyed the "niceness" of spending time with friends, and making new ones, whilst doing something fun.

> But it, like it was fun it was, and I suppose it was coming up to the first men's World Cup and…. So, I mean I think we probably went into it a bit naively in that we didn't realise until either when we got there or very close to the time that we got there that it was basically a sort of a competition for most of the national teams from Europe. Yeah and we did alright yeah that was it but yeah. So, it was, but it was really good fun and sort of everybody was really nice, I mean there were some teams that were harder than others but they were friendly at the same time and I think they were just harder because half of them were sort of ice hockey players from Finland by the looks of it.
>
> (Blocktopus Interview, 8 January 2016)

During the 2016 season, TIL went on another of these "tours", to play a tournament in Brussels. There was the same sense of fun and enjoyment, but this was an A-team game, and the skaters were different (only Jason and I went on both trips), and hence the focus was very different. As this event took place during my official period of observation, I was well placed to observe, as well as discuss the event in interviews afterward. This enabled a better sense of immediacy, since

Belonging and inclusivity 91

everyone's experience of Malmo was seen through the filter of time and distance, leading to a potentially more "rose-coloured" experience. I interviewed Coogan about two weeks after we returned, Frank about three months after, and Stuntman, four. Their responses were framed by the question "tell me about some of your favourite moments with TIL?", and for various reasons, they were keen to present a positive image of the team. Nevertheless, these explanations showed the depth of impact this experience had for them.

> I came back from Brussels, I tried to explain to people the experience that I'd gone through and found myself woefully falling short of any kind of mark on trying to even begin to explain to people how much of a gooder experience it is. It's like when people talk about doing drugs like I did so and so drugs, like I wasn't there, I didn't experience it, I can't relate to you. It's, you know I feel, I'm empathising with you but to truly feel that you have to be there, you have to do in the experience and those are the best ones. When you are in the same place as someone else doing the same thing. But particularly it's having the other side of it 'cos sport's so much about, well it's a social thing....
>
> (Coogan Interview, 31 May 2016)

The event was framed as a triumph, despite losing both games. The focus was on having the same experience, being together, and doing well despite small numbers. Coogan also explained that he felt the low numbers helped people feel more together, that it was more likely they all experienced the games in a similar way as there were so few of them. It is clear here that community building is key. Even for Coogan, despite comments he made about roller derby being primarily a sport for him, and not a place to make friends, this experience was not just about playing a sport. There was a belief in shared goals and the sense of closeness that came from shared experiences (Stone, 2017).

Additionally, skaters were open about the emotion they felt during the games, seeing crying during the game as a positive thing.

> Brussels was incredible. We went to Brussels, and we thought we'd have about 10 people, thought, yep, take a decent team, and then Hoof broke his ankle. Prince left. I think we had somebody who couldn't afford it, and then we're down to like six or seven. We got there, as the magnificent seven, plus bench and line-up, Zoya and Wilma. And you ... and then first minute of the first game we play, Fin sprained an ankle, so we're down to six. The end of the first game, Stuntman wasn't feeling his best, so we were potentially down to five, but luckily Stuntman soldiered on, he was okay, and the fact that we faced De Ronny's at the time, many of them part of an international team, and they gave us quite a good going over, but we held our own, kept going. And by the second we played, it was just six of us, and we held them to a draw after normal time, which is incredible to say that we had – By that point, by

the end of the game, I think we had four people because two had fouled out. I had been back blocked, so I had gone off, and I was so tired, I went and cried in a corner. I was like, "Can't do it anymore," came back for the overtime jam and Zoya said, "No you need to go on." It just hurt so much; I was pretty sure I suffered whiplash from that. It was painful for about five, six weeks afterwards. But the whole journey was just really fun.

(Frank Interview, 17 August 2016)

Brussels for me was a huge personal kind of thing as well ... the two games were an emotional and physical wall I had to get through. Because I hurt myself in the first game. Or rather I got hurt in the first game. And I didn't think I could get through and it was – I felt I'd let the team down. I actually got upset. That's the only time I've ever cried in a roller derby game. I gave – literally gave blood, sweat and tears in that game. And actually it's come out as one of the best experiences, because I kept going, kept pushing. Uhm but it was just an incredible experience.

(Stuntman Interview, 13 September 2016)

The Brussels trip was a shared affective experience that served to both include and exclude (Clark, 2006). Unlike Clark's discussion of the football chant, not only did this experience "serve to act as a boundary marker to differentiate the collectivity from the opposition" (2006, p. 500), but also highlights the existence of multiple collectivities within the team. One such collectivity might be characterised as the Magnificent 7. Members who went to Brussels discussed a feeling of closeness to each other and a deep sense of belonging within the team for some time afterwards, effectively creating a team within a team, where members who could not go were excluded. Even within the Magnificent 7, there were different groups. The bulk of the ten people who went spent the day before the games together on a pub crawl (the specific details of which I chose not to record, with the exception of the banter involving me; see Donnelly, 2014), but Zoya, Wilma, and Foggy went off in a smaller group to visit tourist attractions. These three were excluded from one affective experience, whilst remaining included in the wider experience.

Acceptance

The first rule of roller derby is, always talk about roller derby.

Roller derby saying (apocryphal)

Academic studies of roller derby frequently quote the saying 'roller derby saved my soul' (Breeze, 2014, 2015; Pavlidis and Fullagar, 2014). As suggested, my participants tended to eschew what is sometimes felt to be manufactured and trite affect. Instead, I choose to open discussions on how accepting men's roller derby is with this bastardisation of the line from *Fight Club*: "The first rule of Fight Club is: You do not talk about Fight Club" (Fincher, 1999). Roller derby is inclusive and welcoming, and members of its community sometimes talk about very little else. In the words of one former member of TIL, "it is simultaneously the most welcoming place in the world, and the biggest clique I've ever come across" (Daddy Longlegs Interview, 3 October 2016). The tendency to be so focused on the sport and surrounding community made it very difficult for ex-members to stay connected to those who still moved within the community. One reason for this was the discovery that besides a love for roller derby, members often had very little in common, which at times made it harder to maintain the front of being united. The reverse of this is that roller derby believed itself to be very tolerant of quirks and oddities, and the community was very diverse, at least in certain specific ways. Whilst the next chapter discusses the impact of exclusion on marginal individuals, and ways in which TIL was not always as inclusive as it seemed, in this section I discuss some of the ways in which the roller derby community more generally, and TIL specifically, showed acceptance.

Women's roller derby was created out of a desire to give women opportunities to play sport that they would otherwise not have had. In the US, despite the passing of Title IX in 1972 (requiring gender equity for all educational programmes attracting federal funding, thus aiming to ensure girls and boys had equal funding for school sports), the uptake of sport amongst adult women remained low. It was linked to the Riot Grrrl movement and alternative DIY cultures (Duncombe, 1997), and leagues prided themselves of being women-owned and operated (Beaver, 2012).

Roller derby strived to be inclusive, to be a sport that welcomed anyone, regardless of size or shape or prior sporting experience. In the early days, there certainly was a sense that if you had never done sport before there was a place for you. When I joined a team in 2010, the global picture was beginning to change, but in my home city, the women's team was full of the sort of people who hadn't done team sport before, or often any sport outside of school. Roller derby culture of the time, in the form of blogs, and league websites tended to make it clear that in this context, anyone really meant any woman. Nevertheless, leagues could not flourish without support, and many officials in the beginning were men, drawn in through relationships with participants, or because they too felt marginalised from mainstream men's sports in some way.

TIL grew out of this culture, and also aimed to be inclusive. In the early days, the team welcomed those who had, like Stuntman and Phally, if not outright rejected sport, at least followed a different path; the kind of person who probably would not have been one of the "cool" kids, or an "alpha male" type. Breeze (2014) questioned whether roller derby was a "sport for women who don't like sport" (p. 16), and that's certainly what it seemed to be when I joined. Perhaps men's roller derby was becoming a sport for men who did not play sport. In a single issue of UK roller derby magazine *Lead Jammer*, there was an article discussing the negative effect of co-ed derby on the women's game (Proven, 2014),

94 Belonging and inclusivity

alongside coverage of the first Men's Roller Derby World Cup, and my own article on my research into men's roller derby (Fletcher, 2014a). This was a reflection of how views that were very resistant to the idea of men's derby (Ford, 2015; Racey, 2014) were giving way to positive representations (Copland, 2014; Flood, 2013; Goodman, 2016) focused on its potential to be inclusive.

In discussing the way such non-sporting men are vital to the inclusive nature of a team, and by extension, supporting the development of acceptable masculinities, Oblivion used the example of the "Phally jam" to explain Phally's impact on the team. The importance of that event for several interviewees suggested that Phally embodied team spirit.

Growing up, Phally found it hard to get interested in sports, but always saw roller derby as more of a game, like a grown-up version of Tag or Bulldog. He was drawn to the shared humour. Humour ran through Phally's interview more than any other. His memories and descriptions of events were shot through with asides and jokes, and the word "brilliant", and I laughed more during this interview than any other. Even when describing the banter aimed at him, which at times must have been near constant, he was in fits of giggles. He described wearing hot pants for the first time as a joke.

> And um it started off as a joke and I know at the time of the B-team game um, it was loads of people who literally just passed [minimum skills] and I think up until a couple weeks before, we were sort of worried, "are we gonna have enough players", like, "we need more people to pass" sort of thing so the mins got hammered just so we'd have enough players to do it. So everyone was like really working hard, um, and I know there was Pi and Whack and quite a few people were scared 'coz obviously they'd never done it before, and they'd only just passed, so they'd only just got to scrim like in the months coming up. So everyone was a bit scared and um, I remember talking to Rex, and saying, "Oh no, we'll just keep it light-hearted and just try and keep peoples' um spirits up" 'coz he was captain and I was vice-captain.
>
> (Phallic Baldwin Interview, 25 January 2016)

He goes on to discuss this decision further, as outlined in Chapter 3, and though he positions this choice as "a joke", it also served to help other skaters relax and feel less nervous about their first game. This light-hearted, silly side of roller derby is where Phally was comfortable and happy. He called the serious, athletic mindset "Team No Fun". Humour and silliness spilled over into whatever Phally did. Roller derby was very positive for Phally, and helped give him confidence.

> Starting off I was incredibly shy and quite withdrawn really and it's one of those where meeting lots of people and doing lots of things and travelling to other cities and playing with lots of people sort of brought me out of my shell a little bit and uh, I think it was mainly because everyone was there to have a

laugh at the start. There was no pressure and it was just like, "I'm just going to go talk to this person, coz they're on skates, they're a like-minded person".
(Phallic Baldwin Interview, 25 January 2016)

Being part of the roller derby community could be very positive for people who were shy or socially awkward, as it gave them access to a whole group of people who were, sometimes, as shy and socially awkward as they were, but who had a shared interest, and therefore, plenty to talk about. Stuntman explained that he found this to be the case, when filming a documentary about event planning in SSRD:

> Something from *The Shredding Planner*, actually talking to people like Buzzkill and Anne Grr, who said we are completely socially difficult. You know, backwards to some extent. We wouldn't do this. And I remember, really – we used it at the end of the documentary for a heartfelt hard screen moment. Anne Grr said "I've got Asperger's, I wouldn't talk to people, I'd sit in a room, I didn't see the point. And actually, this has got me out of it. Talking to people, started doing things". You know, and I think that's the great thing about Roller Derby as well. It – it does bring people together, even though it can be destructive at times as well. Because you're always gonna be, when you get that amount of people in a room.
> (Stuntman Interview, 13 September 2016)

Near the end of his interview, Blocktopus and I were joined by his partner and my housemate, both members of SSRD. We were talking about how sometimes the politics within SSRD can seem anti-male, using the examples of two male bench staff who were rumoured to have been chased out purely for being male. I suggested that, despite Blocktopus being SSRD's bench manager for years, no one had ever referred to him being male.

DU:(LAUGHS) HE IS!
BLOCKTOPUS: (laughs) No I think I agree and I said as much, maybe not particularly with SSRD in mind, but certainly with Team West Indies, but I'd never made a secret of it, and that I....
DF: What? that you're not a woman?
BLOCKTOPUS: No, the....
MS: I don't know, he tried to disguise it that time he wore a skirt.
(Blocktopus Interview, 8 January 2016)

From this point, Blocktopus continued to explain how he was more invested in women's derby but would happily step aside and allow a woman to bench, if they wanted it. DU and MS continued to interject, on tape, giving an insight into the dynamics of our friendships, but also highlighting the "oddness" of all of us. We acknowledged Blocktopus' place within SSRD as an "honorary woman" and discussed how, over time, Blocktopus had become the individual with arguably the biggest influence over SSRD, without any of the members expressing concerns about a man being in charge, despite that being a sticking point for other male members. This was precisely because he did display many "feminine" traits, which support the ethos of inclusion. Grievous referred to him as "the least threatening male presence on the planet" (Grievous Interview, 15 January 2016), and this, perhaps accounts for why Blocktopus is sometimes referred to as SSRD's "mum".

Grievous referred to skaters as boys and girls, and referred to the "A" teams as big boys and girls. This infantilising and childish language was in part perhaps a product of his role working with a school reception class, and partly a way of speaking which reflected his view of roller derby as a ridiculous sport that should not be taken too seriously, and the perils of forgetting "that you're all just dickheads on skates" (Grievous Interview, 15 January 2016). He also explained how he felt sympathetic to the way some people felt about men in derby, but suggested that men were always going to be involved in some way. The friendships and the links with the women's team were the most important parts of roller derby for him.

> I can see how derby would be great for guys that aren't going to be part of your regular sports team, you know like Phally, or you know Blocktopus is never gonna go and play football is he? I might do, or Jarvis might do, or take up cycling, but a lot of these guys aren't ever gonna go and do a regular sport for lack of a better word, so it's great that they've got something.
>
> (Grievous Interview, 15 January 2016)

It is interesting to note that though members (and former members) recognised the "oddness" in each other, being aware of others' inability to fit within a mainstream, traditional sporting environment, it was rarer for members to recognise it in themselves.

When discussing one of the TIL members who was a former rugby player, Grievous said that he did not think "that mentality" had a place in roller derby, and valued the sport as a place for non-conventional men.

> I mean, I think male [derby] definitely attracts outliers. You know, I think it definitely attracts or at least it did attract guys that weren't conventional athletes, you know what I mean? As we said, you know, can you imagine Phally going and joining a football team? Umm, and then, and yes, so I think it does attract those outliers and then also has the beneficial effect of reinforcing some sort of norms and values by being around women.
>
> (Grievous Interview, 15 January 2016)

Grievous seemed unaware that he is also considered to be non-conventional, positioning himself as more of a conventional athlete. Both Blocktopus and Grievous demonstrate that roller derby offers a space that allows men to engage with masculinity differently (Messner, 2002).

Belonging and inclusivity 97

There were contrary ideas about how inclusive the sport could or should be. For Bollock Obama, the acceptance stemmed from the fact that roller derby was a niche sport, and therefore did not attract many elite athletes, meaning that it could be more inclusive:

> My brother has an athletic history very similar to mine. He said roller derby is interesting because it seems like the sport in which the ceiling is low enough that it is possible to excel as a reasonably competent athlete and I thought, that's a good point. I could never be a national quality basketball player, certainly not at 38 years old, because I'm just not athletic enough ... whereas at roller derby, because it's such a small sport and because so many of the real elite athletes are elsewhere, it's a combination of my skill set and the low ceiling means that I can excel in it. That's something that Spectral said years ago, we were talking about it and he said he had no illusions that he wasn't a moderately competent athlete in an extremely niche sport.
>
> (Bollock Obama Interview, 24 August 2016)

Many roller derby players were keen for the sport to grow. Bollock wondered if, as the sport grew, and more athletic men were attracted to roller derby, the raised ceiling would change the profile of the sport and affect how inclusive it could be, which reflects Breeze's (2014) conclusions on women's roller derby. Coogan argued that

> there is a massive thing of your freaks and your runts coming into roller derby thinking this is an alternative sport for alternative people and they get there and they realise that it's not like it was back in the DIY days when it first started, it is a proper developing sport. People compete to win.
>
> (Coogan Interview, 31 May 2016)

A view that was in marked contrast to Phally's. Coogan came from a sporting family and had played many sports, though not at a high level, considering himself to be a "jack of all trades". He said that he liked sport, but that roller derby was the first sport he loved. He claimed it was a sport more than anything else. His enjoyment came from playing the sport and working as a team. He argued that he was not interested in "alpha-male bullshit" in life, but in sport, it was all about the win. Again, this contrasts sharply with Coogan's comments about the trip to Brussels, which suggests roller derby was not all about the win for him, but that he valued the community too.

Despite claiming the DIY days were behind us, as chair of TIL for a year (April 2015–April 2016), Coogan contributed a lot to the running of the league. Coogan had clear ideas about how the sport should develop and distance itself from its DIY beginnings. He argued that derby could still retain its "family feeling", but that it needed to be more clearly open to people who were not "alternative". He recognised the tension between broadening the membership base and ensuring space remained for people who sought a place in roller derby because it accepted them for who they were, but he did not necessarily have an answer for that. Instead, he suggested that the way forward was to reach and engage people who had played other sports, to help them see roller derby as a viable alternative.

> It's just a case of people understanding that it's an acceptable thing for them to do. Just as it's an acceptable thing for me to go, oh I fancy trying something else, I'm gonna try cricket. Oh, shit I'm quite good at this, people aren't gonna laugh at me for playing cricket, well they might do but you know, there's a preconceived notion whenever I've spoken to people it's a lesbian sport.
>
> (Coogan Interview, 31 May 2016)

Roller derby is not the only sport facing issues of whether to foreground inclusivity or competition. Cohen *et al.* (2014) discuss how the sport of Quidditch is competitive but inclusive, and explore how the shift towards competition and commercialisation can lead to a loss of enjoyment and increased dropouts in sport. Even within Quidditch, "intrinsic factors, such as inclusivity and equality, often take a back seat to extrinsic motives such as desires to win and success on the playing field when there is opportunity for recognition and notoriety" (Cohen *et al.*, 2014, p. 232). Coogan articulated an issue facing roller derby, and Quidditch; the issue of how to engage with the mainstream of sport, without losing the inclusivity that makes them different.

Stuntman, lacking much in the way of sporting background, talked extensively about the inclusivity of roller derby and TIL. His initial involvement was not athletic, but creative. After becoming aware of roller derby through filming his documentary, he was swiftly drawn into the sport as an active member. Stuntman argued that inclusivity was not just about ticking boxes, but about acceptance. He said it was a community and "it is there for a lot of people and it does give people a lot" (Stuntman Interview, 13 September 2016).

The way inclusivity was understood changed over time. Bollock talked about how roller derby used to be "far more inclusive of people who don't know how to play it and don't know anything about it" (Bollock Obama Interview, 24 August 2016), but Stuntman explained how the focus had become much more about sport:

> it's come from a side show spectacle to something more sincere. And I think that's been orchestrated from within. And correctly so. It's still inclusive. It still accepts everyone. But it's people with sports interests coming in as opposed to someone who thinks it's cool, because they saw it on Murder, She Wrote or whatever it was.
>
> (Stuntman Interview, 13 September 2016)

Belonging and inclusivity 99

He acknowledged that roller derby was largely white and middle class, but he was also proud to be a part of the team as he believed it did not replicate the "bravado masculinity" of more traditional sports, and was open to men like him, with "camp genes". For Stuntman, ultimately, inclusivity was about acceptance of people as they were, and the freedom to be yourself:

> But I guess people [...] perhaps don't behave how society believes you should in a sport. I don't know how to rephrase that. I think it just gives you – for all the people like me and you who didn't do sports, perhaps. That's a great way to put it. It gives you the sport to do. Because there are athletic people, who want to do it, but they feel alienated by other sports. And this sport kind of has a positive stigma attached. What's the word? Positive thing attached to it, which people assume and know that it's all right to be who you are. And I think that's more – I think that's a better way to put it, rather than saying, "Masculine, feminine, gay, straight." And this, that and the other. You can be who you are. Because you're just playing a sport. And you won't get alienated or begrudged or focused on for that.
>
> (Stuntman Interview, 13 September 2016)

The freedom to be who you are was also cited by Nuke as a reason why TIL was inclusive and reflected in Fin's experience as a newcomer. It is likely that this feeling of inclusivity was more possible precisely because the team was smaller. In discussing the period during which TIL had a successful A- and B-Team, Daddy Longlegs highlighted the negative impact of ego:

> I think what happened with the A-Team is, all the talented people ended up in the A-Team, but with the talent came ego, so it also had all the people with ego, so instead of it being, it started to lose its way, and instead of being about a team, it became about individuals. So, the bickering got more. The tantrums got more.
>
> (Daddy Longlegs Interview, 3 October 2016)

This suggests that competitiveness negatively impacted feelings of inclusion and belonging, and the lack of competition for roster spots within TIL during the observation period made it much more possible to include everyone.

Stuntman reflected on the negative impact of elitism within SSRD, and was concerned to ensure TIL did not go back to that:

> I'm intrigued to see how TIL approach next season. I think, you know, we need a professional and focused training, but I also think we need to be inclusive and make sure it stays fun or else it's going to be – it'll drop off again.
>
> (Stuntman Interview, 13 September 2016)

This increased desire for inclusion and equality has been positively linked with gender inclusive experiences in sport (Cohen *et al.*, 2014; Gubby and Wellard,

100 Belonging and inclusivity

2015), and in the openness of OTA and MRDA's policy, roller derby clearly demonstrates this potential.

The need to belong

In roller derby, inclusive was often used in the context of gender (Mullin, 2012), and the WFTDA update of their gender policy in 2016 (WFTDA, 2016), generated lot of discussion about how trans inclusive the sport had become. Whereas previous literature on transgender sport participation finds negative experiences, barriers, and a lack of inclusion (Cohen and Semerjian, 2008; Hargie *et al.*, 2017; Jones *et al.*, 2016; Semerjian and Cohen, 2006), I found positive and welcoming practices in roller derby. In addition to its non-discrimination policy, the MRDA made explicit reference to roller derby as a *community*, thus including everyone.

> With encouragement from the Women's Flat Track Derby Association (WFTDA), MRDA hopes to build a strong and influential organization like WFTDA. Our aim is to complement their contributions to the sport of roller derby and offer new perspectives to the derby community.
>
> (MRDA, 2017)

It was not merely rhetoric, a trick of language. Men's leagues offered something genuinely different in terms of belonging and inclusivity in roller derby. The MRDA position made it clear that you could be yourself in men's roller derby, the importance of which should not be understated (Farrance, 2014).

In Chapter 3, I explored how "inclusivity" was a discourse used to create a good impression and position TIL as a team that is accepting, however, in Fletcher (2020), I focus on how this notion of inclusivity works in everyday practice, with an extended case study of Fin's lived experience. Fin was both newcomer to TIL and had recently come out as non-binary and transmasculine, embarking on a very public transition (Le Fin, 2016). The discussion in this article highlights the importance of the strategies discussed in this chapter in enabling Fin to create a sense of belonging, but also the work done by other TIL members to make the league a place where Fin felt a sense of belonging.

Using the language of action and "doing" emphasises that belonging and acceptance are processes; roller derby was an ever-changing and evolving community, and levels of inclusivity changed over time. Roller derby was a place where people could find acceptance, but though inclusivity may have been the ideal, exclusion and the setting of boundaries were also necessary. Both Goffman and Jenkins attempt to account for difference within groups; they argue that it is not necessary for every group member to think or act the same: Jenkins maintains that "it is possible for individuals to share the same nominal identity, and for that to mean very different things to them in practice, to have different consequences for their lives, for them to 'do' or 'be' it differently" (2014, p. 46). That may have been the case within TIL, but it nevertheless created tension. Carter and Baliko

Belonging and inclusivity 101

call for "a reconceptualisation of community that is based on complexity and struggle" (2017, p. 696), foregrounding the importance of recognising community as a space which is both inclusive *and* limiting, pointing out the transformative possibilities of a notion of community fraught with tension and always in flux. TIL members struggled to reconcile the desire to be inclusive with a drive to be competitive and to take the sport more seriously, which was complicated further by contradictory notions of the very meaning of inclusivity.

The inclusivity that existed tended to be gender-based (Mullin, 2012), or based on intangibles such as acceptance of perceived oddness. Inclusion based on more usual markers such as class or race was not only inadequately provided for, but sometimes actively disregarded as not the sense in which inclusivity was meant. This is problematic in itself, but even to take the view that inclusivity was possible within the boundaries of white and middle-class runs up against several obstacles. Concepts of belonging and inclusivity were open to a multiplicity of interpretations and there existed a difference between the ideal type and how this was experienced in everyday practice. Banter, for example, allowed people to feel they belonged, except when it did not. It was a way of including people under the banner of the group, except when it was distracting and unhelpful. Such practices belied the inclusive claims, offering instead an exclusive reality (Adjepong, 2015; Burdsey, 2008; Rannikko *et al.*, 2016). The practice of banter may have been shared (McHugh *et al.*, 2015), with everyone at least given the opportunity to participate and reciprocate (Mynard *et al.*, 2009), but the values placed on this practice differed, with different members having varying understandings of what the banter represented (Wichmann, 2015).

Spracklen (1996) argues that community is associated with shared meanings and mutual knowledge (see Cohen, 1982, 1985), but points to a polarisation within rugby communities between traditionalists and expansionists (rugby league) and between professionals and amateurs (rugby union). Such a divide creates tension as different meanings come into conflict. This is evident within TIL in the similar divide between traditional and alternative approaches to sport, and the divide between those who were serious and those who refused to be. The B-Team was, by default, more inclusive. The existence of Zom B Cru allowed a situation to arise where the team was split between those who were generally more serious, more athletic, and more likely to subscribe to traditional views of masculinity on the A-Team and sport and those who were non-sporting and non-traditional on the B-Team. Although tension existed between the A- and B-Teams, The Inhuman League as a whole was able to manage this better when members were forced, through declining numbers, to be one single team once more.

TIL members enjoyed being TIL members most when they were working as a team. The problem with this is that it was inextricably connected with newness, and the excitement of creating something free of preconceived notions. The excitement in the beginning, therefore, was mirrored by the excitement Zom B Cru skaters experienced in their first few games. Thus, just as TIL had a difficult middle period, TIL skaters often experienced the same. This sometimes led to skaters discontinuing membership. Where it did not, they had to find fresh challenges. For a few TIL members, the challenge of skating short provided this excitement. However, as the team strove to become more professional and hence more serious, whilst there was a clear path towards gender inclusivity, ways to continue to include and accept the less serious, and the non-sporting were murkier. The "feeling" of belonging (Stone, 2017) could be absent at the margins. Selection made roller derby less inclusive. Breeze (2013, 2014) posited this as necessary for the development of the sport. But within TIL, there was a clear desire to maintain the identity of the group as a community, not just a sport.

The ways in which belonging was experienced, sometimes as a deep sense, and sometimes brief and fleeting (McHugh *et al.*, 2015), by members of TIL highlight the importance of being part of something. Skaters felt they had more freedom to be other than stereotypical sportsmen, given the acceptance of oddities and quirks, thus supporting Messner's (2002) arguments about the freedom to be found at the margins of sport. It did not necessarily matter how "true" this was – and no one had done surveys etc. – but it was believed to be true, and several participants expressed the view that they and the team were inclusive and accepting; the belief in shared values (McHugh *et al.*, 2015) and experiences strengthened the bond between team members, which could render more negative experiences invisible.

Observing TIL suggested there was something more at work than could be explained through concepts such as inclusive masculinities (Anderson, 2009), or masculinities in transition (Robinson, 2008), or mischievous masculinities (Nichols, 2016). How the men in roller derby did friendship and intimacy was very different to the experience discussed by Messner (1992), and Anderson's explication of sport as a negative and damaging "near-total" institution within orthodox masculinity (Anderson, 2009, p. 47). Robinson considers how men interact with each other in relationships; that how men "do" friendship can be deep, lasting, and intimate (Robinson, 2008), which is similar to what I saw in TIL. However, there was an unusualness to the ways the members behaved towards each other. The acceptance of others' quirks, or oddness was different. Belonging and not belonging were inextricably interconnected. In men's roller derby, they were having to learn how to belong in the absence of stable reference points. Members made sense of roller derby and their experience of it through whatever reference point they had. Symbols were shared but understood individually (Cohen, 1985), allowing multiple contested meanings (Pavlidis, 2013) to coexist in an understanding of sport that was both traditional, and alternative. In this context, the "but" of "yes, I belong, but ..." is inevitable.

In the years since Fin joined The Inhuman League, the team became ever more open, reflecting the wider MRDA community. Although nominally still called "Men's" roller derby, most MRDA teams became open to members of all gender identities, including, controversially, cisgender women. This has implications for theories of gender integration in sport. It is a "common sense" view that women can never be as strong as men, or as fast as men, and this is often the excuse for not viewing female sport as on a par with men's (Kessler and McKenna, 1978).

Belonging and inclusivity 103

This still seems to be the case in the "money sports" (Messner, in Messner and Sabo, 1994), but contrary to the organisation of football, basketball, hockey, etc., roller derby was, in its dominant structure and values, a *feminine* construction. The "proof" of men's superiority may in part lie in the value placed on "sports that favour whatever biological advantage men as a whole maintain" (Anderson, 2009, p. 29), but what of a sport that was argued to favour the biological advantages of women?

In calling for an examination of the current system, Messner and Sabo (1994) recommend asking "fundamental questions about the kind of athletic experiences we want to create for ourselves and society" (p. 172). The athletic role can be dehumanising to men, and so equal opportunity in sports, as they are currently constructed, is not necessarily unambiguously positive: as Connell (2009) notes, the masculine domain of sport is just as dangerous for men as for women. Despite this, Messner and Sabo (1994) partially reject the Left/counterculture criticism of sport as "a threat to a healthy self-image, as a barrier to intimacy between men, and as an impediment to building an egalitarian, cooperative community" (p. 183). Taking this position further, locating his work in "emancipatory research" and advocating for change, Anderson (2009) calls for academic examination of gender-integration, arguing that it benefits both men and women. Messner also advocates a social justice model of equity in sport, "adopting a simultaneous quest for simple fairness and equal opportunities for girls and women *along with* critical actions aimed at fundamentally transforming the centre of men's sports" (2002, p. 153). This transformation involves change in other power institutions, such as law, education, and the media, and confronting the sport–media–commercial complex, and its ideological model, the televised sports manhood formula (Messner, 2002, p. 153).

Into this debate, comes a new sport. In its embrace of all genders, roller derby clearly demonstrates the benefits of gender integration, not just for men and women, and not just for cisgender people, but for transgender and non-binary athletes too. Robinson (2008) offers a counter to this perspective, concluding that higher participation of women does not necessarily mean they are valued, but as a DIY sport that was created around the strengths of women, roller derby offers new possibilities for both physical and emotional health for all participants. However, in its reproduction of traditional sporting practices through "seriousness" and "professionalism" roller derby also demonstrates how exclusive and dehumanising the sport can be.

The notion of skills capital does have similarities with Anderson's discussion of masculine capital, especially given that "boys at the top of the masculine hierarchy are actually provided more leeway to temporarily transgress rigid gender boundaries that few other boys are willing to challenge" (2009, p. 43). However, the way this plays out differs from Anderson's (2009) theory of inclusive masculinity and orthodox masculinity because, unlike in his research, within TIL, more traditional forms of masculinity are hegemonic. The traditional masculinity espoused by those with high skills capital is not necessarily desired or aspired to

104 Belonging and inclusivity

by other men, but it is respected and deferred to. This capital also gave the bearers the ability to ignore decisions around reducing banter and to be more explicitly sexual in their use of language. This was accepted by other members, yet still subverted where possible into something more abstract. The acceptance of different forms of masculinity was possible because they were engaged in the wider project of roller derby, which meant however many differences there were, there was this one big similarity – within limits. These limits are discussed further in Chapter 5.

References

Adjepong, A. (2015) "We're, like, a cute rugby team": How whiteness and heterosexuality shape women's sense of belonging in rugby. *International Review for the Sociology of Sport*, 52(2), pp. 209–222. DOI: 10.1177/1012690215584092.

Alexander, J. (2016) *On the Outskirts? Exploring the Sydney Roller Derby Scene*. PhD thesis, Western Sydney University.

Anderson, E. (2009) *Inclusive Masculinities*. London, Routledge.

Beaver, T. D. (2012) By the skaters, for the skaters: The DIY ethos of the roller derby revival. *Journal of Sport & Social Issues*, 36(1), pp. 25–49. DOI: 10.1177/0193723511433862.

Bennett, J. (2015) "Snowed in!": Offbeat rhythms and belonging as everyday practice. *Sociology*, 49(5), pp. 955–969. DOI: 10.1177/0038038515589299.

Bourdieu, P. (1990a). *In Other Words: Essays Towards a Reflexive Sociology*. Stanford, CA, Stanford University Press.

Bourdieu, P. (1990b) *The Logic of Practice*. Cambridge, Polity Press.

Breeze, M. (2013) Analysing "seriousness" in roller derby: Speaking critically with the serious leisure perspective. *Sociological Research Online*, 18(4), p. 23. DOI: 10.5153/sro.3236.

Breeze, M. (2014) *Just a Big, Sexy Joke? Getting Taken Seriously in Women's Roller Derby*. PhD thesis, University of Edinburgh.

Breeze, M. (2015) *Seriousness and Women's Roller Derby*. London, Palgrave Macmillan.

Burdsey, D. (2008) Contested conceptions of identity, community and multiculturalism is the staging of alternative sport events: A case study of the Amsterdam World Cup football tournament. *Leisure Studies*, 27(3), pp. 259–277. DOI: 10.1080/026143608 02127235.

Carlson, J. (2010) The female significant in all-women's amateur roller derby. *Sociology of Sport Journal*, 27(4), pp. 428–440. DOI: 10.1123/ssj.27.4.428.

Carter, C. and Baliko, K. (2017) "These are not my people": Queer sport spaces and the complexities of community. *Leisure Studies*, 36(5), pp. 696–707. DOI: 10.1080/02614367.2017.1315164.

Channon, A., Dashper, K., Fletcher, T., and Lake, R. J. (2016) The promises and pitfalls of sex integration in sport and physical culture. *Sport in Society*, 19(8–9), pp. 1111–1124. DOI: 10.1080/17430437.2016.1116167.

Clark, T. (2006) "I'm Scunthorpe 'til I die": Constructing and (re)negotiating identity through the terrace chant. *Soccer and Society*, 7(4), pp. 494–507. DOI: 10.1080/14660970600905786.

Cohen, A., Melton, E. N., and Welty Peachey, J. (2014) Investigating a coed sport's ability to encourage inclusion and equality. *Journal of Sport Management*, 28, pp. 220–235. DOI: 10.1123/jsm.2013-0329.

Cohen, A. P. (1982) Belonging: The experience of culture, in A. P. Cohen (ed.), *Belonging: Identity and Social Organisation in British Rural Cultures*. Manchester, Manchester University Press, pp. 1–19.

Cohen, A. P. (1985) *The Symbolic Construction of Community*. London, Routledge.

Cohen, A. P. (1986) *Symbolising Boundaries: Identity and Diversity in British Cultures*. Manchester, Manchester University Press.

Cohen, J. H. and Semerjian, T. (2008). The collision of trans-experience and the politics of women's ice hockey. *International Journal of Transgenderism*, 10(3), pp. 133–145. DOI: 10.1080/15532730802297322.

Connell, R. W. (2009) *Gender in World Perspective* (2nd edn). Cambridge, Polity Press.

Copland, S. (2014) "Roller derby could herald a revolution for gender equality in sport". *Guardian Online*. Available from: www.theguardian.com/lifeandstyle/2014/jun/18/could-the-men-of-roller-derby-become-sports-first-male-feminists (accessed 27 August 2015).

Delanty, G. (2010) *Community*. London, Routledge.

Donnelly, M. K. (2014) Drinking with the derby girls: Exploring the hidden ethnography in research of women's flat track roller derby. *International Review for the Sociology of Sport*, 49(3/4), pp. 346–366. DOI: 10.1177/1012690213515664.

Duncombe, S. (1997) *Notes From the Underground: Zines and the Politics of Alternative Culture*. London, Verso.

Dynel, M. (2008) No aggression, only teasing: The pragmatics of teasing and banter. *Lodz Papers in Pragmatics*, 4(2), pp. 241–261. DOI: 10.2478/v10016-008-0001-7.

Farrance, L. (2014) "Roller derby changed my life": Sport as emancipatory potential. *Proceedings of the 2014 Australian Sociological Association Annual Conference held at the University of South Australia, Adelaide*.

Fincher, D. (1999) *Fight Club*. [DVD] Los Angeles, 20th Century Fox.

Fletcher, D. (2014a) Roller derby: A ladies' sport, for ladies? *Leadjammer*, 9, p. 28.

Fletcher, D. (2014b) Co-ed roller derby. *Inside Line*, 14, pp. 35–36.

Fletcher, D. (2020) The positive impact of trans inclusion in team sports: Men's roller derby, in R. Magrath, J. Cleland, and E. Anderson (eds.), *Handbook of Masculinity and Sport*. London, Palgrave Macmillan, pp. 171–187.

Flood, J. (2013) "Roller derby provides a model for pro sports in accepting openly gay men". *Huffington Post*. Available from: www.huffingtonpost.com/jim-flood/roller-derby-provides-a-model-for-pro-sports-in-accepting-openly-gay-men_b_3212721.html (accessed 14 January 2017).

Ford, C. (2015) "Why some sports should remain a women's game". *Daily Life*. Available from: www.dailylife.com.au/health-and-fitness/dl-sport/why-some-sports-should-remain-a-womens-game-20150519-gh53a2.html (accessed 14 January 2017).

Goffman, E. (1959) *The Presentation of Self in Everyday Life*. London, Penguin.

Goodman, E. (2016) "Meet the men of roller derby, a niche sport within a niche sport". *Vice Sports*. Available from: www.vice.com/en_us/article/xybdq7/meet-the-men-of-roller-derby-a-niche-sport-within-a-niche-sport (accessed 27 March 2019).

Gubby, L. and Wellard, I. (2015) Sporting equality and gender neutrality in korfball. *Sport in Society*, 19(8), pp. 1171–1185. DOI: 10.1080/17430437.2015.1096261.

Hargie, O., Mitchell, D., and Somerville, I. (2017) "People have a knack of making you feel excluded if they catch on to your difference": Transgender experiences of exclusion in sport. *International Review for the Sociology of Sport*, 52(2), pp. 223–239. DOI: 10.1177/1012690215583283.

Haugh, M. (2010) Jocular mockery, (dis)affiliation, and face. *Journal of Pragmatics*, 42(8), pp. 2106–2119. DOI: 10.1016/j.pragma.2009.12.018.

Haugh, M. (2014) Jocular mockery as interactional practice in everyday Anglo-Australian conversation. *Australian Journal of Linguistics*, 34(1), pp. 76–99. DOI: 10.1080/07268602.2014.875456.

Haugh, M. and Bousfield, D. (2012) Mock impoliteness, jocular mockery and jocular abuse in Australian and British English. *Journal of Pragmatics*, 44(9), pp. 1099–1114. DOI: 10.1016/j.pragma.2012.02.003.

Jenkins, R. (2014) *Social Identity* (4th edn). London, Routledge.

Jones, B., Arcelus, J., Bouman, W., and Haycraft, E. (2016) Sport and transgender people: A systematic review of the literature relating to sport participation and competitive sports policies. *Sports Medicine*, 47(4), pp. 701–716. DOI: 10.1007/s40279-016-0621-y.

Kessler, S. J. and McKenna, W. (1978) *Gender: An Ethnomethodological Approach.* Chicago, IL, University of Chicago Press.

Kotthoff, H. (2006) Gender and humor: The state of the art. *Journal of Pragmatics*, 38(1), pp. 4–25. DOI: 10.1016/j.pragma.2005.06.003.

Le Fin, T. (2016) *Switching Teams.* [Film] Sheffield, E.D.E.N. Film Productions.

May, V. (2011) Self, belonging and social change. *Sociology*, 45(3), pp. 363–378. DOI: 10.1177/0038038511399624.

McCann, P. D., Plummer, D., and Minichiello, V. (2010) Being the butt of the joke: Homophobic humour, male identity, and its connection to emotional and physical violence for men. *Health Sociology Review*, 19(4), pp. 505–521. 10.5172/hesr.2010.19.4.505.

McHugh, T. F., Coppola, A. M., Holt, N. L., and Andersen, C. (2015) "Sport *is* community": An exploration of urban Aboriginal peoples' meanings of community within the context of sport. *Psychology of Sport and Exercise*, 18, pp. 75–84. DOI: 10.1177/1049732318759668.

McManus, J. (2015) "Transgender athletes find community, support in roller derby". *ESPN*. Available from: www.espn.com/espnw/athletes-life/article/14110104/transgender-athletes-find-community-support-roller-derby (accessed 14 January 2017).

Messner, M. (1992) *Power at Play: Sports and the Problem of Masculinity.* Boston, MA, Beacon Press.

Messner, M. (2002) *Taking the Field: Women, Men and Sports.* Minneapolis, MN, University of Minnesota Press.

Messner, M. and Sabo, D. (1994) *Sex, Violence & Power in Sports: Rethinking Masculinity.* Freedom, The Crossing Press.

Morgan, G. (2013) "Bonnie Thunders, roller derby star, on the sport's acceptance of LGBT players". *Huffington Post.* Available from: www.huffingtonpost.com/2013/05/15/bonnie-thunders-roller-derby-gay_n_3280263.html (accessed 27 March 2019).

MRDA (2017) "About". *MRDA.* Available from: http://mrda.com/about (accessed 5 November 2017).

Mullin, K. (2012) *Neither Butch nor Barbie: Negotiating Gender in Women's Roller Derby.* MA dissertation, Loyola University Chicago.

Murphy, S. P. (2017) Humor orgies as ritual insult: Putdowns and solidarity maintenance in a corner donut shop. *Journal of Contemporary Ethnography*, 46(1), pp. 108–132. DOI: 10.1177/0891241615605218.

Murray, G. (2012) *The Unladylike Ladies of Roller Derby? How Spectators, Players and Derby Wives Do and Redo Gender and Heteronormativity in All-Female Roller Derby.* PhD thesis, University of York.

Mynard, L., Howie, L., and Collister, L. (2009) Belonging to a community-based football team: An ethnographic study, *Australian Occupational Therapy Journal*, 56, pp. 266–274. DOI: 10.1111/j.1440-1630.2008.00741.x.

Nichols, K. (2016) Moving beyond ideas of laddism: Conceptualising "mischievous masculinities" as a new way of understanding everyday sexism and gender relations. *Journal of Gender Studies*, 27(1), pp. 73–85. DOI: 10.1080/09589236.2016.1202815.

Packington, E. (2012) "Roller derby saved my soul … O RLY?". *TEDx Sheffield*. Available from: http://tedxsheffield.com/2012/erica-packington (accessed 21 July 2018).

Pavlidis, A. (2013). Writing resistance in roller derby: Making the case for auto/ethnographic writing in feminist leisure research. *Journal of Leisure Research*, 45(5), pp. 661–676. DOI: 10.18666/jlr-2013-v45-i5-4368.

Pavlidis, A. and Fullagar, S. (2014) *Sport, Gender and Power: The Rise of Roller Derby*. Farnham, Ashgate.

Piedra, J., García-Pérez, R., and Channon, A. (2017) Between homohysteria and inclusivity: Tolerance towards sexual diversity in sport. *Sexuality & Culture*, 21, pp. 1018–1039. DOI: 10.1007/s12119-017-9434-x.

Plester, B. A. and Sayers, J. (2007) "Taking the piss": Functions of banter in the IT industry. *Humor: International Journal of Humor Research*, 20(2), pp. 157–187. DOI: 10.1515/HUMOR.2007.008.

Racey (2014) "In her hips, there's revolution …". *Rollin' News*. Available from: http://rollinnews.com/post/in-her-hips-theres-revolution (accessed 14 January 2017).

Rannikko, A., Harinen, P., Torvinen, P., and Liikanen, V. (2016) The social bordering of lifestyle sports: Inclusive principles, exclusive reality. *Journal of Youth Studies*, 19(8), pp. 1093–1109. DOI: 10.1080/13676261.2016.1145640.

Robinson, V. (2008) *Everyday Masculinities and Extreme Sport: Male Identity and Rock Climbing*. Oxford, Berg.

Semerjian, T. Z. and Cohen, J. H. (2006). "FTM means female to me": Transgender athletes performing gender. *Women in Sports and Physical Activity Journal*, 15(2), pp. 28–43.

Spracklen, K. (1996) *"Playing the Ball": Constructing Community and Masculine Identity in Rugby: An Analysis of the Two Codes of League and Union and the People Involved*. PhD thesis, Leeds Metropolitan University.

Stone, C. (2017) Utopian community football? Sport, hope and belongingness in the lives of refugees and asylum seekers. *Leisure Studies*, 37(2), pp. 171–183. DOI: 10.1080/02614367.2017.1329336.

Mynard, L., Howie, L., and Collister, L. (2009) Belonging to a community-based football team: An ethnographic study, *Australian Occupational Therapy Journal*, 56, pp. 266–274. DOI: 10.1111/j.1440-1630.2008.00741.x.

WFTDA (2016) "WFTDA Gender Statement". *WFTDA.com*. Available from: https://wftda.com/wftda-gender-statement/ (accessed 2 May 2018).

Wichmann, A. (2015) Participating in the World Gymnaestrada: An expression and experience of community. *Leisure Studies*, 36(1), pp. 21–38. DOI: 10.1080/02614367.2015.1052836.

Chapter 5

Barriers to belonging

The previous chapter included an in-depth exploration of inclusive practices. Inclusivity is discussed as a contested "ideal" (Breeze, 2014, p. 166), and there are factors compromising a league's attempts to be inclusive. One of these is the drive to be competitive. Breeze suggests that for her league, "there's a sense that inclusivity was where the league began, and competitiveness was where it is going" (Breeze, 2014, p. 173). As discussed in Chapter 3, TIL also, at times, strove to be serious and competitive. As part of this drive for competitiveness, leagues take steps such as implementing attendance policies, as TIL did on more than one occasion.

> Developing an attendance policy was a question of how to encode and enact an ideal of "fairness" or *inclusivity*. Even as team selection is about inclusion, it is also about exclusion and the definition of boundaries.
>
> (Breeze, 2014, pp. 170–171, emphasis in original)

Attendance policies in effect exclude those with responsibilities beyond the league, who cannot always make roller derby a priority. The term "inclusive" is used very specifically in roller derby to talk about including different types of women who may not be particularly athletic, or skilled at the game. It is about including those who are different shapes and sizes, and different age groups. Although there is a pervasive idea in roller derby that anyone can play with "enough hard work and determination" (Cotterill, 2010, p. 27), it is openly apparent that this is not the case in practice. In her research, Cotterill found that "multiple participants talked about women joining for the 'wrong reasons'" (2010, p. 32). Roller derby therefore is not open to everyone, identity is policed, and self-expression is limited (Cohen, 2008; Pavlidis, 2013).

Within TIL, however, a feeling of exclusion was sometimes the result of failing to demonstrate sufficient skill, either through patchy attendance, or differences in ability between the strongest and weakest skaters. At times, skaters expressed frustration at this, but during 2016, TIL were too few in number to abide by an attendance policy. Inclusivity became the default position, and even the weakest skaters were almost guaranteed a roster spot, although it could be argued that this was out of necessity, and therefore, weaker skaters could at times feel that their sense of belonging was insecure. Therefore, although the group identity was inclusive, members experienced this differently through, for example, the treatment they received from others. This is in line with Jenkins' (2014) argument that members of a group do not necessarily experience and understand a nominal identity, in this case an inclusive league, in the same way. Additionally, Jenkins' assertion that fragile membership status results in greater conformity (2014, p. 152) would suggest that these weaker skaters are less likely to speak out about any negative feelings or events.

Exclusion, however, is written into the very fabric of this community. The WFTDA's mission statement itself promoted this:

> Founded in 2005, the Women's Flat Track Derby Association (WFTDA) promotes and fosters the sport of women's flat track roller derby by facilitating the development of athletic ability, sportswomanship, and goodwill among member leagues.
>
> The governing philosophy of the WFTDA is "by the skaters, for the skaters." Female skaters are primary owners, managers, and/or operators of each member league and of the association. Operational tasks include setting standards for rules, seasons, and safety, and determining guidelines for the national and international athletic competitions of member leagues.
>
> All WFTDA member leagues have a voice in the decision-making process, and agree to comply with the governing body's policies.
>
> (WFTDA, 2016)

As discussed in Chapter 2, it may be unintentional, but the "by the skaters, for the skaters" ethic undermines efforts to include those who do not skate: the non-skating officials, announcers, photographers, etc. who work just as hard as skaters do, often for less "reward" (Fletcher, 2017). Despite WFTDA changing their mission statement to remove this phrase, its impact continued to be felt, and though the MRDA made explicit reference to "community" (MRDA, 2017), within TIL there was still a divide between skaters and volunteers.

As far as this study goes, these issues arose continually through the data, representing significant barriers to belonging. Particular individuals had a major impact within the team, which, when negative, created tension for all members. Whilst some members had a very positive experience within TIL, and talked about the team's inclusivity, other members had less positive experiences, and talked about the downsides of membership. These tensions played out on an individual basis, but affected the whole group. Through detailed case studies, this chapter will explore the barriers to belonging in key areas. First, I discuss the impact and influence of one member, whose behaviour and actions created tension within the league, leading some to leave, and others to feel less welcome. I theorise this as a clash between different types of masculinity, with Donald Thump (a pseudonym I have chosen to protect this member's anonymity; see Introduction) functioning as an embodiment of hegemonic masculinity pitted against the more inclusive masculinity of most members. The next section explores how this hegemonic masculinity plays out in an attitude towards referees, which impacts upon their feelings of belonging, and explores their position at the boundary of the TIL community (Barth, 1969; Cohen, 1985). Whereas Chapter 2 considers the lack of officials from an institutional and logistical perspective, this chapter explores the issue from a more individual perspective, and therefore includes my personal account of acting as a referee during fieldwork. Finally, I consider an outsider perspective, that of a photographer, to draw links between practices I have observed within TIL and those of the larger community, whilst also considering how community was experienced at the boundary.

A variety of studies on the broad themes of community and identity in sport have concluded that, although many sporting spaces, especially alternative ones, make claims for inclusiveness (Adjepong, 2015; Burdsey, 2008; Rannikko *et al.*, 2016), such spaces often reproduce exclusion. This exclusion occurs through adherence to the dominant gender order (Burdsey, 2008) and hegemonic masculinity (Rannikko *et al.*, 2016) or norms of race (Adjepong, 2015). Such findings suggest the existence of boundary maintenance and group identities based on a collective internal definition, but also that the question of whose definition counts is still a matter of power (Jenkins, 2014). Such research consistently reveals the marginalisation of those who do not fit the heteronormative masculine ideal.

Rannikko *et al.* (2016) make connections between subcultural capital and the display of hegemonic masculinity, despite the continued existence of an ideology of equality, which reflects the findings of my own research (Fletcher, 2019) that members with high skills capital had more freedom to behave in ways that replicated traditional sports models, and that within TIL, the ethos remained one of inclusivity, regardless of whether the practice could always be judged as such. Although Rannikko *et al.* (2016) identify significant differences in the roller derby community due to its explicit aim to provide a space for women and non-stereotypically athletic bodies, my experience more accurately reflects Spracklen's (1996) discussion of rugby as a space where expressions of male identity tend towards the hegemonic. Women in the game express masculinity, but, despite this, are the recipients of banter, including abuse, hostility, and sexist remarks. Like Mary, a female referee who "has had to face abuse and disinterestedness at every step of her refereeing career" (Spracklen, 1996, p. 191), I experienced difficulties refereeing for a men's team.

Every team has one

During my time with TIL, I experienced conflict with one member in particular, and this spilled over into my work as head referee of SSRD. This member also refereed, but never accepted my authority as HR, choosing to talk over me and ignore things I said whilst refereeing, and to argue my calls and shout penalties at me whilst he was playing. Initially, this made attendance at TIL sessions difficult and stressful.

> This antagonistic feeling seems to be worse since I've started doing fieldwork. Maybe I've noticed more all the little things he does to show disrespect and make me feel isolated and unwelcome, or maybe it's because I'm dwelling on it a lot. Is his presence really such a huge part of everything, or are there many more stories I'm missing?
>
> (Field notes, Saturday 16 January 2016)

It became apparent that I was not the only person with tales of difficulties working with this member. Observation and interviews strongly suggested that the influence of one member could have massive implications for the team as a whole, so whilst the influence of Donald Thump was not the only story within TIL, it was an important one, and should be considered.

Thump's identity as TIL's dark secret (Goffman, 1959) has been discussed in Chapter 3, as an aspect of the league which was incompatible with their ethos and image as inclusive. In Fletcher (2019), I discuss Thump's behaviour as an expression of high skills capital and expected sporting masculinity (Wellard, 2016). He was very secure in his membership at the centre of the community, allowed greater freedom for non-conforming or deviant behaviour (Jenkins, 2014) as a direct result of his skills capital and in contrast to the conformity of less secure members. He was considered to be "too valuable to lose" (Fletcher, 2019, p. 5). Possibly for this reason, current members were much more cautious about saying anything negative, one referring to his poor behaviour as "nonsense" and suggesting anyone with an issue should take it up with him, rather than talk about him behind his back. The respect other members had for Thump was shown by focused attention during the sessions he coached, and most members regarded him as an effective coach, despite his long-winded explanations of drills, and discussions of examples of when he had used the skills in question successfully and how great things were "back in the day". Thump seemed to expect other coaches to run the sessions just as he did and explain every aspect of a drill. But if they chose not to, he would attempt to derail the session and encourage others not to listen, which meant that, by comparison, his sessions ran more smoothly, simply because people listened.

But many members did have issues with Thump, and on occasion did try to raise them with him. Thump had previously been subject to a disciplinary for his behaviour towards other members, but refused to accept the legitimacy of any complaints, instead attacking the process itself. The recommendations of the disciplinary were not particularly harsh, simply insisting Thump follow the code of conduct, specifically: take part in warm up and cool down; wear a helmet; pay attention to coaches and in drills; do not undermine officials; be considerate to his teammates. However, this disciplinary seemed to cement a division between Thump, who seemed to be aggrieved, and the committee, who felt that too much of their time was spent dealing with issues around Thump, and not enough spent developing the team.

This tension meant that his coaching style was not appreciated by everyone.

> If we are going to have training sessions that are the Donald Thump show again, with lots of Donald Thump talking and lots of Donald Thump showing us how to do things and lots of me standing around and waiting, then I might find something else to do.
>
> (Bollock Interview, 28 August 2016)

Bollock expressed dislike of Thump's coaching style and explained how he preferred to have a drill explained one-to-one if necessary, whilst other skaters continued with the drill. Bollock also suggested that Thump demanded similar levels of attention when he was not running training, and this was another negative.

> I dislike playing with Donald Thump because he always makes everything about himself. Even when he's not in the drill, he has taken himself out of the drill to go away somewhere else so that we can see that he has taken himself out of the drill to go away somewhere else.
>
> (Bollock Interview, 28 August 2016)

In roller derby, there is a penalty for "unsporting conduct", or misconduct:

> **All participants in a game of roller derby must be respectful of one another.** This includes but is not limited to Skaters, Team Staff, Officials, mascots, event staff, and spectators. When Skaters or Team Staff behave in an unsporting manner, they should be penalised accordingly.
>
> Unsporting conduct can take many forms. Examples include deceiving or ignoring Officials, engaging in dangerous and illegal actions that pose a real danger to oneself or another, or being abusive toward another person; other unsporting conduct may also be penalised.
>
> (WFTDA, 2019, emphasis in original)

Although this rule sets out some specific examples of unsporting conduct, the final phrase remains fuzzy, and open to interpretation. As a referee, I was often in a position to see such tactics being used. Thump often used them.

> Last jam – although skaters may not have realised it was the last jam, they knew it was near the end. Thump lone wolfing at the front (in exactly the way he's told others not to), facing off against LRT jammer. Jammer comes towards him, and I (as front IPR) see Thump lift his hand to his face, scream, and go down, before there is any contact from the jammer. Classic Donald Thump.
>
> (Field notes, Sunday 15 November 2015)

This tactic was rarely called.

> Thump did another flopping thing – Afa was blocking him, Andy called OOP, and Thump threw himself to the floor and shouted, "OOP block, surely?" neither of us called anything, so Thump got up and carried on. I said afterwards to Andy that it was a clear case of embellishment, but he said he didn't think it was, that it was Afa counter blocking, which assumes Thump went down as a result of the block. It was so clear, I was 100% certain it was embellishment. I didn't call it, mostly because I couldn't be bothered with the hassle it would inevitably cause – Thump would argue it and things would become unpleasant.
>
> (Field notes, Sunday 8 May 2016)

In field notes, I acknowledged my reluctance to call such a penalty, for fear of unpleasantness, which again supports Jenkins' (2014) discussion of conformity by those on the edge of a community, but I was also frustrated that these actions did not seem to be recognised by other referees either. It was difficult to know whose refereeing was at fault, given that despite such a lengthy ruleset, it was often subjective and depended upon the individual referee's positioning and perspective on the game.

It was interesting to note the differences in referee responses. In examples of on-track behaviour I noted in field notes as "flopping", most other referees simply ignored the action. However, referees who were also friendly with Thump consistently called penalties on the other skater. In one scrimmage:

> Thump'd be doing something clearly obvious – falling over in a way that was obviously fake, and then Pa Corr, every time, Pa Corr was calling a penalty on the other skater. Even when it was blatantly obvious that Thump was flopping.
>
> (Field notes, Sunday 7 August 2016)

It is important to acknowledge that my personal feelings may have impacted the way I saw such actions, and that, as a referee, if I was 100% sure about the initiator and impact of an illegal action, I should have called a penalty. In the next section I discuss in more detail the various reasons why I did not do so, but here I explore further what I did see.

My perspective was that Thump created unnecessary tension in scrimmages, through his actions and words. In field notes, I noted when such things occurred: "The scrim got a bit scrappy and messy. Thump was throwing a few revenge hits in and shouting things to refs – Shouting a lot at his team, both when on track and off" (Field notes Sunday 8 May 2016). On such occasions, I tried to speak to other team members to see what sessions looked like from another perspective and record their responses in my field notes. During this session, for example:

> Dorny recognised the game was not calm. We discussed before the end whether or not we should call it early – mainly to avoid further injury, and

114 Barriers to belonging

messiness. We called "captains" in to have a word, and they did calm down a lot. I asked Fin later if it was obvious the game wasn't calm from a skater's perspective too, and they said yes. Which is interesting.

(Field notes Sunday 8 May 2016)

The kind of gameplay used in the game against CTB, discussed in Chapter 3, continued to be used throughout the year I observed TIL. One of the other referees of that game told me that she had not refereed a men's game since, having had such an unpleasant time at that one.

Skaters, however, maintained the front (Goffman, 1959) that they had been calm and "played their game". This playing style had negative impacts on the whole team. There was a rise in both needless aggression and unsporting behaviour from other team members, and in "targeting" skaters during training (Fletcher, 2019, p. 9). I noted that in one scrim:

Wilma seemed to be targeted by Thump quite a bit. He hit her in the face one time, and twice more in other (legal) target zones. Each time he'd apologise, once actually hugging her, but still, the hits seemed deliberate.

(Field notes, Sunday 20 March 2016)

This sometimes seemed to be a style of training Thump employed, being tough on skaters to encourage them to improve, but it was not always seen as beneficial.

If you're playing another team you obviously look for the weak link ... but within your own team, I don't think you need to make the point of continually attacking the same person and beating them down time after time after time after time to try and get the reaction of them to improve.

(Blocktopus Interview, 8 January 2016)

At other times, it seemed to be less about a training opportunity, and more a sign of frustration. Often occurring in tandem with flopping, Thump shouted and swore at other skaters on track, and often at the referees as well.

Jason did something, blocked him in some way, which probably was perfectly legit. I heard Thump shouting to him "what is your fucking problem?" Actually, probably should've called him on a misconduct for that, but I didn't.

(Field notes, Sunday 7 August 2016)

Sometimes the frustration was justified. I had noted several times, that this aggression occurred after a penalty had been missed. Frequently I note this because I was the referee who missed the penalty, which led to feelings of guilt on my part. In one example though:

That guilt evaporated in the rest of the half as it became clear that Thump was out to get Circe big time. Revenge hit after revenge hit – not sporting, not necessary. I think there was one pass where Thump let the opposing jammer straight through because he was so intent on hitting Circe. Also, at least one hit caused Circe to go down and take another skater with her, leading her to get a penalty.

(Field notes, Friday 1 April 2016)

After the trip to Brussels, Thump left. This was a surprise since the trip had been such a positive experience, and served to build bonds and bridges between members, including, it seemed at the time, Thump. Nevertheless, TIL felt much more relaxed whilst he was gone. I discuss in Fletcher (2019) some of the potential reasons for Thump leaving, and how then chair Frank shared with me the disagreements he had had with Thump over committee decisions (p. 9). This marks a turning point in TIL management. Coogan had largely agreed with Thump over issues of how to run the league and they worked together well during the time that Thump was vice chair. Given Frank's more inclusive, democratic style of leadership, it was perhaps inevitable that there would be conflict between him and Thump. The rest of the team, however, was still willing to allow Thump to take the lead, and as soon as he returned, things carried on much the same. He immediately began making comments on training and suggesting improvements as though he had never been away – talking about the team as "we" and making no reference to his disappearing act after Brussels. He quickly assumed authority again, suggesting Nuke for a fill-in line-up manager (LUM) when the regular LUM was unable to make a game, and running training sessions.

Thump's attempt to take control was short-lived and his behaviour quickly became problematic once more. Stuntman believed that "Thump's heart [was] always in the right place", but he did seem to be struggling to maintain involvement. During his absence, the league had had to restructure training and, therefore, other team members were running sessions in a much more open way than Thump had previously. Questions and discussions were more welcome, there was a more mutually respectful atmosphere. No longer being the sole voice of authority meant Thump had to work with others; not a position he appeared comfortable with, choosing instead to sit on the sidelines and criticise:

Zoya gives a skater some tips, saying "remember …" Donald Thump parrots her, adding "it's me who taught them that", to his son. He seems to be behaving in a very petulant and childish manner. Beat goes over to talk to Donald Thump, but they end up arguing (quietly, but it's definitely not friendly). Donald Thump says "dunno what she's doing here" meaning Zoya. Beat says she's here because she's bench manager. Donald Thump says he's the one who's been here (over the last few weeks, he has run training, and Zoya has been away with, partly, family issues). Beat points out that, at the moment, he's just watching. After Beat leaves him, suggesting he joins in,

Donald Thump continues making snide comments, loud enough for Beat to hear. Beat turns, but doesn't respond or engage with Donald Thump further. Nobody else does either, for the rest of the session.

(Field notes, Sunday 2 October 2016)

Thump's difficulties coincided with my withdrawal from the field, so I was not there to see what happened next. Later, I was told by more than one member that Thump had been asked to leave, although it is unclear to me whether he was formally expelled from the league or made the decision himself. Current TIL members were reluctant to discuss negatives and were keen to assure me that everything within the league was wonderful. Having withdrawn from the league almost entirely for a period of time, I was now an outsider, and therefore someone from whom certain things must be hidden (Adler and Adler, 1987; Beere, 1979).

Most of the interviewees who expressed negative opinions of Thump were ex-members. Overwhelmingly, they cited Thump himself as one of their main reasons for leaving. These negative experiences echo what Pavlidis and Fullagar characterise as the "dark side" of belonging in roller derby (2014, p. 83).

> Just to make sure it's on record obviously as well, you know, I don't want to underplay, Donald Thump is you know, if Thump wasn't in TIL, I would potentially still be at TIL. And I can think of a number of people that would say exactly the same thing. You know, you had a person here that, you know, I can think maybe like three or four people that had said in private that the reason they left was because of Thump. You have referees that left, you had one of the founding members who was ostracised from attending, you had a relationship with our sister league that was broken and this is all because of one person and I think part of it for me, was a kind of umm, how can you lot not see how malignant an element this person is, and allow him to stay in your league?
>
> (Grievous Interview, 15 January 2016)

For some ex-members of TIL, Thump came to embody all that was wrong with TIL.

> I just feel like he damages the lives of a lot of people. I don't mean to be – [sigh]. I don't feel like I'm exaggerating there. Roller Derby is such a huge part of people's identities and people's lives and he's literally taking it away from people by driving them out, and that's awful. Some people can find other places in it but I think what he did to Phally was pretty awful … [he] would often be like, "You know, if you would just transition better, that would have been an easier drill for you".… But never in front of anyone. Only after the drill was done and he also just physically – one of the good things for Donald Thump is that he was so aggressive to everyone that it was hard to tell when he was bullying someone physically, but he also physically bullied Phally.
>
> (Oblivion Westwood Interview, 19 August 2016)

In his interview, Phally made no mention of this, and was largely positive about Thump. It was not always clear whether some interviewees had greater insight into Thumps' actions, or whether personal feelings led to bias against him and therefore over-reporting of his shortcomings. Ex-chair Daddy Longlegs, for example, argued that Thump was a massively disruptive influence.

> Donald Thump refused to basically interact with the committee for most of it. He was very vocal in public, in public forums and social media about asking questions. Which in essence weren't anything wrong with the questions he asked, but then wouldn't accept the explanation you'd give him. And I can't really think of a specific, but it would be something would be done, the committee would do something and then it would be, I don't know.... Classic one would be, we'd be late publishing minutes, so he'd start, "Where's the minutes? where's the minutes? where's the minutes?" Put the minutes out, he'd read the minutes and gone, "Why have you done that? Who said you could do that?" Well, we've done it because it's part of the committee's role. "Well, you didn't ask the team." And it would just go round and round in circles. While on the flip side, being a very good coach, just, we spent far too much time in committee talking about Donald Thump, with a committee full of people who weren't prepared to act.
>
> (Daddy Longlegs Interview, 3 October 2016)

Daddy recognised that the committee was at fault, and acknowledged weaknesses of leadership, but it remained clear that Thump was problematic, causing significant issues for individual members and the league as a whole.

> And certainly cost me Omar. It cost me Grievous. It cost me probably Brad, Al. But I definitely know they all left and packed in committee because of their interaction with Donald Thump. Al, who took on head of coaching, Thump wouldn't talk to him. He refused to interact with him at any level.
>
> (Daddy Longlegs Interview, 3 October 2016)

Frank talked about TIL's reputation "for being arseholes" as a result of the environment created by Thump's actions. The disrespect shown towards opposition skaters and officials, and sometimes even teammates, was not popular outside of the team and was at odds with TIL's desire to be seen as a nice, inclusive league. This attitude reflected normative ideas of masculinity and sport (Messner, 2002; Numerato and Baglioni, 2011), which privilege practices of hegemonic masculinity (Atencio *et al.*, 2009).

The way in which hegemonic masculinity continued to be rewarded within TIL was strongly connected with the impact of skills capital, and the power of those with high levels of it to be able to control the direction of the team. Although there was a sense that such negative and damaging behaviours ought to have been challenged and dealt with sooner, there were many factors that prevented this.

During our interview, I explained to Grievous that the committee had been calm and much less fraught since Thump had been voted on to it.

> That's a tough one isn't it, because that makes it sound like Thump was the solution, when all of those times the problem was that Thump was the problem.... So he created this whole year of problems, and then comes in, joins the committee and everything gets sorted, as if he's somehow been the white knight, even though all the problems were.... That's really, that's bizarre.
>
> (Grievous Interview, 15 January 2016)

Andy summed up the feelings of many when he said, "I just don't find him a likable person ... I find his cynicism and his sarcasm, and his sense of humour really destructive" (Andy Social Interview, 18 October 2016).

During fieldwork, I observed Thump to be directly instrumental in making skaters feel that they did not belong. During one session, Thump was particularly harsh towards Broot. I noted that: "I was in the process of preparing to move the benches because they were in the way and dangerous. Thump skates by, knocking Broot (deliberately?) over into the bags left there" (Field notes 14 February 2016). Broot told me at this session that he desperately needed new skates because his were falling apart, but that he had been struggling to pay his membership dues, and therefore could not afford to both save for new skates and pay for membership. He had decided to try to focus on refereeing for a while, to stay involved, and felt that his current skates might hold up to that better than scrimmaging. However, Thump told Broot he was not needed to ref, so he stood in the penalty box instead and watched as three people struggled to referee a scrimmage that could have used four. He did not continue attending training for long after that. Despite the belief that TIL was an inclusive league, the treatment of Broot supports points made by several researchers that roller derby is not inclusive for everyone (Cohen, 2008) and that there might not be a place for someone who is not the right kind of person (Krausch, 2009).

The referee's decision is final

In teams, as defined by Goffman, there is the same separation of insider and outsider as discussed by Cohen (1985). "Logically, *in*clusion entails *ex*clusion, if only by default" (Jenkins, 2014, p. 104, emphasis in original). Goffman outlines a variety of discrepant roles, which complicate the binary of insider/outsider, and suggest the existence of individuals who are neither audience nor performer. One of these roles is the confidant: "confidants are persons to whom the performer confesses his sins" (1959, p. 158). As a researcher, I functioned in this way. But as a participant, there were things it was necessary to hide. This section lays bare some of the issues I had during my observation.

Researchers argue that it is not enough to recognise that there can be "situated knowledge", but that knowledge must also be accountable (Downes, 2009;

Stanley, 1997), which means a deliberate recognition of the stance of the observer. Trying to keep a check on my emotional responses required "faking" (Beere, 1979; Klein, 1983). In roller derby, so much is shared publicly, and there is such pressure on members of the community to show positive images of the sport, such faking is inevitable. Skaters within the team environment sometimes "faked" socially desirable and acceptable responses. Klein recommends recognising that "faking" occurs, and incorporating it into research methods, and that "by accepting and taking it seriously, we accept and take ourselves seriously" (Klein, 1983, p. 91). The importance of faking in a roller derby context is twofold. First, insiders want to present a positive view of the sport to outsiders, presenting a front to those who are not members (Adler and Adler, 1987; Goffman, 1959), and second, insiders may sometimes choose to fake emotions and responses to other insiders.

Thurnell-Read (2011) discusses how draining it can be to manage "ambivalent emotional responses to our participants" (p. 44), turning to the practicalities of embodiment – his dress, presentation of self, his "embodied masculinity" (p. 44) – in managing the impression he creates. Leigh (2013) borrows the phrase "dirty secret" from Morriss (2014) to explain the desire to keep things back from her participants: "In this context, my dirty secret involved not wanting to show participants my analysis of their words for fear (or shame) that I would disappoint them or fail them in some way" (Leigh, 2013, p. 123). In my own research, faking occurred when I disagreed with some of the practices of my participants, and for much of the time during early field work, my "dirty secret" was that I would much rather not have been there, and found engaging with several members of the team, especially Donald Thump, rather difficult and emotionally challenging and it became necessary to find ways to manage my emotions (Holland, 2007; Thurnell-Read, 2011).

As outlined earlier, the conflict I experienced in TIL spread into further roller derby communities. Shortly after I became head referee of SSRD, Thump started showing up to referee at training. In an attempt to boost the number of officials, and the skill level of existing officials, I was running a referee training programme. Thump would only occasionally engage, but when he did, his actions undermined my coaching and session plan. During scrimmage, I felt that he undermined me at every turn – calling penalties I was in a better position to see, telling me calls I made were wrong, calling pack definition/penalties as an OPR (which is not usually done), changing referee positions after I had organised them. In part because of this, he made me feel nervous and unsure and my confidence in refereeing plummeted whenever he was at training. I felt a sort of imposter syndrome, a discomfort that was heightened the more the environment reflected a "traditional" model of sports. I did eventually talk to Blocktopus (head of training) and the chair of SSRD about it, and they were broadly supportive, but offered not actually that much practical help. He disappeared for a time, but even when he was not at training, there was always a bit of a cloud over things for me, expecting Thump to turn up every session and not really relaxing until about halfway through the session when it became clear he would not. This did not last though, and at around the point I had started to relax, Thump came back.

Throughout most of the observation period, Thump and Zoya were close friends, working together frequently. Having some months with both Thump and Zoya in my referee crew was hard. They would skate around talking together for most of the session, joining up to chat between most jams and at every time out. They would frequently join in a little group with whoever else was reffing the scrim, effectively isolating me, as I did not feel comfortable joining such a close group. They would both overrule my calls, and contradict what I was saying. In any referee discussion, they would agree with each other in opposition to me. Thump would try to lead official reviews and take it upon himself to perform the duties of a head referee, or tell me what I should be doing, when I was head referee. In any rules discussion, they would confidently assert their position, and would frequently explain the rules to me as though I did not know them. This destroyed my confidence, even though I noticed that Thump and Zoya were both wrong, or I was right, often enough to demonstrate that there was no need to feel this way. Nevertheless, my perception of Thump and Zoya's behaviour towards me was such that I had no confidence in making referee calls when they were present. In this routine behaviour, it could be said that Thump and Zoya were doing belonging (Bennett, 2015). They were engaged in practices of inclusion, and exclusion. In my distress, I reacted by withdrawing further, isolating myself even more.

It was not only members of TIL who made things difficult. SSRD skaters were equally hard to work with. It was difficult to be the head referee when skaters liked to shout at you and tell you that you were wrong. This made for an, at times, uncomfortable training atmosphere. Combined with the lack of communication around events, I began to feel isolated and unappreciated. Again, the refrain of "by the skaters, for the skaters" reinforced this feeling, this lack of belonging, and by centring skaters, it demonstrated that I was on the margins of the group at best.

This lack of communication with officials stemmed from the needs of officials, and the need for officials, simply not occurring to most skaters – often skaters who were tasked with organising training, games, and travel. As such, volunteers seemed to become invisible, or to become a role rather than a human being. I am unsure how much my feelings about SSRD impacted on my feelings about TIL or vice versa, or how much my feelings were impacted by my researcher status or my referee status, but there were so many negative experiences all together that my overall emotions at this time were sadness, rejection/isolation, and anger, and these feelings spilled out over all of roller derby.

Taking all of these feelings into the observation of TIL made things very difficult. As I was negotiating official entry into the league, I was simultaneously dealing with these issues at SSRD training. Thus, as I was explaining my plans to the league, and explaining how, in return for allowing me to observe, they would have a regular referee at training (something which had long been an issue as noted in Chapter 2), I was struggling to fulfil this obligation because of feeling so

Barriers to belonging 121

undermined and therefore not wanting to be at training. Strengthening this feeling at the time were occasions when other TIL skaters came to SSRD training to ref – such as Coogan and Frank. They deferred to Thump and huddled with Thump and Zoya, further isolating me, and becoming involved in a situation where my refereeing skills were belittled and undermined, which then translated into a similar attitude towards me at TIL training.

I had absolutely zero confidence in my refereeing skills when I was at TIL training. During drills, I heard Coogan shout at me to ref things, whilst skaters who were coaching, or resting from the drill skated in front of me blocking my view so I could not ref. Skaters regularly reffed their own drills, partly because they'd had to for so long because they hadn't had enough regular referees, and partly for ongoing feedback and coaching as they run drills. It became a vicious cycle that I felt undermined, so my refereeing suffered, so skaters picked up the slack and learned not to rely on me, so I felt undermined … it was difficult to know where it started, and it was difficult to see a way back. I never knew in training sessions what coaches wanted me to do in drills – make the full call, or just say "Jason, watch your elbows", or if the skaters noticed I was there to ref, or needed me there at all. Regularly in training sessions, it took nearly an hour for the coach to ask me to do something. I felt useless at training partly because of the lack of confidence, but also because there seemed to be no provision for the referee's needs. The league wanted referees there to help them but had given no thought to what benefit attendance could have for the referees – it was a totally one-sided arrangement.

There were serious problems with this approach seen from a referee perspective. Being ignored by coaches and skaters was boring and isolating. Drills were set up to facilitate skater improvement, not referee improvement. There were many drills that were impossible to referee, and so it was difficult to work out how to get involved. Skaters were told exactly what to do and why to do it for a drill, but no one told the referees what to do or why to do it. Again, as any referees attending training were largely self-taught, we had to figure it out for ourselves most of the time. Skaters were often told they should drill as though it was for real, but referees were told not to call penalties because it was only a drill, making drills an ineffective learning experience. Skaters were encouraged to fail as part of the process of learning, but referees were expected to be perfect from the start. The impact on referees of decisions made about how to structure training was never considered, making training a very hostile environment in which to learn to referee.

Despite these things, skaters would sometimes ask why there were not enough referees at training, why referees did not want to come to training, or how to get more referees. Not enough thought was given, however, to how to retain the referees that were already there, as if those referees did not count, did not exist, or were somehow defective, and not worth bothering with. I became part of the problem, because I was the person who should be making refereeing a supportive environment for new trainee refs, but I no longer had the time or the inclination to chase down the plans so I could organise things for the refs.

Refereeing for TIL games was also hugely problematic. I felt that, although skaters shouted at referees a lot, TIL skaters saved the worst of it for me, and that it was somehow personal. This made attending a training session the day after a game where several league members had shouted at me, or criticised the refereeing from the bench, very difficult. I did not subscribe to the view that referees should be less sensitive. I did not believe that feeling passionate about a game was a reasonable excuse for being horrible to people who are supposed to be your friends, and I found it upsetting that in some ways, when I was dressed as a referee, I ceased to be seen as a person for the duration of a game.

In what I saw as a further attempt to undermine my position as head referee of SSRD (and at the time, the only HR in Sheffield), Donald Thump talked Frank into arranging "Sheferees in the Pub", an event for Sheffield-based referees to discuss specific aspects of the rules, with drinks. He arranged this on a Tuesday evening, so it would clash with SSRD training, and I could not attend. Eventually, I lost the desire to fight for continued involvement, because I felt at best invisible and at worst victimised. Also, despite having stood for HR of SSRD twice, I did not actually want to be in charge. What I wanted was for people to be able to work together, without egos and competitiveness, towards a common goal, without sniping, or back-stabbing, or one-upmanship. But I did not know how to make that happen. In August 2016, I stood down as HR of SSRD, and instead shifted focus to the *observation* part of my participant observation for the remainder of fieldwork.

Despite attempting to perform an identity of experienced referee and TIL member, it is likely that I gave off (Goffman, 1959) too many impressions to the contrary. My negative feelings resulted in tension and apprehension that may have given off the unintended impression that I felt like I did not belong, as noted earlier in this section. Such a failure in terms of impression management thus may have defined my role as an outsider. Not least because, as unserious as I often was, the front of experienced official (presupposing a performance of professionalism) was difficult to maintain. Therefore, my identity was not validated by Thump, or Zoya, or either team, and it was their definition that counted (Jenkins, 2014). In addition, taking on the discrepant role of confidant (Goffman, 1959), compounded the difficulties of giving a successful performance as a member of TIL.

Andy Social, a fellow referee, and also TIL's secretary and finance officer, was more resilient than I had been, and had a much more relaxed take on the tensions and criticisms that arose.

> You have to rationalise it and put it in perspective. I think, whose making those criticisms and how much do I think of their opinion and actually where do I look for my validation and stuff. If there's issue is to do with the committee, I think well if you want it different get yourself on the committee or do it formally, come to the committee and put a motion and don't just slag people off behind their back.
>
> (Andy Social Interview, 18 October 2016)

Having quite a stressful job, Andy saw roller derby as a hobby; he did it for fun, and so did not take it seriously.

However, Andy talked about his experience of refereeing in a way that validated my own. Andy did suggest that his views on officiating would not be listened to by the team.

> I don't think I'm seen with any authority and I don't know if that's because I haven't been a skater and I'm not a brilliant skater, but there are a lot of referees that aren't brilliant skaters, that are respected.
>
> (Andy Social Interview, 18 October 2016)

I asked if Andy felt he was respected at TIL, and he said, "No, I don't think I do". I suggested that this lack of respect for officials might have had an impact on their attendance at training.

> Well, I mean, yes, it's been a strange time at work and other things; I can make excuses, but some of it's down to it's not as enjoyable if you're not appreciated and like I said I'm not after appreciation but if it doesn't come then it doesn't motivate you to put yourself out.
>
> (Andy Social Interview, 18 October 2016)

Andy also talked about the place of officials in training, or rather, the lack of a place.

> I certainly don't feel that they use, well, I'll talk about me but probably the same as you, they don't use the referee officials that are there in a positive way or a constructive way. They're not asking you to can you go and do, can you watch them, can you do this, we're looking for this, we're practising this, it tends to be the officials going to the people leading the training, well, what do you want us to do?
>
> I mean, it's not difficult to do but I think it's a subtle difference and not being incorporated into that practice, you're almost an additional thing that they gotta to deal with rather than an integral part of the session.
>
> (Andy Social Interview, 18 October 2016)

Andy alluded to the behaviour of skaters towards officials and how that tended to put potential officials off volunteering at training sessions.

Despite his involvement with the team as referee and as committee member, Andy talked of TIL as "they" rather than "we". He supported the team, and enjoyed seeing them play well. He enjoyed the excitement of the sport, but did not consider himself to be one of them. In describing the camaraderie of the refereeing side of things, it seemed clear that amongst like-minded officials is where Andy felt he belonged. Officials had, or Andy believed they had, shared values and practices. This belief in similarity led to a feeling of belonging, as discussed by McHugh *et al.* (2015) and Stone (2017). However, he still wanted to be respected by the members of TIL, and to feel part of the team.

> I'd like to think that the home league was where I belonged. I'm not always sure that's the feeling I get back. That's probably why I've not been to prac- tise as much. I think if I – I don't know whether it'll change. I used to go very regularly and never missed. Yes. I don't know if it was that different. But there are different people there now, and some of the people I really enjoy being with and rub along with well. Yes, apart from Thump there's no one that I would struggle to get along with. I can't think of anyone. I suppose if it was an ideal, I would enhance my skills and my skating and be seen as a ref at TIL by TIL and from outside. Whether, that means me dedicating myself a bit more, and doing –
>
> (Andy Social Interview, 18 October 2016)

However welcoming the referee community could be, it was important to feel val- ued and respected by the people with whom he spent most of his time in roller derby.

Andy talked of working to develop his refereeing skills. I asked if he thought TIL would give him the support he needed.

> That's the million-dollar question isn't it? Because the officiating role is going to be put out to – put out to people again along with a few other roles. I'm in two minds as to whether to put my name forward because I might get shot down in flames. Then if no one else does it, a bit like the treasury role and the secretary role and it's a more visible role, it's a more active role.
>
> (Andy Social Interview, 18 October 2016)

Andy stressed that appreciation was key to recruiting and retaining volunteers, from officials to committee members. In many ways then, despite his more relaxed approach, Andy's feelings mirrored my own. He identified the importance of being valued and respected, but as referees lacking in skills capital, we both occupied a marginal space within the team, and therefore had limited opportunity to have an impact upon the team's ethos and training.

Roller derby through a different lens

Because I wanted to gain an insight into how roller derby and The Inhuman League was experienced from a different point of view, I interviewed the pho- tographer behind Roller Derby on Film (RDOF), who had been involved in the margins of the sport for the last eight years. He had worked with many roller derby teams and had covered events in a number of countries. Initially loosely affiliated with SSRD, he was in the unusual position of being neither insider nor a complete outsider.

It was quite interesting in how if they had someone else, a partner or someone who was in the team who was a photographer, it meant that sometimes you were then overlooked, so you weren't really part of it because they're quite happy to shift who is doing that role to make someone else feel good.... You're part of the team when they want something but not part of the team when someone else has got some sort of in into the role you're doing.

(RDOF Interview, 19 October 2016)

It was clear that RDOF had experienced many frustrations through his years as a volunteer. He suggested that the skaters got a lot out of the sport but failed to consider the effort involved "around the edges" to help the teams become successful.

It's interesting about what I get out of it but if I go and shoot a bout I could end up coming back with 3,000 photographs. I have to sit down, usually a day after, because I know people want to see them quite quickly afterwards, to edit them. That can take between four and six hours – depends how quick I am working and how much coffee I have had. Post the pictures up and you edit as best as you can to make everyone look good.... They like ones that have got their friends in, they'll comment on, they'll make little conversation between friends. The number of people that actually go, "thanks for taking photographs", I can count them on one hand or probably less than one hand to be honest. And they're people I know personally, everyone else doesn't care, it's always like, we don't care what else is going on. They don't say thanks or anything. In those sorts of circumstances, it's a bit demoralising.

(RDOF Interview, 19 October 2016)

RDOF talked about the roller derby community in general. The problems he outlined and the experiences he discussed were not limited to one team alone. This suggested that the issues present in The Inhuman League were not unusual. He talked about the attitude and behaviour of skaters towards officials and towards each other as being less than supportive, and suggested that the only surprising thing about a fight that broke out between members of two teams at the MRDA Championships that year (2016) was that it was discussed and dealt with, rather than swept under the carpet and ignored.

I also think the trouble with the management in Roller Derby teams is because – you know it seems like every year they vote a new committee in different roles and stuff there's no consistency to start seeing those trends. Everyone is starting fresh and it's like, it's a clean slate for everybody so this behaviour starts to perpetuate. Also, that thing of going like, if they are your best player who's going to turn around and say you are not playing?

(RDOF Interview, 19 October 2016)

126 Barriers to belonging

This suggests that the impact of skills capital is recognised and there is an awareness of how it functions, at least by those on the fringes of roller derby. As RDOF had a broader view of the sport than players engaged with the minutiae of league politics, he was more able to see how certain aspects played out again and again in different teams.

Talking to RDOF, it was clear that women's roller derby was the form of the sport with which he was most interested in being involved. When asked why, he said, "probably because I've had more issues with men's roller derby", referring to the behaviour and attitude of people involved in the men's sport. RDOF did not have a high opinion of The Inhuman League, but it did not seem to be any worse than his view of men's roller derby in general.

> The Inhuman League. It does come down to who is actually involved, individual personalities. There are certain people in The Inhuman League that totally piss me off. There are others I get on with. The trouble is that the people that piss me off are people that seem to have more sway within the team. Because it's on a totally voluntary basis you can just go, "sorry I'm not gonna".... There are people out there that dedicate a lot of time and effort; so you got the NSOs that go for all the training, likewise with the refs. When you get to that level where you can pick and choose what you want to do, you're not going to start picking the stuff where people will annoy you.
>
> (RDOF Interview, 19 October 2016)

RDOF argued that there were no mechanisms for resolving issues within the league (or other leagues). Outsiders were simply ignored.

This was another reason for volunteers choosing not to be involved with TIL, and indicates that skills capital may play a part beyond skaters, in that experienced and skilled photographers, for example, have greater ability to demand fair treatment. RDOF suggested that this picture would not change until the sport became professional, or at least semi-professional.

> What they don't see is the whole emotional side of what it does to people so, "If we do this we piss off this person, they don't come back". They don't really care about it. If you say it, "If you did this you piss this person off and you lose 200 quid" they would care about it. I think until it becomes a professional, semi-professional sports where there're easily quantifiable gains or losses, no I don't think it's going to happen.
>
> (RDOF Interview, 19 October 2016)

This is an interesting perspective on roller derby that seems to differ from my findings, which suggest that players find roller derby more inclusive when there is not such a focus on professionalism. This indicates an additional area of tension between players and volunteers. Despite this, RDOF talked about a positive side to volunteering in roller derby.

The fact that people are participating and they'll come out with a lot more skills, and actually they'll be able to achieve stuff in their own personal life that they probably wouldn't've done if they hadn't been involved with it. Perhaps that's the real story to take out of the whole sport.

(RDOF Interview, 19 October 2016)

This is an encouraging note to finish on. The development of skills, and the range of experiences and achievements that are possible through an involvement with roller derby are immensely rewarding even for those who never quite feel they belong. RDOF, Andy, and I placed value on these aspects despite existing on the fringes or at the boundary of the roller derby community. It may be that those at the boundary can negotiate their position more effectively than those who fail to belong but would otherwise expect to find a place at the centre. For people like Broot and Foul Out Boy, a lack of belonging may be even more disappointing, because of their position as skater in the league, which ought to have afforded them a greater level of belonging than those of us who volunteer.

One way of analysing the experiences detailed in this chapter is through the lens of hegemonic masculinity (Connell, 2005), with which TIL appeared to have a curious relationship. On the one hand, members of TIL replicated some of the problems of men's sport, whilst on the other, members were trying to create a different way of playing sport, which was more cooperative and open, and reflected a more inclusive masculinity (Anderson, 2009). Thus, the community of TIL was a site of struggle (Carter and Baliko, 2017). The difficulties inherent in dealing with hegemonic masculinity as embodied by Donald Thump mirrored the difficulty the wider community of men's roller derby had in dealing with "toxic" masculinity. This struggle could be thought of in terms of what Connell (1987) termed "crisis tendencies".

An example of this struggle occurred during the 2018 Men's Roller Derby World Cup in Barcelona. The four-day event showcased the best of men's roller derby, with 24 national teams competing. Every member of every team I worked with (as one of the track managers) was unfailingly polite, respectful, and appreciative of the work I, and the other volunteers, had put in, and was keen to present men's roller derby as inclusive, and supportive. Team USA was the only exception, perhaps because they were the most successful team there, and favourites to win. Failing spectacularly to read the mood of the competition, three Team USA skaters and one of their bench staff played the final sporting the number 23 on their legs, in recognition of a skater who had withdrawn from the competition due to allegations of sexual assault. In the days that followed, after much discussion and criticism on social media of both the team, and men's roller derby in general, both Team USA and the MRDA announced suspensions of these individuals (MRDA, 2018; USA Men's Roller Derby, 2018b). Although a very different situation from any that arose within TIL, this action was discussed as resulting from "unfortunate cultural norms" (USA Men's Roller Derby, 2018a) and is suggestive of the hegemonic practices present in high-level men's roller derby, which are characterised by, in this instance especially, male privilege and misogyny.

128 Barriers to belonging

Again, within TIL, skills capital was gained through successful performances of masculinity, which in many cases meant performances of hegemonic masculinity, and was therefore denied to those who practised a different type of masculinity. So, although there may have been some circumstances in which deviating from norms was worth the risk (Risman *et al.*, 2012), such as wearing boutfits and expressing emotion, that risk often did not pay off in terms of increased skills capital and secure group membership. Instead, due in part to the complicity of other members, displays of more inclusive styles of masculinity still resulted in marginalisation. In many examples throughout this chapter, the time and effort given to the sport was not necessarily rewarded. Instead, skill was the main measure of inclusion. High skills capital enabled non-conforming behaviour, which in turn led to the exclusion of others (Fletcher, 2019).

It is important to note that there was an unspoken hierarchy within the roller derby community. Given the endurance of the "by the skaters, for the skaters" ethic, unsurprisingly, skaters are at the top of that hierarchy; below that are coaches (who are often skaters or ex-skaters), bench staff, high-level referees, high-level NSOs, low-level referees, announcers, photographers, medics, low-level NSOs, staff and crew. Membership of a group or community implies a recognition of similarity (Barth, 1969), but by the very nature of their role, referees were positioned as different. They stand outside the game, "punishing" infractions of the rules. Referees are playing the game in a very different way, and it could therefore be argued that they are not part of the group. However, recognition of the multiplicity within communities (Cohen, 1985) allows for their continued inclusion. It is worth reiterating though that, as a result of their fragile membership status on the edge or boundary of the group, referees, like other less secure group members, are thus more likely to conform and therefore not speak out about negative treatment.

By the time I completed fieldwork, Thump was no longer associated with TIL. His behaviour had become too erratic and damaging for the current committee to accept. There was recognition that he had been the catalyst for dwindling membership and low attendance, and his skill as a skater was no longer seen as enough to offset the negative impact he could have. Officials were beginning to see an improvement in their treatment. The team had begun to recognise their importance. Potentially, as time goes by, commitment may become as important as skills capital in terms of belonging within the league. Breeze (2014) asserts that professionalism and seriousness are about hegemony and dominant ideology, and this view indicates that roller derby is increasingly reproducing norms of sport. However, the belief that roller derby is inclusive (Becker, 2010; Mullin, 2012) offers the possibility that the sport may continue to do things differently (Messner, 2002).

References

Adjepong, A. (2015) "We're, like, a cute rugby team": How whiteness and heterosexuality shape women's sense of belonging in rugby. *International Review for the Sociology of Sport*, 52(2), pp. 209–222. DOI: 10.1177/1012690215584092.

Barriers to belonging 129

Adler, P. A. and Adler, P. (1987) *Membership Roles in Field Research*. Newbury Park, Sage.

Anderson, E. (2009) *Inclusive Masculinities*. London, Routledge.

Atencio, M., Beal, B., and Wilson, C. (2009) The distinction of risk: Urban skateboarding, street habitus and the construction of hierarchical gender relations. *Qualitative Research in Sport and Exercise*, 1(1), pp. 3–20. DOI: 10.1080/19398440802567907.

Barth, F. (1969) *Ethnic Groups and Boundaries*. Boston, MA, Little Brown.

Becker, S. (2010) Fishnets, feminism, and femininity: Resistance, construction, and reproduction of femininity within sport. *Proceedings of the 2010 American Sociological Association Annual Meeting held at the Hilton Atlanta and the Atlanta Marriott Marquis, Atlanta*.

Beere, C. (1979) *Women and Women's Issues: A Handbook of Tests and Measures*. San Francisco, CA, Jossey-Bass.

Bennett, J. (2015) "Snowed in!": Offbeat rhythms and belonging as everyday practice. *Sociology*, 49(5), pp. 955–969. DOI: 10.1177/0038038515589299.

Breeze, M. (2014) *Just a Big, Sexy Joke? Getting Taken Seriously in Women's Roller Derby*. PhD thesis, University of Edinburgh.

Burdsey, D. (2008) Contested conceptions of identity, community and multiculturalism is the staging of alternative sport events: A case study of the Amsterdam World Cup football tournament. *Leisure Studies*, 27(3), pp. 259–277. DOI: 10.1080/0261 4360802127235.

Carter, C. and Baliko, K. (2017) "These are not my people": Queer sport spaces and the complexities of community. *Leisure Studies*, 36(5), pp. 696–707. DOI: 10.1080/ 02614367.2017.1315164.

Cohen, A. P. (1985) *The Symbolic Construction of Community*. London, Routledge.

Cohen, J. H. (2008) Sporting-self or selling sex: All-girl roller derby in the 21st century. *Women in Sport and Physical Activity Journal*, 17(2), pp. 24–33.

Connell, R. W. (1987) *Gender & Power: Society, the Person and Sexual Politics*. Cambridge, Polity Press.

Connell, R. W. (2005) *Masculinities* (2nd edn). Cambridge, Polity Press.

Cotterill, M. S. (2010) *Skating the Metaphorical Edge: An Ethnographic Examination of Female Roller Derby Athletes*. MA dissertation, University of Delaware.

Downes, J. (2009) *DIY Queer Feminist (Sub)cultural Resistance in the UK*. PhD thesis, University of Leeds.

Fletcher, D. (2017) "Or are you just pleased to see me?": The role of the boutfit in men's roller derby. *Sheffield Student Journal for Sociology*, 1, pp. 120–136.

Fletcher, D. (2019) Skills Capital and Inclusivity in Men's Roller Derby. *International Review for the Sociology of Sport*, Online First. DOI: 10.1177/1012690219855733.

Goffman, E. (1959) *The Presentation of Self in Everyday Life*. London, Penguin.

Holland, J. (2007) Emotions and research. *International Journal of Social Research Methods*, 10(3), pp. 195–209. DOI: 10.1080/13645570701541894.

Jenkins, R. (2014) *Social Identity* (4th edn). London, Routledge.

Klein, R. D. (1983) How to do what we want to do: Thoughts about feminist methodology, in G. Bowles and R. D. Klein (eds), *Theories of Women's Studies*. London, Routledge, pp. 88–104.

Krausch, M. L. (2009) Feminism(s) in practice: The sport, business and politics of roller derby. *Proceedings of the 2009 American Sociological Association Annual Meeting held at the Hilton San Francisco, San Francisco*.

Leigh, J. (2013) *Constructing Professional Identity in Child Protection Social Work: A Comparative Ethnography*. PhD thesis, University of Salford.

McHugh, T. F., Coppola, A. M., Holt, N. L., and Andersen, C. (2015) "Sport *is* community": An exploration of urban Aboriginal peoples' meanings of community within the context of sport. *Psychology of Sport and Exercise*, 18, pp. 75–84. DOI: 10.1177/1049732 318759668.

Messner, M. (2002) *Taking the Field: Women, Men and Sports*. Minneapolis, MN, University of Minnesota Press.

Morriss, L. (2014) *Accomplishing Social Work Identity in Interprofessional Mental Health Teams Following the Implementation of the Mental Health Act 2007*. PhD thesis, University of Salford.

MRDA (2017) "About". *MRDA*. Available from: http://mrda.com/about (accessed 5 November 2017).

MRDA (2018) Facebook post 20 April 2018. Available from: www.facebook.com/theMRDA/posts/1646223008788359 (accessed 2 May 2018).

Mullin, K. (2012) *Neither Butch nor Barbie: Negotiating Gender in Women's Roller Derby*. MA dissertation, Loyola University Chicago.

Numerato, D. and Baglioni, S. (2011) The dark side of social capital: An ethnography of sport governance. *International Review for the Sociology of Sport*, 47(5), pp. 594–611. DOI: 10.1177/1012690211413838.

Pavlidis, A. (2013). Writing resistance in roller derby: Making the case for auto/ethnographic writing in feminist leisure research. *Journal of Leisure Research*, 45(5), pp. 661–676. DOI: 10.18666/jlr-2013-v45-i5–4368.

Pavlidis, A. and Fullagar, S. (2014) *Sport, Gender and Power: The Rise of Roller Derby*. Farnham, Ashgate.

Rannikko, A., Harinen, P., Torvinen, P., and Liikanen, V. (2016) The social bordering of lifestyle sports: Inclusive principles, exclusive reality. *Journal of Youth Studies*, 19(8), pp. 1093–1109. DOI: 10.1080/13676261.2016.1145640.

Risman, B. J., Lorber, J., and Sherwood, J. H. (2012) Toward a world beyond gender: A utopian vision. *Proceedings of the 2012 American Sociological Association Annual Meeting held at the Colorado Convention Center and Hyatt Regency, Denver*.

Spracklen, K. (1996) *"Playing the Ball": Constructing Community and Masculine Identity in Rugby: An Analysis of the Two Codes of League and Union and the People Involved*. PhD thesis, Leeds Metropolitan University.

Stanley, L. (1997) Methodology matters, in V. Robinson and D. Richardson (eds), *Introducing Women's Studies*. Basingstoke, Palgrave Macmillan, pp. 198–219.

Stone, C. (2017) Utopian community football? Sport, hope and belongingness in the lives of refugees and asylum seekers. *Leisure Studies*, 37(2), pp. 171–183. DOI: 10.1080/02614367.2017.1329336.

Thurnell-Read, T. (2011) "Common-sense" research: Senses, emotions and embodiment in researching stag tourism in Eastern Europe. *Methodological Innovations Online*, 6(3), pp. 39–49.

USA Men's Roller Derby (2018a) Facebook post 9 April 2018. Available from: www.facebook.com/usamensrollerderby/posts/1921488761257978 (accessed 2 May 2018).

USA Men's Roller Derby (2018b) Facebook post 19 April 2018. Available from: www.facebook.com/usamensrollerderby/posts/1934659689940885 (accessed 2 May 2018).

Wellard, I. (2016) Gendered performances in sport: An embodied approach. *Palgrave Communications*, 2, 16003. DOI: 10.1057/palcomms.2016.3.

WFTDA (2016) "Mission Statement". *WFTDA.org*. Available from: https://wftda.org/mission (accessed 2 May 2018).

WFTDA (2019) "Rules". *WFTDA.com*. Available from: https://rules.wftda.com/ (accessed 21 December 2019).

Chapter 6

Skills capital and acceptable masculinities

This book has focused on four key areas: Community and engagement, image and identity, belonging and inclusivity, and barriers to belonging. Through discussion of these areas, it is clear that identities are a continual process, and that the individual and the group are closely connected. The central concern of these members was to "get roller derby right", and hence to get masculinity and identity right. The difficulties faced stemmed from the constantly shifting nature of roller derby. As the sport evolved, what constituted "right" also changed. Thus, a perfect state of "rightness" was unattainable, and members settled for moments of being "good enough". Within these moments, there were opportunities for doing identity and masculinity differently, but also moments of engagement with traditional forms of masculinity.

Both observation and interviews pointed to members' conscious desire to be better at roller derby. This was exemplified through a successful performance of a roller derby persona, which was achieved through the successful performance of the game, training and drills and a focus on strategy. It was also demonstrated through knowledge about roller derby and fitting in with the current ethos of the community. A successful roller derby persona implied a successful performance of identity, and also necessitated a successful performance of masculinity, although few members deliberated on this as consciously as Fin, the only trans member of the team. This performance (Goffman, 1959) involved developing a feel for the game and comfort in the habitus (Bourdieu, 1977, 1990a, 1990b). Though there were pressures to conform, these also stemmed from the desire to get roller derby right. Members had an idea of what roller derby was *supposed to be*, which differed from person to person, though to form a working consensus, it was only necessary that they be right enough – there was room for flexibility. There existed a notion of being able to simultaneously do roller derby right for your team, and right for yourself.

Crisis moments occurred when TIL found itself at odds with the prevailing roller derby ethos of the wider community; or when a critical mass of members found their own idea of what roller derby should be, their self-image, was at odds with the ethos of TIL, and its public image. This was seen in the struggle between individuals' performances of identity and the drive for professionalisation, and in the gap that existed between the team's ethos and how the administration of the league functioned in practice. The response to this was a redefinition of what TIL was and what the league stood for, which involved issues of continuation and change. Such moments of redefinition entailed a struggle between ideals of inclusion and the very real exclusion that members sometimes felt, which was especially visible in the divide between officials and players.

This ethnographic study suggests that identity, belonging, and community in men's roller derby hinges on two main practices: successful performances of a roller derby persona, and everyday constructions of community. Cultural capital in the form of skills capital was attained through successful masculine performances, which in turn enabled deviant behaviour. However, roller derby also enabled men to construct more accepting masculine identities, to prize acceptable masculinity above hegemonic masculinity, and to accept difference. Successful performances of a roller derby persona involved taking a risk, which could intersect with the freedom engendered by skills capital. Doing masculinity differently could lead to a more inclusive space, where the new and exciting created a sense of togetherness and deepened friendships. I theorise these ways of being and doing as "acceptable masculinities". The desire for inclusivity within men's roller derby was ever-present, but the tension between acceptable masculinities and skills capital rendered a commitment to inclusivity problematic and difficult to achieve in practice.

TIL provided a space for different ways of doing masculinity. On the one hand, members with a high level of skills capital, like Thump and Coogan, subscribed to a more hegemonic style of masculinity in which strength, aggression, and violence were prized. Time after time, these characteristics were noted in my fieldnotes and in interviews regarding Thump's actions especially. However, members of TIL also gained closeness, intimacy, and respect with more inclusive masculinity, offering support and feelings of belonging to a diverse group of people. The importance of the team and "teamliness" and the range of strategies employed to ensure continued feelings of belonging to acceptable masculinities, were in turn linked to a commitment to inclusivity. Prizing those with high skills capital was linked to exclusion and a traditional sports model that offered less freedom of expression. Identity is a process and a performance – one that must be validated by others. Communities, likewise, are created through both thinking and doing. Conducting ethnographic observation and interview allowed for an understanding not only of how my participants conceptualised identity and community, and how they did it in practice, but also of power dynamics at play, and an awareness of whose definition of a situation counted.

Individual and group identity is inextricably linked, but although groups and communities involve shared understandings, they also incorporate difference. Therefore, a distinction can be made between the two, and it is possible to account for conflicting ideas and positions taken on matters of interest to the community. It is also clear that communities involve processes of both inclusion and exclusion. This book has explored how the boundary is maintained within the research

134 Skills capital, acceptable masculinities

field, and how notions of belonging and barriers to belonging are experienced by members of the community.

Successful performances of a roller derby persona

Members of TIL sought to subvert both the roller derby ethos and ideals of mainstream sports, albeit in different ways. The satirical treatment of "skate" names and the refusal to accept the importance of such names implied a rejection of the dominant roller derby ethos. However, the resistance to more mainstream ways of doing sport suggested that the members of TIL wanted to create something different, something new; neither roller derby as a *women's* sport, nor roller derby as a mainstream sport. This was *men's* roller derby, and it refused to take the history and conventions of roller derby seriously, but it also refused to take sport too seriously.

Conversely, how different men's roller derby could be depended upon a few individuals. In terms of community and engagement, a narrowing focus enabled those with higher skills capital to dominate, to become a big fish in a small pond. The increased confidence and capital that helped create the conditions for independence from the women's league also granted them the power to define the situation as they saw fit. Skilled skaters and established members even had the power to name others. Additionally, some members were immune from becoming the recipient of banter. Those with high skills capital controlled the discourse and controlled what was said and how it was said.

Members of TIL consistently worked towards the successful performance of a roller derby persona, but on their own terms. This "doing" of identity was impossible to separate from "doing" gender. Though West and Zimmerman (1987) argue that there are negative consequences for not doing gender appropriately, in TIL acceptable masculinity was performed in ways that challenged normative ideas of masculinity. The experience of members of TIL supports Messner's (2002) argument that opportunities exist for doing gender differently in sports that are away from the centre. Roller derby is considered to be a niche sport, and men's roller derby occupies an even more marginal place within that.

My participants took risks in deviating from accepted notions of masculinity and what men should be (Eckert and McConnell-Ginet, 2013; Risman *et al.*, 2012). This was especially apparent in the wearing of boutfits, but also in the close friendships and intimacy that developed amongst some TIL members, argued to be much less likely in men's sports (Messner, 2002). This research supports arguments that position roller derby as a sport that offers participants opportunities to challenge gender norms and heteronormativity (Cotterill, 2010; Werhman, 2012), allowing participants to cross gender boundaries (Gieseler, 2012) and if not actively break gender binaries, to at least question them.

The notions of body-reflexive practices (Connell, 2005) and body-reflexive pleasures (Wellard, 2012) are intelligible in participants' performances of a roller derby identity, as seen through the adoption of boutfits. In many of the responses regarding boutfits, skaters valued the opportunity to challenge hegemonic notions of masculinity. Though this was more apparent in those who identified as non-heterosexual and non-cisgender, an understanding of the way clothing could allow a skater to play with gender expectations was apparent in responses from cisgender and heterosexual skaters, such as 4D. Whilst sometimes positioned as a "joke", like Phallic Baldwin did, there was an undercurrent of seriousness in terms of the positive impact this joke could have on other skaters. These practices are suggestive of inclusive masculinity as discussed by Anderson (2009).

The negative connotations of boutfits expressed by some participants highlight the "risk" (Lyng, 1990; Robinson, 2014) associated with these clothing choices when the sport attempts to become legitimate. At such times, skaters were discouraged from expressing themselves more freely, and instead expected to conform to a single team image. This suggests that transgressive acts are only possible when participating in an activity itself seen as transgressive, such as roller derby was before the drive to "professionalise" the sport, or when individuals possess a high level of skills capital and therefore are permitted more freedom. It is apparent that more skilled skaters had more freedom to play with boutfit choices, and that there was substantially less risk for them in terms of capital. In many ways, those with high skills capital actually gained from experimenting with their gender presentation.

The impact of skills capital is apparent in other ways, such as when highly skilled skaters reproduce practices at odds with the inclusive ethos of the league, yet this behaviour becomes hidden under a collective definition of inclusivity. As one participant said in reference to such a member, "he's an arsehole, but he's our arsehole". This behaviour became accepted through the narrative of inclusivity. Deviant behaviour becomes accepted because the skater is too skilled to lose. In this way, the interconnection of skills capital and acceptable masculinities becomes clear. The imperative to accept and include all forms of masculinity results in a space that is less inclusive. However, the eventual expulsion of Thump suggests that there are limits.

Wellard (2002) argues that attempting to do masculinity differently still tends to reproduce established practices. Within TIL, it was clear that this was not always the case. When the team's focus was on seriousness and competitiveness, such as during Coogan's chairship or after the team meeting at the end of the 2016 season when TIL were promoted to Tier 1, then established practices of mainstream sport and hegemonic masculinity came to the fore. This was seen in the drive to eradicate banter (which in TIL's case works to cement bonds between team members), the encouragement to wear "uniform" clothing, and the focus on maintaining a front of "calm". In such situations, the difficulty of escaping from the established social role of "sportsman" became apparent, as skaters replicated the exclusive practices of competitive sport. This reflects Wellard's (2016) more recent discussion of expected sporting masculinity, in which he critiques inclusive masculinity theory (Anderson, 2009), arguing instead for the continuing existence of a belief

136 Skills capital, acceptable masculinities

in one single authentic form of masculinity that is aligned with hegemonic and exclusionary ways of being.

Within TIL, skills capital granted the freedom to engage in this style of masculinity. Although it was not prized, and so those with low skills capital were punished for behaving in this way, high skills capital essentially enabled some to do whatever they wanted. The hierarchy created by the constant, enduring dictum that roller derby is both by and for skaters, casts non-bouting skaters to the margins. As such, they frequently lack capital and therefore have less freedom to speak, and to act. This results in increased marginalisation of officials and volunteers as their need to belong goes unrecognised.

However, at other times, practices were much more inclusive, such as when skaters demonstrated closeness and intimacy. Consequently, the ethos of TIL remained in constant flux. The switch between discourses and the type of image and definition of the situation projected happened quickly; the impact of one individual could have an undue influence and other members were complicit in their silence (Messner, 2002).

Constructions of community in everyday practice

In terms of roller derby, it is more accurate to speak of communities in the plural sense. These communities were always shifting, and the "rules" around membership shifted also. The Inhuman League could be both inclusive, offering support and feelings of belonging to a diverse group of people, and excluding. TIL demonstrated what I refer to as "acceptable masculinity" in several ways. In their opening up of membership, tied to the MRDA non-discrimination policy that refuses to constrain and restrict masculinity to narrow definitions, TIL was very deliberate in its intent to include trans skaters, and women. This was about making space for all types of masculinity, both for those who were striving for seriousness and professionalism, and those who were less serious and focused on having a fun hobby.

My participants valued togetherness. The team and "teamliness" were important concepts. Even after problems and difficulties, which in some cases led to members leaving the team, this is what interviewees chose to focus upon. Although I asked questions about good and bad memories, the responses were deeper and more heartfelt when discussing what brought these people together. Grievous talked at length about the value and importance he attached to times spent with Zom B Cru and the Crucibelles. Dr Blocktopus and Stuntman told me stories of times they had played in France and Sweden. Even Coogan, who was at pains to stress that roller derby was not "friend club", talked of the emotion he felt when the team went to Brussels. Discussions of these events strongly indicate that positive emotions regarding togetherness are felt more keenly in the act of creating something. It was the "new" and the "exciting" that captured the hearts of members. The trip to Toulouse represented a first: TIL's first international game. The small collection of skaters who went over had the feeling of being part of something bigger than themselves or their team. The trip to Malmo was Zom

Skills capital, acceptable masculinities 137

B Cru's first international tournament. Although by the time of the tournament in Brussels the skaters for TIL had been on several such trips, this event was important in that it demonstrated the possibility of doing well with only a very few skaters. It was very unusual for a team to attempt a tournament with only seven skaters, half the standard number. The result was that Brussels also felt like something new.

Over and above the sense of togetherness created by going away as a group, this sense of being part of something larger, of creating something worthwhile, of going where no sports team had gone before, deepened friendships and forged links that continued long after returning home. Messner (1992) argues that in mainstream sporting environments, men lack deep, meaningful and lasting friendships, but in these experiences, the members of TIL demonstrated the capacity to do just that. As roller derby is currently far removed from the centre of sport, as outlined by Messner (2002), it has the potential to provide a different model of masculinity, for skaters to do gender differently. Far from the Lombardian ethic that winning is the only thing, roller derby rankings systems are set up to reward even a loss, if the losing team played well. Additionally, there are frequent games and tournaments where mixed teams play for the sheer enjoyment of competing, and "winning" encompasses things such as communicating well as a team, playing cleanly, having fun, and achieving personal goals, not simply the final score. This structure of sport allows male athletes to gain a sense of closeness, intimacy, and respect that can be lacking in the "centre" of sport (Messner, 2002) yet found in more alternative sports, such as rock climbing (Robinson, 2008).

That said, spending time together was also very important in generating a feeling of belonging, and sustaining these levels of togetherness and "teamliness" was harder in everyday practice, especially when attendance was low. Members of TIL employed a range of strategies to ensure continued feelings of belonging. Friendships were strengthened through the use of banter and jokes, which often arose through participation in events away from home, such as Phally and I describe. Banter functioned as a symbol of belonging, and as such, reinforces arguments made by Cohen (1982, 1986) about how communities are created symbolically. This banter was often obscure and more than a little ridiculous. It could be near the bone but felt good, and ultimately served to mark you out as part of the team.

The team practised acceptance of non-traditional men and attempted to create a "family feeling" (Coogan Interview 31 May 2016). This allowed for recognition of both difference and similarity (Jenkins, 2014). However, there was a different idea of what inclusivity meant. In its ethos, TIL was open to anyone, but in practice, the team was only open to those who sought it out. Thus, members of TIL demonstrated what could be termed inclusive masculinity (Anderson, 2009). There was a lack of homophobic and transphobic discourse. In fact, as the experiences of Fin attest to, there was a marked improvement in inclusive discourse. Members displayed positive attitudes to women, welcoming them into the team and expressing a desire to work more closely with women in roller derby – reflective, and going beyond the findings, of Pavlidis and Connor (2015). There was a greater freedom to express different forms of masculinity, seen through boutfits, and the close, supportive ties of several members.

Breeze (2013) argued that exclusion was necessary for the development of roller derby into a legitimate sport, but this indicates a very traditional notion of sport, as though the centre, the mainstream, of sport, is where roller derby should strive to be, and a belief that serious recognition is incompatible with revolutionary practices. A notion which is itself contested (Messner, 2002). Although this was evident at times during the research, the desire for inclusivity was ever-present. The challenge team members faced was in continuing to live up to their inclusive ideals as the sport developed. This tension was never resolved during my time with TIL and continued to remain problematic. Rather than a solution, what this research offers is additional evidence that there are possibilities to do sport differently. But also, that the choice is never simple. Messner and Sabo (1994) suggest that it is important to consider the athletic experiences we want to create, and TIL members were clear that they wanted to be inclusive but were not clear about how to make that happen. Different ways of leading were shown to be possible as Coogan and Frank chaired the league differently. Their experiences demonstrate that, regardless of leadership and capital, there was a sense of being in it together and facing the same issues.

However, in analysing what separated and what joined members in a community, it was clear that who is part of the community was contested. Regardless of the wording of documents, experiences suggested that "feelings" mattered, reflecting argument made by other researchers (McHugh *et al.*, 2015; Stone, 2017). Officials often reported a lack of "feeling" of belonging, which meant they were less likely to consider themselves part of the team or remain so. Participants talked about a sense of joy, teamliness, and community. They told me about how "nice" TIL was, and how accepting they were. There was an acceptance of oddness, but it was possible to be too odd. Acceptable masculinity had its limits.

Attempts to be inclusive also included hegemonic practices, as Rannikko *et al.* (2016), Burdsey (2008), and Spracklen (1996) found. Adherence to ideals of inclusivity meant that members whose behaviour was more closely aligned with hegemonic masculinity continued to be made welcome. Strong personalities who demanded respect and created conflict through more traditional ways of doing sport were accepted as part of the league. The league did not have structures in place to deal with such issues. In welcoming disruptive elements, the league became less inclusive. Giving a good impression involved maintaining the line – creating and curating an image of TIL that focused on this inclusivity and protected the "dark" secrets, both the inclusion of those who were too good to lose, and the exclusion of those who were too odd to stay.

My participants' experiences suggest that DIY participation is not easy, and that there can be significant barriers to creating and sustaining a grass-roots sports team, which complicate the relationship between what participants would like to do and what is possible. Specific issues affecting TIL were venues, lack of money, and lack of engagement. Members valued involvement with TIL when it gave them opportunities to be part of something bigger, but TIL itself was a very small community, and often very inwardly focused. Lack of engagement meant that TIL was largely invisible to the surrounding community. During my research I frequently met people who had no idea roller derby existed, and if they did, they were unaware of any men's teams. Several existing members of the team lacked either interest or the time to be involved beyond skating, and with such a small and stretched committee, lack of promotion meant it was difficult to recruit new members. Although members valued their place in the team, they did not successfully articulate to outsiders why they might want to join a men's roller derby team. It was clear that members of TIL wanted more for the sport, and the team, but were not necessarily inclined to work towards getting it.

After withdrawing from the field, I remained hopeful about the possibilities for inclusivity in roller derby. A crisis point occurred within TIL soon after I completed fieldwork. Not long after their successful Champs performance and promotion to Tier 1 precipitated a more serious and focused training ethos, several of the league's strongest skaters quit the team. TIL played in Tier 1 during the 2017 season, losing all their games, but seeming to become more stable, more pleasant and democratic, more engaged, stronger, kinder, and more fun in the process. This coincided with Donald Thump's alleged "expulsion" from the league. TIL had made the decision that skills capital was not sufficient to offset problems caused by non-conforming behaviour such as Thump's, and had decided to focus on being inclusive, and to deal decisively with issues that might impact that goal, even if that meant not winning.

The following year, TIL were demoted to Tier 2 for the 2018 season, but changes within the Champs structure meant that they would again be competing in Tier 1. This news coincided with the chair, Frank, quitting the league, and the discovery that league finances were in disarray. TIL's future was again in doubt, and the remaining team members had to work together to redefine the league once more. At this juncture, it is interesting to note that TIL made a conscious decision to celebrate difference and work towards cooperation, fully embracing the DIY ethics of modern roller derby's origins, in sharp contrast with women's roller derby and the WFTDA's move towards a more "masculinist" and traditional approach (Pavlidis and Fullagar, 2014). Although it is not clear how those decisions will play out in time, for TIL, at least, a rejection of traditional norms of sport was necessary in order for them to regain a sense of inclusion. It was a hard road to get there, and the inclusion they created involved an acknowledgement that it was inseparable from exclusion, and that boundaries must be maintained. The Inhuman League are currently small, tightly knit, and focused on inclusivity. Their story suggests that alternative sports can offer alternative ways to "do" gender, identity, and community.

Conclusion

This book adds a new dimension to the growing body of empirical research on roller derby. For the first time, the perspective of male skaters has been explored, and men have been given the opportunity to share their experiences. Roller derby is theorised as both a feminised sport, and a sport that gives women space to be masculine, but my research opens out the discussion to explore how roller derby also gives men the opportunity to redefine what it means to be masculine within sport, and to experiment with femininity. It demonstrates that it is just as important for men to experience belonging and to have safe spaces within which to explore their identity. The research also identifies strategies that may be employed to create this space, such as banter and tours, and reinforces the necessity of time spent together in fostering a sense of community and belonging. The fieldwork suggests that safe spaces are possible within a fringe sport. Although this research cannot capture how possible safe spaces and this level of inclusion are within mainstream sport, it suggests ways in which this might be discussed and explored.

Current debates around "toxic masculinities" focus on the negatives of male-dominated environments, but this research suggests that alternative spaces exist where it is possible for men to relate to each other differently, and for all genders to engage in mutual support, although it also highlights significant challenges. The existence of mainstream sport cannot be ignored, and neither can its impact upon alternative sports. Widespread, common-sense beliefs about sporting masculinities result in the reification of those who are able to succeed in sport; they are granted freedom of behaviours, and when they abuse that freedom to engage in practices that exclude others, they are not sanctioned. In this way, the challenges of men's roller derby are the same as women's; non-typical men lose out, whilst those who really like sport (Breeze, 2015) are more highly regarded. Thus, tensions between inclusivity and professionalism can be seen to play out similarly in both incarnations of roller derby, although it remains to be seen whether skills capital functions in women's roller derby in the same way (Fletcher, 2019).

This book contributes to methodological discussions of insider research, specifically in terms of the difficulties of dealing with a disruptive presence within the field. In terms of accountable research (Downes, 2009; Stanley, 1997), I add to the discussion of what is ethical in the inclusion of material that represents a risk (McKenzie, 2017). This research offers a variety of perspectives on one situation, representing my "journey" as much as that of my participants. I do not claim to offer an autoethnography, and yet, the discussion involves much that is autoethnographic. Although the methodological concepts referenced in this book are not new, the freshness of the context in which they are applied speaks to their continued relevance. In considering situated knowledges, I have demonstrated that the researcher's perspective, or rather *perspectives*, are multiple, varied, and subject to change. This provides additional support to feminist methodologies that argue against the use of traditional notions of "objectivity" as an available tool for research. And I have continued to trouble the insider/outsider boundary with discussion of the place of referees within the sport.

How applicable the research findings explored in this book are beyond this specific context is a pertinent question. Although I have explored how these people, in this place and time, construct their community, it would be interesting to explore how these same issues and practices play out in other sports teams and other communities. I have opened up the field of roller derby research to explore the experience of MRDA skaters and considered the experiences of marginal members such as referees, but further research is required to expand knowledge beyond this context.

Additionally, I have demonstrated the possibility for transgender skaters to be fully included within what remains a largely cisgender sporting environment. Through the involvement of transgender athletes, cisgender skaters can learn to be more inclusive, to use more inclusive language, and to become more accepting of difference. This can lead to changes in membership policies and a recognition of the value of difference in creating a strong team. Although it must be acknowledged that these are findings from one small team, the conclusion remains valid and useful.

Despite the work that has been done thus far, roller derby continues to offer potential for further research. Trans inclusion is increasingly on the public agenda, and the difficulty of opening up sporting spaces to the trans community has been established. I argue that the sport of roller derby is a space that offers strong potential for trans inclusion. This needs further exploration, through a larger, more focused analysis of the experience of trans skaters in other leagues, and other organisations, to more fully understand how far alternative sports can demonstrate gender inclusion as a possibility, and, as desirable. Analysis points to the possibility that the presence of trans teammates has a positive impact on cisgender members, and the inclusive ethos of a team. This also requires further research.

Other research points towards significant barriers to inclusion for young transgender people in sport. Though this book focuses on the experiences of adults, it does raise pertinent questions that could be explored in a study of junior roller derby. In Sheffield, as in other teams, junior roller derby is open to members of all genders, up to the age of 17. Training is split by skill level, not age or gender. There is a case, therefore, for studying junior roller derby to answer questions about the possibility of gender inclusion. The experiences of young people of all genders who play a full contact sport *together* could offer invaluable data to bodies such as Sport England, and to schools.

References

Anderson, E. (2009) *Inclusive Masculinities*. London, Routledge.
Bourdieu, P. (1977) *Outline of a Theory of Practice*. Cambridge. Cambridge University Press.

142 Skills capital, acceptable masculinities

Bourdieu, P. (1990a). *In Other Words: Essays Towards a Reflexive Sociology*. Stanford, CA, Stanford University Press.

Bourdieu, P. (1990b) *The Logic of Practice*. Cambridge, Polity Press.

Breeze, M. (2013) Analysing "seriousness" in roller derby: Speaking critically with the serious leisure perspective. *Sociological Research Online*, 18(4), p. 23. DOI: 10.5153/sro.3236.

Breeze, M. (2015) *Seriousness and Women's Roller Derby*. London, Palgrave Macmillan.

Burdsey, D. (2008) Contested conceptions of identity, community and multiculturalism is the staging of alternative sport events: A case study of the Amsterdam World Cup football tournament. *Leisure Studies*, 27(3), pp. 259–277. DOI: 10.1080/02614360802127235.

Cohen, A. P. (1982) Belonging: The experience of culture, in A. P. Cohen (ed.), *Belonging: Identity and Social Organisation in British Rural Cultures*. Manchester, Manchester University Press, pp. 1–19.

Cohen, A. P. (1986) *Symbolising Boundaries: Identity and Diversity in British Cultures*. Manchester, Manchester University Press.

Connell, R. W. (2005) *Masculinities* (2nd edn). Cambridge, Polity Press.

Cotterill, M. S. (2010) *Skating the Metaphorical Edge: An Ethnographic Examination of Female Roller Derby Athletes*. MA dissertation, University of Delaware.

Downes, J. (2009) *DIY Queer Feminist (Sub)cultural Resistance in the UK*. PhD thesis, University of Leeds.

Eckert, P. and McConnell-Ginet, S. (2013) *Language and Gender* (2nd edn). Cambridge, Cambridge University Press.

Fletcher, D. (2019) Skills capital and inclusivity in men's roller derby. *International Review for the Sociology of Sport*, Online First. DOI: 10.1177/1012690219855733.

Gieseler, M. (2012) *Performances of Gender and Sexuality in Extreme Sports Culture*. PhD thesis, University of South Florida.

Goffman, E. (1959) *The Presentation of Self in Everyday Life*. London, Penguin.

Jenkins, R. (2014) *Social Identity* (4th edn). London, Routledge.

Lyng, S. (1990) Edgework: A social psychological analysis of voluntary risk-taking. *The American Journal of Sociology*, 95, pp. 851–886. DOI: 10.1086/229379.

McHugh, T. F., Coppola, A. M., Holt, N. L., and Andersen, C. (2015) "Sport *is* community": An exploration of urban Aboriginal peoples' meanings of community within the context of sport. *Psychology of Sport and Exercise*, 18, pp. 75–84. DOI: 10.1177/1049732 318759668.

McKenzie, J. S. (2017) "You don't know how lucky you are to be here!": Reflections on covert practices in an overt participant observation study. *Sociological Research Online*, 14(2), pp. 1–10. DOI: 10.5153/sro.1925.

Messner, M. (1992) *Power at Play: Sports and the Problem of Masculinity*. Boston, MA, Beacon Press.

Messner, M. (2002) *Taking the Field: Women, Men and Sports*. Minneapolis, MN, University of Minnesota Press.

Messner, M. and Sabo, D. (1994) *Sex, Violence & Power in Sports: Rethinking Masculinity*. Freedom, CA, The Crossing Press.

Pavlidis, A. and Connor, J. (2015) Men in a 'women only' sport? Contesting gender relations and sex integration in roller derby. *Sport in Society*, 19(8–9), pp. 1349–1362. DOI: 10.1080/17430437.2015.1067781.

Pavlidis, A. and Fullagar, S. (2014) *Sport, Gender and Power: The Rise of Roller Derby*. Farnham, Ashgate.

Rannikko, A., Harinen, P., Torvinen, P., and Liikanen, V. (2016) The social bordering of lifestyle sports: Inclusive principles, exclusive reality. *Journal of Youth Studies*, 19(8), pp. 1093–1109. DOI: 10.1080/13676261.2016.1145640.

Risman, B. J., Lorber, J., and Sherwood, J. H. (2012) Toward a world beyond gender: A utopian vision. *Proceedings of the 2012 American Sociological Association Annual Meeting held at the Colorado Convention Center and Hyatt Regency, Denver.*

Robinson, V. (2008) *Everyday Masculinities and Extreme Sport: Male Identity and Rock Climbing.* Oxford, Berg.

Robinson, V. (2014) Risky footwear practices: Masculinity, identity, and crisis. *NORMA: International Journal for Masculinity Studies*, 9(3), pp. 151–165. DOI: 10.1080/18902138.2014.950501.

Spracklen, K. (1996) *"Playing the Ball": Constructing Community and Masculine Identity in Rugby: An Analysis of the Two Codes of League and Union and the People Involved.* PhD thesis, Leeds Metropolitan University.

Stanley, L. (1997) Methodology matters, in V. Robinson and D. Richardson (eds), *Introducing Women's Studies.* Basingstoke, Palgrave Macmillan, pp. 198–219.

Stone, C. (2017) Utopian community football? Sport, hope and belongingness in the lives of refugees and asylum seekers. *Leisure Studies*, 37(2), pp. 171–183. DOI: 10.1080/02614367.2017.1329336.

Wellard, I. (2002) Men, sport, body performance and the maintenance of "exclusive masculinity". *Leisure Studies*, 21(3–4), pp. 235–247. DOI: 10.1080/0261436022000030641.

Wellard, I. (2012) Body-reflexive pleasures: Exploring bodily experiences within the context of sport and physical activity. *Sport, Education and Society*, 17(1), pp. 21–33. DOI: 10.1080/13573322.2011.607910.

Wellard, I. (2016) Gendered performances in sport: An embodied approach. *Palgrave Communications*, 2, 16003. DOI: 10.1057/palcomms.2016.3.

Werhman, M. M. (2012) Response to Cohen: Separating sport from sexuality in women's roller derby. *Women in Sport and Physical Activity Journal*, 21(1), pp. 71–78.

West, C. and Zimmerman, H. (1987) Doing gender. *Gender and Society*, 1, pp. 125–151. DOI: 10.1177/0891243287001002002.

Index

abuse: towards referees 31, 110
acceptance 77, 92–100, 100–4, 137, 138;
  and acceptable masculinity 2; and
  identity 3, 82; of bodies 55; and boutfits
  56; of change 69
aggression 28, 63–5, 71, 114, 116, 133
alternative sports 55, 97, 102, 139, 140, 141;
  drive to become mainstream 8, 37–8, 45;
  and inclusivity 110; model of 62–3
Anderson, E. 2, 70, 76, 102, 103, 135
attendance 36, 128, 137; at another
  league's training 31, 35; and
  membership 16; officials 121, 123;
  policies 11, 108

banter: banning of 83, 135; and capital
  134; failure of 79; and humour 94; and
  kindness 83; and masculinity 78; and
  naming 51, 69; sexualised 79–80, 82,
  104; as a symbol of belonging 77, 79,
  81–2, 101, 137, 140; *see also* jokes
belonging: and banter 81, 82, 83, 137;
  barriers to 110–28; and boundaries 85;
  and conflict 110–18; the "dark side"
  of 116; feeling of 28, 78, 89, 92, 102,
  133; and identity 69; and inclusivity
  67, 136; lack of 120, 127, 138; and
  membership 16, 40; as a practice 45,
  76–7; as a process 30, 100; and referees
  33, 118–24; and roller derby 4, 6, 13;
  search for 26
boundary work 41, 44, 71, 110, 127, 128;
  and identity 30; masculine/feminine 79;
  and risk 7
Bourdieu, P. 1, 69, 70
boutfits 55–62, 70, 79, 138; and identity
  18; and mainstream sport 9; and risk
  128, 134–5; *see also* hot pants

Breeze, M. 8–9, 108
British Championships 12, 30, 42, 44
British Roller Sports Federation 11, 41
B-Team *see* Zom B Cru
"by day, by night" 50
"by the skaters, for the skaters" 5, 30, 45,
  109, 120, 128

calm 49, 63–4, 65, 71, 113–14, 135
capital 58, 59, 62, 138; cultural; 1; high
  skills capital 45, 55, 60, 64–5, 110–11,
  128; low skills capital 52, 60, 64, 124;
  masculine 60, 70, 103; skills capital 1–3,
  70, 103–4, 126, 133–6, 139; social 1–2;
  subcultural 110; symbolic 1, 55
change 34–5, 40, 63, 70–1, 87–8; and
  identity 69, 13–14, 54; and image 18,
  67–8; and ritual 32–3
clothing *see* boutfits
Cohen, A.P. 71, 137
committee 16–17, 31–3, 38–40, 117–18,
  128; and banter 79; and boundary work
  43–4, 67–8; and engagement 29; and
  image 65–6
community: and banter 83; and boundary
  work 40, 44, 45; and conflict 11, 35–6,
  100–1, 119–20; constructions of 29–30,
  45, 62–3, 69–71, 85–6; and exclusion
  109–10, 125–8; and inclusivity 7–8,
  56–7, 67, 93; as linked communities
  25–8, 41–6; margins of 30, 113;
  policing 52–3
competitiveness 4, 8, 11, 98–9, 108; and
  masculinity 80, 135–6; and seriousness
  52, 70, 82, 88, 101
conflict 35–6, 101, 110–18, 119–20, 138;
  and identity 52–3, 70; and boutfits 55,
  58–60

Index 145

conformity 28, 111, 113, 128, 132, 135
Connell, R. 103, 127
Connor, J. 10
consent 16–17, 49, 67
costumes *see* boutfits
crisis 12, 15, 127, 132, 139
Crucibelles 27, 136

Dead Meat 40, 45
DeLyser, D. 14–15
derby names *see* skate names
deviance 70, 111, 133, 135; disruptive
   presence 63–4, 110–18, 138; *see also*
   non-conformity
"Devil" Dan Policarpo 4–5
difference 27–8, 49, 69, 100–1, 133,
   137–41
disciplinary 111–12
discourse 40, 45–6, 49, 58, 62–5, 70–1;
   inclusive 137, 67–8; and skills capital
   134, 136
DIY 5, 7, 37–40, 97–8, 138–9; and boutfits
   61; and insider research 14; *see also* "by
   the skaters, for the skaters"

edgework 7, 55–6; *see also* risk
emotion 84, 89–92, 126, 136; labour 32;
   researcher 14, 50, 119, 120
engagement 31, 37–9, 43; lack of 29, 33,
   39, 45–6, 139
ethics 16–17, 67, 140
ethos 5, 45, 132–3, 134, 139; inclusive 96,
   110–11, 135, 137, 141; *see also* DIY
excitement 15, 84–6, 88–90, 101–2,
   133, 136
exclusion 92, 100–1, 108–10, 128, 133,
   139; and competitiveness 8, 135–6, 138;
   and referees 118–20
experience: negative 31, 102, 115–18,
   120; positive 56–7, 60, 115; shared 27,
   78, 89–92

Facebook *see* social media
faking 119
"family feeling" 27, 97, 137
femininity 6–8, 15–16, 56, 58–60, 79, 140
fieldwork 12, 14, 17–18, 28, 122
Fletcher, D. 56–7, 60, 61, 100, 111, 115
friendship 51, 77, 89–92, 95–6, 102, 137;
   and research 15, 50, 67; "friend club"
   84, 87, 136
front 59, 66, 70, 114, 119, 122, 135
Fullagar, S. 76, 116

fun 34, 60–2, 84–5, 88–90, 99, 136–7
fundraising 38, 39

gender: doing gender 7–10, 15, 25, 49,
   56–9, 134–5; identity 67, 132; mixed
   gender 10, 29, 34–5, 43–4, 67–8, 84; *see
   also* OTA; norms 6–7, 15, 48, 55, 70;
   policies 8, 44, 67, 100; transgender and
   non-binary inclusion 8, 68, 77, 102–3,
   136, 141
Goffman, E. 51–2, 66, 118

habitus 2, 69, 70, 76, 132
Haraway, D. 12
homophobia: lack of 76, 78, 80, 138
hot pants 15, 55, 57–8, 61, 70, 94; *see also*
   boutfits
humour 59, 80–1, 83, 94; destructive 118;
   see also banter

identity: collective 7, 29–30, 68, 87–8;
   doing identity 10, 15, 25, 134; gendered
   67–8; individual 50–4; as a performance
   13, 55–9, 81–2, 122; as a process 18, 48,
   69–71, 132–3
image 70, 79; good impression 62–3, 66,
   138; impression management 48, 49, 63,
   65, 67, 70, 122; inclusive 64, 111; public
   40, 48, 55, 87; team 49, 135, 138
inclusivity 1–3, 7–9, 71, 92–9, 127–8;
   discourses of 62–8, 137; gender
   inclusive 10–11, 35, 43–4, 100–1; lack
   of 108–10, 118; as a practice 76–7,
   93–9, 133, 135–6
independence 27, 29–30, 40, 45, 85, 135
injury 13–14, 28, 65, 113
interviews 49–50, 66, 84
intimacy 3, 78, 102–3, 133, 134, 137

Jenkins, R. 48, 51–2, 66, 69–71, 100–1
Jerry Seltzer 4, 5
jokes 57, 78–80, 83, 87, 90, 94; *see also*
   banter

leadership 10, 29, 38–9, 45, 87, 117, 138;
   autocratic 39, 71; democratic 71, 115
leggings *see* boutfits
Leo Seltzer 3–4
Lyng, S. 55

mainstream sport 9, 38, 54, 135, 137, 140
masculinities 10, 58, 81, 102; acceptable
   masculinity 2–3, 94, 132–3, 134–8;

Index

masculinities *continued*
  getting masculinity wrong 55, 59, 69;
  hegemonic masculinity 16, 103, 110,
  117, 124–8; inclusive masculinity theory
  76, 103, 127, 135, 137–8;
  non-conventional men 94, 96–7
May, V. 76
McKenzie, J.S. 17
membership 16, 26, 39, 41, 43–4, 45;
  insecure 118, 128; policies 67–8, 136,
  141; secure 65, 111, 128
Men's Roller Derby World Cup 1, 94, 127
Messner, M. 77–8, 103, 137
minimum skills 11, 12, 34, 85, 94
misconduct *see* unsporting conduct
MRDA 9–10, 41, 43–5, 100, 102, 127;
  non-discrimination policy 43, 67–8,
  136; suspension from 125
multiplexity 28, 45
multiplicity 13, 17, 62, 76, 101, 128

negotiation 18, 55, 62–3, 127; and identity
  51, 58–60, 68–70, 87; and masculinity
  55–6
non-conformity 65, 70, 111, 128, 139; *see
  also* deviance
nostalgia 27, 34, 84
numbers 50–1, 53–4, 69, 127

oddness 95–6, 1, 101, 102, 138
officials 30–3, 44–6, 93, 119–20, 136;
  and identity 2, 122; impartiality 14;
  lack of respect for 123–4, 125; *see also*
  referee
OTA 10, 68, 99–100
outsider 45, 61, 66, 83, 118–19, 124–6;
  researcher as 14, 49, 116, 122

Pavlidis, A. 10, 76, 116
performance 25, 70; failed 122; of gender
  10, 16; of an identity 49–50, 51–2, 59;
  performativity 6–7, 55; successful 82,
  128, 132–3, 134–5; team 64–6
personas 7, 50–2, 79, 82, 132–3, 134–6
pleasure: body-reflexive pleasures 58,
  134–6
practice: belonging as a 45, 76–7, 120,
  137; body-reflexive practice 58, 134–6;
  everyday practice 3, 18, 25, 66, 101–2;
  hegemonic 83, 117, 127, 135, 138;
  naming 51–3; risky practices 55; shared
  values and 27, 123–4
presentation of self 2, 58, 119

professional 4, 5, 60–2, 101–2, 126;
  professionalisation 3, 9, 132–3, 135;
  professionalising the personal 15
pseudonyms 16–17, 109

quidditch 98

recognition 8–9, 11, 61, 138
recruitment 36, 38, 39–40; of officials and
  volunteers 32–3, 124; *see also*
  Dead Meat
referees 5, 26, 80, 128; and emotion
  113; and gender 44, 110; negative
  experiences 31–3, 63–4, 110, 114,
  121–3; referee community 124; referee
  school 32, 119–20; researcher position
  14–15, 17, 120–1; *see also* officials
reflexivity 12, 17, 67
reputation 63, 66, 117
researcher 14, 17, 120, 140; as an identity
  2, 81–2; as insider 12, 14, 140; as
  participant 14, 118
resistance 52, 134; boutfits as a form of
  57, 60–1
risk 15, 55–62, 69–70, 128, 133, 134–5;
  and ethics 140; risky practices 55
Robinson, V. 55–6, 102–3
rollergirl 6, 8–9, 52
routine 25, 32, 120

safe space 7, 67, 68, 140
secret: dark secret 64, 111, 138; "dirty
  secret" 119
seriousness 48, 88–9, 101, 135, 139; and
  banter 82, 83; and boutfits 58, 60–2;
  and exclusion 8–9, 30; refusal to accept
  58, 69, 94, 96, 134; and skate names
  51–2, 70
sexual harassment 80, 127
SheEOs 5
Sheffield Steel Roller Derby 11, 13, 26–9,
  122; conflict with TIL 66, 84–6; and
  training 31–3, 34–5, 120–1
situated knowledge 12–13, 118, 140
situational analysis 17, 49–50
skate names 48, 50–4, 69, 134; and ethics
  16; and seriousness 9, 70
skater-owned and operated 5; *see also*
  women-owned and operated
skills capital *see* capital
social media 16, 38, 40, 66, 117, 127
Stone, C. 30

Index 147

team spirit 60, 94
teamliness 84, 88–9, 133, 136–8
televised sports manhood formula 103
Texas Rollergirls 5, 7
togetherness 27, 29, 78, 81, 133, 136–7
toughness: referees 31, 33; skate names 48, 53; training style 114
tours 86, 90–2, 140
traditional sports: environment 96; ideologies 52, 99; model 46, 62, 64, 110, 133; organisations 7; practices 103
transphobia: lack of 138

UKRDA 8, 11, 41–4, 45, 67; sanctioned game 11, 42; affiliated official 14
underdog 49
unsporting conduct 63–4, 71, 81, 112–14

venues 27, 34–7, 44–5, 66, 139
volunteers 30–3, 109, 120, 123–4, 125–7, 136; *see also* officials

Wellard, I. 58, 135–6
WFTDA 5, 37, 43–4, 54, 67, 112, 139; gender policy 8, 100; mission statement 30, 109; rules 5–6; separation from MRDA 10
women-owned and operated 93; *see also* skater-owned and operated
women-only 1, 7–8, 9–10, 15, 34, 84

Zom B Cru 11, 13–14, 53, 79, 87–90, 101; and the Crucibelles 27–8, 136–7; the end of 28, 40, 62, 88; and Phallic Baldwin 15, 88–9

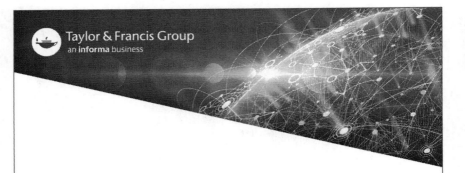